A MAN'S GAME

A MAN'S GAME

Masculinity and the Anti-Aesthetics of American Literary Naturalism

JOHN DUDLEY

THE UNIVERSITY OF ALABAMA PRESS

Tuscaloosa

Typeface: AGaramond

∞

The paper on which this book is printed meets the minimum requirements of American
National Standard for Information Science–Permanence of Paper for Printed Library
Materials, ANSI Z39.48-1984.

Library of Congress Cataloging-in-Publication Data

Dudley, John, 1965–
A man's game : masculinity and the anti-aesthetics of American literary
naturalism / John Dudley.
p. cm. — (Studies in American literary realism and naturalism)
Originally presented as author's thesis (doctoral)—Tulane University, 2001.
Includes bibliographical references (p.) and index.
ISBN 0-8173-1347-8 (cloth : alk. paper)
1. American fiction—20th century—History and criticism. 2. Naturalism in literature.
3. American fiction—Male authors—History and criticism. 4. American fiction—African
American authors—History and criticism. 5. African American men in literature.
6. Masculinity in literature. 7. Aesthetics, American. 8. Men in literature. I. Title.
II. Series. PS374.N29 D83 2004
813′.50912—dc22
2003018414

British Library Cataloguing-in-Publication Data available

Contents

Acknowledgments

This book has its origins in a dissertation completed under the direction of Donald Pizer, whose patient, but insistent, guidance and encouragement allowed this project to emerge and develop. I extend to him my deepest thanks. I can only hope to emulate his professional integrity and intellectual rigor in my own career as a teacher and scholar. Also instrumental in the design of this project were Rebecca Mark and Felipe Smith, who offered generous amounts of advice and support over the course of my years at Tulane University. Among many wonderful and supportive friends and colleagues at Tulane, Kristina Busse, Bill Mullaney, and John Halbrooks in particular, served as valued readers and confidants at the early stages of this project, for which I am very grateful. Earlier versions of material included in Chapters 1 and 4 appeared in *College Literature* 29.1 (2002), and an earlier version of Chapter 2 appeared in *American Literary Realism* 34.2 (2002). A brief section of Chapter 3, dealing with the Spanish-American War, was published in an earlier form in *Convergencias Hispanicas: Selected Proceedings and Other Essays on Spanish and Latin American Literature*, ed. Elizabeth Scarlett and Howard B. Westcott (Newark, DE: Juan de la Cuesla, 2001). Among the many people who have provided valuable assistance throughout the subsequent development of this work, I would like to specifically thank Gary Scharnhorst for his very useful comments and strong support, as well as the anonymous readers whose insightful readings and concrete suggestions improved the manuscript in many ways. I am also extremely grateful to Sondra Guttman for her patience and astute observations on many occasions. Any flaws or inconsistencies in the following pages reflect my own shortcomings in the face of the exemplary efforts of many wonderful people.

The staff at The University of Alabama Press offered invaluable support at all stages of the publication process and guided this project with admirable skill and judgment. I completed much of the work on this book at Southern Arkansas University during a research fellowship in the summer of 2001, thanks to the efforts of James Willis and the other members of the Faculty Research Committee. For their expertise, encouragement, and assistance, I am also grateful to my colleagues of the SAU faculty, in particular Elizabeth Davis, Stacy Clanton, Lynne Belcher, Shannin Schroeder, Ben Johnson, and Paul Babbitt.

Special thanks must go to my parents, Dr. and Mrs. Edward Dudley, who have maintained a relentless faith in my capabilities in spite of periodic evidence to the contrary and who have given me more than they could ever know.

Finally, I am unable to describe my debt to Judy Zwolak, who has made everything possible, and to Sophia and Owen, who have made everything worthwhile.

A MAN'S GAME

Introduction

"Life, Not Literature"? Naturalism and Anti-Aesthetics

We don't want literature, we want life!
—Frank Norris

In 1904, one year before the publication of *The House of Mirth* would establish her as a commercially successful novelist, Edith Wharton published a volume of short fiction, *The Descent of Man and Other Stories*. The book's title story tells of a dedicated entomologist, Professor Samuel Linyard, who, quite by accident, becomes the best-selling author of a pseudoscientific monograph offering a series of banal homilies on the human condition. Initially conceived by the professor as a "skit on the 'popular' scientific book" (15), the treatise, ironically entitled "The Vital Thing," catapults Linyard to national prominence after a publisher convinces him to present the book as a serious work. Thinking that his secret knowledge of the book's satirical intent will only enrich the joke, Linyard instead finds himself both distracted and exhilarated by the fame and wealth his "skit" generates.

Its title notwithstanding, "The Descent of Man" eschews a conventionally naturalistic exploration of Darwinian themes. Unlike such works as Frank Norris's "Lauth" and "A Case for Lombroso," which present fictional scenarios that demonstrate the evolutionary theories of Cesare Lombroso and Joseph LeConte, Wharton's story does not focus on the combination of genetic and environmental forces that determine human destiny. Such sociological explorations, conventionally used to define the thematic boundaries of naturalist fiction, seldom attracted Wharton's attention. This story, however, does explore the specific problems of writing and publishing in turn-of-the-century America and, in this regard, raises a number of issues crucial to an understanding of the aesthetic goals that characterize Wharton's understanding of her place within the discourse of American literary naturalism.

Wharton's title recalls, of course, Darwin's famous work of the same name, and the narrative offers an ironic commentary on the impact of evolutionary science within the popular arena.[1] Upon realizing the popular demand for slapdash scientific writing, Professor Linyard laments that "the inaccessible goddess whom the Professor had served in his youth now offered her charms in the market-place" (7). His attempt to lampoon this phenomenon, however, goes astray, and the story chronicles the literal "descent" of a particular man into the abyss of middlebrow capitalist consumption, as Linyard becomes a widely marketed authority, offering opinions on a variety of topics: "These confidences endeared the Professor to millions of readers, and his head passed in due course from the magazine and the newspaper to the biscuit-tin and the chocolate-box" (28). The only deterministic forces at work in this story are those material temptations that compel Linyard to forsake his "serious" projects on such esoteric topics as "the Unconscious Cerebration of the Amœba" (5). Through her satirical representation of the Professor's downfall, Wharton demonstrates her awareness of the absurdity and risk of the literary marketplace and its pernicious effect on the attempt to create meaningful texts.

That Wharton should equate "real" literature with hard science is no coincidence in the context of a society obsessed with the practical applications of cultural and intellectual work. Wharton presents the struggle between purposeful "science" and frivolous literary concoctions within the gendered discourse of her time, which identified all forces as essentially either "male" or "female." Professor Linyard maintains that "he didn't want any women bothering with his beetles" (3) and wishes to keep the male and female realms of his professional and domestic lives entirely separate. With "The Vital Thing," however, Linyard addresses a popular audience composed largely of women. Wharton notes that "everyone now read scientific books and expressed an opinion on them. The ladies and the clergy had taken them up first" (6). As Ann Douglas describes in *The Feminization of American Culture,* such female readers were largely responsible for the growth of commercial publishing during the nineteenth century: "[Women] comprised the bulk of educated churchgoers and the vast majority of the dependable reading public; in even greater numbers, they edited magazines and wrote books for other women like themselves. They were becoming the prime consumers of American culture" (8). By century's end, many critics, authors, and readers simply accepted the notion that popular "literature" had become a distinctly feminine realm, in spite of the continued, albeit somewhat diminished, domination of scholarly and commercial publishing by men. The creative and editorial gains by women, real and perceived, complemented widespread suspicions about the place of artistry in a scientifically obsessed society. Bram Dijkstra, in *Idols of Perversity: Fantasies of Feminine Evil in Fin-De-Siècle Culture,* traces the deep misogyny in turn-of-the-century art and literature and notes that "to be a stylistic innovator in the arts was to use artistic muscle to push aside any potential accusation of artistic effeminacy" (207). Wharton, as a woman embarking on a professional writing career, adopted an attitude of skeptical condescension, if not outright hostility, toward the increasingly feminized literary establishment in both her literary characterizations of the publishing world and her critical assessments of the work of her fellow woman writers. In "The Descent of Man," Linyard's transformation from dutiful man of science into mercenary literary hack is complete when he agrees to write a "series of 'scientific sermons' for the Round-the-Gas-Log column of *The Woman's World*" (25). For Wharton, Linyard's creative degeneration involves a corrupt alliance of the domestic sphere, the pulpit, and the commercial marketplace—all traps that threaten the autonomy and vigor of the true genius, whether scientist or author.

Central to the critique of authorship contained in "The Descent of Man" is the fact that Linyard's surrender to the vulgar marketplace comes about as a result of misinterpretation, specifically the chronic misreading of his satirical attack on pseudoscience by a feminized audience. Such is the perceived effect of the marketplace on art, and Wharton's apprehensive recognition of this phenomenon foregrounds her own literary endeavors. The question of how to produce literature that resists the commodification and frivolity endemic to popular art would continue to preoccupy Wharton, as it did the literary naturalists who emerged in the 1890s. The tendency toward ornamentation, typified by the Art Nouveau movement, which Wharton roundly criticizes in her book *The Decoration of Houses,* saw its literary equivalent in the popularity of the feminized aestheticism of "the decadents," whose influence permeated the intellectual establishment at the close of the nineteenth century.

Indeed, few concurrent literary movements offer such divergent philosophies of art as did English aestheticism and American naturalism at the turn of the twentieth century. Besides Wharton, writers such as Stephen Crane, Frank Norris, and Jack London explicitly defined themselves and their work in rigid contrast to the effete "literary" qualities cherished by an American intellectual establishment that they viewed as increasingly dominated by "decadent" English authors and critics, from Swinburne to Wilde, who adhered to Walter Pater's advocacy of "art for art's sake."[2] Moreover, both Crane and Norris rebelled against a movement in which they had, to some extent, participated. While still a university student, Norris wrote a highly stylized medieval romance, *Yvernelle,* and later developed a number of close friendships with members of the circle of San Francisco aesthetes who produced *The Lark,* a journal modeled on the voice of English aestheticism, *The Yellow Book,* a controversial quarterly magazine founded in London by American expatriate Henry Harland in 1894 and dedicated to the "decadent" art and literature of the day.[3] For his part, Crane lived a hand-to-mouth existence in the bohemian world of painters and writers in New York City before the success of *The Red Badge of Courage.*[4]

In his critical essays, Norris alludes to the inadequacy of the aesthetes' involvement with the rigors and rituals of "life," connecting a perceived artistic failure to the artist's lack of "masculine force." The pervasiveness within naturalist fiction of an artist figure who struggles with issues of masculinity underlines how this unequivocal opposition to aestheticism helped shape an aesthetic doctrine of American naturalism as a literary movement. The goals and principles of naturalist fiction ultimately rely upon a remarkably precarious image of the artist that has nonetheless remained central to the critical understanding of American authorship and to the construction of a canon of suitably "literary" texts. Simply put, naturalists as diverse as Norris, Crane, London, and Wharton, as well as several African-American naturalists, including Paul Laurence Dunbar, Charles Chesnutt, James Weldon Johnson, and W. E. B. Du Bois, sought to define themselves and their literary endeavors in direct opposition to an "unmanly" vogue of decadent aestheticism, and in so doing, they reveal the inherent instability of this opposition. In defining authorship as a "man's game," the naturalists invite critical inquiry into just what the rules of this game are.

The aesthetic properties of American literary naturalism as a movement have been largely ignored as the subject of critical study for a number of reasons. Any unity among the diverse texts conventionally described as naturalistic has often been attributed to a dubious philosophical doctrine of pessimistic determinism rather than to any formal similarities in the texts. The key works associated with naturalism in the United States seem to have little in common stylistically. The stark impressionism of *The Red Badge of Courage,* the grotesque humor of *McTeague,* and the Jamesian wit of *The House of Mirth,* for instance, exemplify widely disparate narrative techniques. Furthermore, the authors in question formed no cohesive "school" around which the movement revolved. Although they supposedly shared a common doctrine, any professional or collegial relationship between these writers was minimal at best. Although the rise of naturalism as a literary attempt to investigate the interplay of heredity, environment, and chance in the determination of an individual's fate might be explained by the cultural forces present in Progressive Era American culture, its persistence as a literary form throughout the subsequent century calls for further examination of the aesthetic doctrines that emerged from this era.

In this regard, an obvious legacy of this generation of naturalists surrounds the construction of a hypermasculine definition of the writer. Although the notion of authorship in the nineteenth century often carried suggestions of effeminacy, such was not the case in the twentieth century, at least not to the same degree. The public persona of the male writer as a virile, robust man of action, from Ernest Hemingway to John Steinbeck to Norman Mailer, reveals the profound influence of Crane, Norris, London, and their contemporaries. Behind this vigorous image, however, lie the same anxieties about the usefulness of fiction that confronted the naturalists of the 1890s. Naturalism, dismissed by some critics as either an extreme outgrowth of realism or an unfortunate philosophical dead end, incorporated the American tradition of anti-intellectualism while reflecting a growing unease about the fate of the individual in a modern, industrial society. The rhetoric of masculinity that accompanied the development of naturalist fiction reflects the sense of impending loss behind this narrative stance, and its persistence in American literature demonstrates the continuing relevance of these anxieties.

Since the 1980s, the widespread acceptance of post-structuralist theory and a resurgent concern for historical contexts have reinvigorated interest in naturalism, primarily as a movement indicative of the cultural ideologies of turn-of-the-century America.[5] A number of texts examine the relationships between race, class, and gender in the genre and suggest the possibilities for a reconsideration of the aesthetic sensibility behind these representations. In *Form and History in American Literary Naturalism,* June Howard applies the psychoanalytic Marxism of Althusser and Jameson to identify and examine two dominant tropes within naturalist writing: the brute and the spectator. In her analysis, naturalism, as the site of contention between these two tropes, occupies a crucial space in the establishment of class distinctions between an affluent literary audience and the symbolic "Other" during the era of industrialization, immigration, and the growth of consumer culture. Howard's book usefully explores the apparently contradictory impulses within naturalism in the context of the social changes of the late nineteenth century, and her study resituates the "antinomies" of naturalism within the form of the text itself.[6]

Amy Kaplan's *The Social Construction of American Realism* further applies the Marxist notion of "strategies of containment" to assert literature's role in shaping social contexts, rather than simply reflecting them. According to Kaplan, the various threats to the social order that occur in texts by William Dean Howells, Wharton, and Theodore Dreiser are ultimately defused by the construction of "social spaces" in these novels that ensure the preservation of class distinctions. Although Howard and Kaplan focus largely on the construction of a race- and class-based Other, Walter Benn Michaels, drawing heavily on Michel Foucault, explores the relationship between naturalism's gender concerns and the market economy of the late nineteenth century. In *The Gold Standard and the Logic of Naturalism,* Michaels suggests two gendered models for writing in the 1880s and 1890s: production (masculine) and consumption (feminine). Because naturalist writers believed they were engaged in a critique of consumer culture, they sought to develop a language of representation that transcends materiality—a language that contains true "worth." Although their effort therefore appears to reject capitalist excess, it actually endorses the masculine, mechanistic model of production over the weaker, feminized model of consumption, represented by the female body.[7] In this way, the capitalist marketplace asserts itself as the dominant system of representation in spite of the oppositional ideals ostensibly at work in the novels.

Recent criticism has also highlighted the emergence of a professional culture of authorship, one that collapsed the image of a writer from that of an upper-class intellectual into something less definite. The writers who dominated this transition sought to preserve what Howard calls the "cultural legitimacy" of authorship while conforming to the standards of professionalism typified by the tightly knit fraternity of newspaper reporters. Christopher Wilson's *The Labor of Words* analyzes the influence of journalism in constructing the aesthetic perspectives of London, Norris, and Upton Sinclair, as well as the relationship of these writers' "literary" output with the muckraking reportage of David Graham Phillips and Lincoln Steffens. Contradicting the traditional critical view that the expanded publishing marketplace had a democratizing effect on the profession of authorship,[8] Wilson maintains that writing, like the fields of social work or academics, underwent a process of professionalization that created a "publishing elite." The trend toward professionalism led to a disappearance of bohemian correspondents with literary pretensions, in favor of reporters such as William Randolph Hearst's who "act" while others "sit idly by" (Wilson 28). Wilson accepts the declared link between novelists such as London and Norris and journalists with whom they claimed allegiance, but to a certain extent it was possible that these writers wanted to be thought of as "reporters" in order to camouflage their primary role as "artists."[9] The credentials of London, Norris, and Crane as journalists are dubious, at best, especially when compared to muckrakers such as Steffens. Crane's career began as precisely the kind of bohemian reporter with aspirations beyond journalism that had been the model in the preprofessional era. It was only after his success and acclaim as a novelist that Crane achieved any status as a correspondent, as was true for London. Norris wrote journalistic pieces for the *Wave* and other publications, but these works are not a major part of his legacy. By and large, the guise of professional reporter proved attractive to these men, who invariably balked at the feminizing label of "author" or "artist."

Also central to the literary stance of naturalist discourse is the Progressive Era construction of manhood, as both an ideal and a set of cultural practices. According to Howard, "The normative perspective from which the Other is defined and authority is asserted is, in naturalism as elsewhere, essentially masculine, and a full understanding of the ideology of professionalism should eventually include an analysis of how it is bound up with gender identity" (140). As Howard points out, the masculinist bias found in naturalist texts is not unique. I would argue, however, that its role in shaping an aesthetic strategy for naturalism not only reveals the gender anxieties of America in the late nineteenth century but also explains both the unresolved tensions inherent in the naturalist notion of authorship and the long-term relevance of this aesthetic strategy in the subsequent development of American literature. In her essay "Men of Color, Women, and Uppity Art at the Turn of the Century," Elizabeth Ammons observes that "the institutionalization of an exclusively white and an entirely or almost entirely male literary canon in the United States" in the twentieth century has its roots not only in the long-standing exclusion of women from academia, but also in scholars' "dedicated labor to establish, reify, and keep in place a controlled, tidy, white, male version of American literature" (28–32). Of course, the literature itself also plays a role in the construction of the notion of American literature as a man's club. Donna Campbell, in *Resisting Regionalism: Gender and Naturalism in American Fiction, 1885–1915*, persuasively argues that the constructed "masculinity" of the naturalists evolved as a strategy for displacing and devaluing the "local colorists," who represented a broader definition of authorship. For the naturalists, Campbell claims, "Their anxieties about art and writing . . . pivot on the issue of gender dominance and the encoding of realism and local color as feminine" (6). Campbell's book establishes the instability in depictions of "Otherness" and the feminine in canonical naturalist works. Indeed, the shaky constructions of masculinity also reveal the radical instability of the "masculine" naturalists' own aesthetic work. In *Language and Gender in American Fiction*, Elsa Nettels notes that "in nineteenth-century criticism, the connotations of *masculine* were rarely negative, whereas *effeminacy* was always bad and *feminine* was at best graceful and delicate, at worst perfervid and shrill" (7). Under this rubric, the "feminine" artist may serve some aesthetic function, however limited or inferior, but the "effeminate" artist—that is, a man with inappropriately gendered aesthetics—has no place whatsoever. Such policing of the boundaries of language and art ensures that any written work emerges into a contentious and volatile arena, albeit one posing as a mere reflection of the "natural" distinctions between men and women. Close inspection of the apparently sturdy banner of naturalism as a manly enterprise therefore reveals a fabric not only fraying at the edges but stretched to its limit by the anxieties of manhood that preoccupied American culture at the turn of the twentieth century.

The late nineteenth-century preoccupation with male sexuality surfaced in such divergent phenomena as the rise of professional spectator sports, the scientific establishment of homosexuality as a category of identity, the post-

Darwinian interest in the sexual component of natural selection, and the obsessive concerns over masturbation and adolescent sexuality among various groups, including adherents of so-called muscular Christianity, psychologists such as G. Stanley Hall and reform-minded health advocates such as Milton Kellogg. Organized athletics, in particular, united the various strains of masculine anxiety and proved significant in shaping Norris's, Crane's, and London's journalistic and literary concerns. As a public performance of manhood, spectator sports began to demand the attention of the American public in the late nineteenth century and contributed to the promotion of hypermasculine virtues in the increasingly sedentary and thus feminized realm of popular entertainment.

In the gender-charged climate of the Progressive Era, it is hardly surprising that American naturalists should express their unequivocal difference from the so-called decadents in sexual terms. As Norris's own flirtation with the aesthetic movement suggests, however, the contrast between these movements was never as conspicuous as he might have hoped. If British observers frequently dismissed the work of writers as diverse as Émile Zola, George Gissing, J. K. Huysmans, Aubrey Beardsley, and Wilde with a common nod toward standards of decency, the editorial gatekeepers of American letters, conscious of the need to establish a credible national literature, were, if anything, even more heavily invested in a genteel tradition that placed such sensational subject matter well outside the bounds of respectability. Perhaps more significantly, naturalism and aestheticism shared an ideal of the artist as a professional, a craftsman whose acquired skills granted access into the expanding cultural marketplace. The fact that the figure of the aesthete, for American naturalists, came to represent the ineffectual languor of a feminized aristocracy can be traced to the divergent paths followed by British and American concepts of masculinity in the nineteenth century and to larger differences in the class structure of these two societies. Ultimately, however, both movements exhibited a deep-seated ambivalence toward the increasing commercialization of art—resisting the middlebrow demands of the marketplace even while assuming prominent roles in the emergent class of professional artists.

Critical appraisal of British aestheticism in general, and Wilde in particular, has consistently conflated issues of identity and aesthetics, whether for the purpose of condemnation or celebration. Lorraine Janzen Kooistra, in a study of the decadents and the commercial viability of illustrated books, summarizes the transformation of the figure of the aesthete from the sequestered ascetic to the subversive dandy:

> The aesthete's credo of "Beauty for beauty's sake" does not . . . signify simply a retreat into an artificially created world. The love of the beautiful and the rare also stages a revolt against the pressures of Victorian middle-class conformity and the dehumanizing aspects of industrialization and crass materialism. The aesthete could surmount the vulgar horrors of Victorian society by refusing to conform—by developing a unique personal style. Thus *style* became of paramount importance to decadent artists, for through style they could launch a highly visible counter-attack to the expectations of the Philistine and the *bourgeoisie*. (35)

Within the context of postindustrialized British society and its simultaneous embrace of mechanized mass culture and an apparently outdated and rigidly stratified class structure, the aesthetic embrace of beauty constituted a considered, if ultimately inadequate, assault on the status quo. In addressing the complementary functions of text and illustration in popular monographs, Kooistra notes that "the contemporary identification of 'aesthete' or 'decadent' with the effeminate and the homosexual ensured that the bitextuality of the art-nouveau book would participate in *fin-de-siècle* sexual discourses" (34–35). In light of contemporary understandings of gender and identity, the decadents emerge as subversives for whom the personal was, indeed, political. One must ultimately perceive this opposition to hegemonic culture, however, as compromised—or at least complicated—by the enthusiastic self-commodification of such artists as Wilde and Aubrey Beardsley. Indeed, the advanced technology of the marketplace made possible their commercial success and subsequent challenge to normative customs. The figure of the dandy stood in stark contrast to the English definition of the gentleman and represented, as Regenia Gagnier notes, a "natural aristocracy" based on artistic standards rather than birthright (98). Wilde's witty self-promotion and worship of beauty provided an audacious critique of the class structure of England; in the United States, however, the successful packaging of aestheticism was seen, by and large, as elitist and exclusionary. In part, the emphatic resistance to aestheticism espoused by American naturalists arose in response to the substantial cult of personality that developed around Wilde in the wake of his 1882 lecture tour of the United States—an event that Jonathan Freedman describes as a "mania" of commercialization (102). For the next several years, so-called decadent art and literature would enjoy significant popularity in the United States, not only among disaffected university students (such as Norris at the University of California and Harvard) but in the realms of interior decorating, book design, and periodical publishing. The most influential source for American aestheticism was *The Yellow Book,* a journal published in England and edited by American expatriate Henry Harland. Gagnier observes that *The Yellow Book* proved an economic success because it was "directed toward an inclusive market beyond esoterica" (55). In fact, for young American artists in the 1890s, aestheticism was an established mode of expression, not an outlet for dissent. Although Pater had espoused a form of aestheticism that maintained a strict distance between art and life, Wilde's spectacle of self-fashioning represented what Leon Chai calls an "externalization of form" (102), in which the artist's own life becomes a part of the art itself. If Wilde's humiliating public downfall symbolizes the hegemonic British response to aestheticism's extreme Romantic individualism, the turn toward Zola's naturalism among some American writers could be said to reflect a similar rejection.

Zola's concept of the novelist as scientist, an objective observer of the actions and reactions of representative characters, combined with increasing cultural currency granted Darwinian ideas, profoundly affected the first generation of American naturalist writers, either directly or indirectly. The naturalists' approach to art thus constituted an even starker rejection of the self-conscious Romantic artist than had the generation of realists before them. Henry James, for instance, in "The Art of Fiction," claims that "the deepest quality of a work of art will always be the quality of the mind of the producer. In proportion as that intelligence is fine will the novel, the picture, the statue partake of the substance of beauty and truth" (21). For the naturalists, however, the relationship between artist, story, and audience was as never before. In his essay "Fiction Is Selection," Norris writes, "The fiction writer of the wildest and most untrammelled fancy cannot get away from real life. Imagination! There is no such thing; you can't imagine anything that you have not already seen and observed" (*Literary Criticism* 52). Instead of the imaginative wellspring of creative realizations or the inspired vessel of divine insight, the naturalist author assumed the role of disinterested intermediary between the concrete facts of experience and an audience separated from this experience by time, space, or—in many cases—race and class. Much of this evolving notion of authorship stemmed from tangible and quantifiable changes in the social and economic conditions under which these writers operated, and the increased professionalism in all fields was reflected in the redefinition of the author as a skilled tradesman who differed little from other workers in the consumer marketplace.

At least as important as Zola's work in its influence over the naturalists' aesthetic doctrine, however, is the adventure writing of such figures as Rudyard Kipling and Robert Louis Stevenson. The adventure genre, produced as "boys' stories" apart from the larger feminized domain of the "literary," offered American writers a model distinctly and explicitly opposed to the aestheticism of what became known as the "mauve decade." *Captains Courageous,* published in 1896, is Kipling's only novel set in America and provided a template for works such as Norris's *Moran of the Lady Letty* and London's *The Sea-Wolf,* in which an effete upper-class youth discovers his true mettle after being rescued at sea by a shipload of experienced sailors and their steely, ferocious captain. In *Captains Courageous* young Harvey Cheyne is transformed from the weak and spoiled son of a railroad tycoon to a robust and vigorous young man worthy of inheriting his self-made father's commercial empire. Kipling's characterization of Harvey captures the anxieties of a generation of privileged young men whose lives had become increasingly alienated from the active, manly labor of earlier generations, and this characterization clearly struck a chord with those writers seeking a career in a profession too closely identified with ivory towers and drawing rooms.

Even more influential on the ideas of Crane, Norris, and London, however, is Kipling's 1891 novel *The Light That Failed,* which articulates an anti-aesthetic ideal that resonated powerfully in the context of a long-standing American anti-intellectual tradition. Through the achievements and disappointments of its hero, Dick Heldar, Kipling explicitly examines the relationship between journalism and art and the struggle of the artist in the marketplace. Dick, a writer and painter, becomes a war correspondent and sketch artist in the Sudan for the "Central Southern Syndicate," and Kipling presents his artistry as a form of labor; his efforts are those of an honest, hard-working craftsman toiling for a large, impersonal company. When his first sketches are accepted for publication, Kipling writes, "Dick was made free of the New and Honourable Fraternity of war correspondents" (21). As a member of this fraternity, Dick is much like the soldiers whose exploits he documents; often, he and his fellow correspondents take up arms themselves and become literal participants in the dirty work of the British Empire. The challenge to Dick's honorable, fraternal code comes through Maisie, whose romantic involvement with Dick tempts him with the prospect of marriage and domesticity. Maisie is also an artist, but a poor one—too beholden to the affectations of the European salons and too absorbed by the pursuit of public acclaim. Ultimately she fails to seduce Dick into giving up either his aesthetic principles or his bachelorhood, even as he slowly loses his eyesight and his ability to paint. As Maisie and Dick argue about brush strokes and the purity of line drawing, Kipling offers the question "Was it not time to leave all this barren wilderness of canvas and counsel and join hands with Life and Love?" (62). Kipling's rejection of the self-conscious notion of "art" as a rarefied and picturesque alternative to the "pure lines" of real life served to codify, in the minds of his American literary heirs, an aesthetic— or anti-aesthetic—sensibility that remains central to our understanding of naturalism.

Certainly the most outspoken supporter of a naturalist aesthetic doctrine, and perhaps the only avowed naturalist among those writers considered central to the movement in the United States, is Norris. In "Novelists of the Future," one of his many essays on the craft of fiction, Norris places gender and race in the foreground of a literary manifesto. Describing novel writing, Norris proclaims,

> It is not an affair of women and aesthetes, and the muse of American fiction is no chaste, delicate, super-refined mademoiselle of delicate roses and "elegant" attitudinizings, but a robust, red-armed bonne-femme, who rough-shoulders her way among men and among affairs, who finds a healthy pleasure in the jostlings of the mob and a hearty delight in the honest, rough and tumble, Anglo-Saxon give-and-take knockabout that for us means life.
>
> . . . Believe me, she will lead you far from the studios and the aes-thetes, the velvet jackets and the uncut hair, far from the sexless crea-tures who cultivate their little art of writing as the fancier cultivates his orchid. (*Literary Criticism* 13–14)

Here, as elsewhere in his critical prose, Norris situates the appropriate work of the novelist within a strictly gendered discourse, shaped by historical exigencies of race and class, but also purposely conceived as a rejoinder to what Norris and others saw as a literary establishment increasingly alienated from its social and ethical responsibilities. As the previous passage demonstrates, Norris struggled to create what Tom Lutz refers to as "a phallic rhetoric that, by privileging action over scholarship or reflection, calls into question his own activity as a writer" (133). This uncertainty over the status of authorship informs the naturalists' unstable self-definition and is reflected in the depiction of intellectual or aesthetic activity in their fictional texts.

This book approaches the masculinist discourse of the Progressive Era not only as the unfortunate byproduct of a misogynist and homophobic cultural perspective, but as an essential element in the formation of American literary naturalism, one that a diverse number of texts employ to articulate a unique set of aesthetic concerns. In so linking artistic ideals with notions of manhood, naturalist fiction, in turn, reveals the contradictory and unstable nature of this aesthetic scheme and constructs an approach to the problem of the artist as both insider and outsider that continues to haunt the persona of the author in American society.

The construction of a naturalist aesthetic sensibility in the 1890s accompanied a complex set of cultural tensions over race, class, and gender, each of which saw its expression through a specific discourse of masculinity. The articulation of these ideas, in turn, helps redefine conceptions of the author and of literary expression in American society at a time of dramatic social upheaval. This expression took shape in two ways. First, American naturalist writers participate in open debate with the theory and practice of 1890s aestheticism as the apotheosis of the European Romantic tradition, placing their own work in direct opposition to this tradition and thus as part of a uniquely American enterprise. Second, these writers construct an aesthetic doctrine in their texts that reveals their desire for active engagement in what Donald Pizer describes as Norris's paradoxical aesthetic doctrine of "life, not literature," as well as the concomitant anxieties about the possibility of such involvement.[10] I focus on a group of distinct authors who created a remarkably diverse collection of texts unified by a common aesthetic tension between the anti-aesthetic sensibilities of naturalism and the more widely accepted notions of artistry. This uneasy perspective of the artist as mediator between spectacle and audience emerges in the male-dominated realm of

Crane's, London's, and Norris's fiction and is subsequently adopted in the works of Wharton, Dunbar, Chesnutt, Johnson, and Du Bois to articulate ideas—specifically those arising from the conditions of women and African Americans—seemingly at odds with the dominant ideology of fin-de-siècle America and with the very idea of American "masculinity" itself. Although all of these authors accept and perpetuate a definition of writing as an essentially male enterprise, their efforts simultaneously reveal significant ambiguities and uncertainties about this connection between authorship and masculinity—ambiguities and uncertainties that exist in this notion of authorship from the very beginning.

Chapter 1 explores the development of a masculinist sporting culture in late nineteenth-century America and its power to illuminate the aesthetic ideals of American literary naturalism. The legalization of boxing, the establishment of professional baseball, and the popularity of intercollegiate football all contributed to a definition of American masculinity that both complemented and complicated the Darwinian sense of purpose offered by naturalism. Not only did organized sports provide these writers with suitably atavistic and survivalist imagery and subject matter (comparable to those offered by combat, the slums, the Klondike, etc.), but it also offers a metaphor for what they viewed as the condition of the naturalist author himself. As mediator between violent events and a middle-class audience, the naturalists' conception of the author occupies an uneasy position between the "masculine" spectacle and the "feminine" onlookers. From its earliest incarnation, therefore, American naturalism sat on unstable ground, both ideologically and aesthetically. Novels such as Norris's *McTeague,* London's *The Game* and *The Sea-Wolf,* and Crane's *The Red Badge of Courage* serve both to elucidate the unique and troubling issues of masculinity at the dawn of the twentieth century and to articulate their views on the ethical and aesthetic responsibilities of the artist. Returning to the metaphorical relationship of sport and the naturalist artist, I examine the surprisingly complementary reactions of London and James Weldon Johnson to the rise of the boxer Jack Johnson, who loomed as a conspicuously black presence on the American cultural landscape in the early decades of this century. Whereas Crane, Norris, and London call for a "masculine" art to uphold the obligations of empire building, James Weldon Johnson, engaged in the construction of a nation within a nation, adopts a comparable cultural stance in direct response to the racially exclusive ideology of the day. The intrinsic instability of this stance did not prevent its adoption by writers with such divergent tasks nor its impact on the definition of authorship during this period and beyond. This instability, however, reveals the crucial anxieties at work in both naturalist discourse and the culture from which it emerged.

Chapter 2 focuses particular attention on selected works of Crane, who displayed a marked interest in the sporting culture of his time as well as in the masculinist ethos it represents. The stories collected in Crane's *Tales of Adventure* document the struggle of an artist to define his role within the restrictions of exclusively masculine rites and rituals and reflect the instability of Crane's conception of the artist in a world of "action," not words. Crane certainly accepts Leo Tolstoy's claim that "man's first and most unquestionable duty is to participate in the struggle with nature to support his own life and that of others" (*I Cannot Be Silent* 96–97). It is precisely this "struggle with nature" that Crane proposes in such stories as "The Open Boat," using the metaphorical language of masculinity in an attempt to resolve the problem of the passive artist as mere spectator. The struggle to become an interpreter, to create meaning from the chaos of nature, is, for Crane, the proper enterprise for the naturalistic writer—a challenge made even more difficult when one confronts the hollowness of the masculine rituals of the cowboy, the soldier, and the adventurer. That these battles for meaning should occur on the various frontiers of American civilization indicates the place of the writer in the definition of an imperial and nationalist agenda. Crane's fictional exploration of the American West, Mexico, and the Caribbean reflects the impact of American expansion and imperialism on the emergent role of the naturalistic artist.

Chapter 3 examines the presence of problematic male protagonists in selected novels by Norris and Wharton. For both authors, issues of race, class, professionalism, and imperialism collide in the figure of the unsuccessful artist, and this recurring figure provides an illustrative negation of the idealized masculine conception of the writer promised by the naturalist sensibility. *The Octopus,* the first novel in Norris's unfinished "Epic of the Wheat," depicts a deep anxiety about the artist as "orientalized" outsider among the hypermasculine impulses that guide the growing economic and political fortunes of the United States. Through a close examination of Presley, the poet and would-be social critic whose experiences among the ranchers of the San Joaquin Valley give shape to the novel's narrative, I explore the extent to which Norris depends on the language and concepts of masculinity in developing a naturalistic aesthetic program in *The Octopus*. Presley's inability to shape an artistic representation of his experience emerges through his reluctance to fully engage in the actualities of experience, and, more specifically, to fulfill Norris's conception of masculinity. *The Octopus* exemplifies the kind of writing Norris proposes to depict the emerging American empire of the late nineteenth century, whereas Presley's conflicting roles, as unreliable artist and insightful observer, represent Norris's repudiation of a misguided aesthetic approach and also reveal the anxieties present in Norris's own work. Likewise, an analysis of Wharton's problematic male protagonists in *The House of Mirth* and *The Age of Innocence* reveals an aesthetic stance both consistent with that of her naturalist contemporaries and indicative of her cultural context. Lawrence Selden, Lily Bart's would-be suitor in *The House of Mirth,* and Newland Archer, whose essential conventionality overwhelms his love for Ellen Olenska in *The Age of Innocence,* have provided consistent challenges to critical analyses of Wharton's novels. Contemporary critics have chiefly viewed Selden and Archer as either villains or victims, a formula that ultimately fails to explain these characters' positions and functions. Rather, it is their dispassionate aestheticism and correlative failure to conform to accepted standards of masculinity that proves disastrous. In architecture and design, Wharton discovers an alternative to the alienated, detached aestheticism that traps and emasculates her male characters and reveals the extent to which her artistic sensibility is informed, and shaped, by the anxieties and tensions present in turn-of-the-century America.

Chapter 4 explores the surprising adoption of literary naturalism as a fictional strategy by African American writers at the beginning of the twentieth century. Given the violent and repressive policies governing the notion of racial difference during this period, naturalist writers such as London and Norris, with their emphasis on heredity and genetic determinism, hardly seem likely aesthetic models for African Americans devoted to challenging the logic of Jim Crow America. Early experiments in naturalism, including Dunbar's *The Sport of the Gods* and Chesnutt's *The Marrow of Tradition,* nonetheless demonstrate the appeal of naturalistic fiction as a tool for social critique. In these works and later novels, such as Du Bois's *The Quest of the Silver Fleece* and James Weldon Johnson's *The Autobiography of an Ex-Colored Man,* African American authors seek to transform the notion of determinism as a cultural and political phenomenon, de-emphasizing the prominent role of biology as well as the scientific discourse present in earlier naturalist texts. In so doing, however, these artists rely upon the hypermasculine definition of artistry put forth by the naturalists. In the context of the black struggle for racial self-definition, the role of the "race man" as both an engaged man of action and an aloof artist presents unique problems that call into heightened relief anxieties not unlike those that haunt white writers, from Crane to Wharton. The imprint of naturalist discourse, therefore, on the African American literary tradition reveals both the power of American literary naturalism as an opportunity for expression and the profound contradictions and anxieties that have defined the genre from its inception.

1 / Inside and Outside the Ring

The Establishment of a Masculinist Aesthetic Sensibility

In short, in life, as in a foot-ball game, the principle to follow is: Hit the
line hard; don't foul and don't shirk, but hit the line hard!

—Theodore Roosevelt, *The Strenuous Life*

The emergence of spectator sports at the end of the nineteenth century—as
commercial enterprise, masculine performance, and nascent profession—
offers a paradigmatic lens through which to understand the artistic ethos of
those writers commonly adjoined under the rubric of American literary
naturalism. Athletic competition functions in several ways as a metaphorical
representation of the ideology of naturalism. If the thematic link between
sports and naturalism—the struggle for survival as entertainment—is self-
evident, given the pervasiveness of social Darwinist thought at the turn of
the century, the aesthetic connection between these phenomena requires
some attention. Although the romantic literary tradition posits the text as
pure invention, springing from the mind of an individual artist, naturalist
writers attempt to redefine the author as intermediary between the characters and events of the text and the detached observation of an audience far
removed from the gritty details of the human struggle.

Just as staged sporting events simultaneously promise both the steady rule
of order and the unpredictable exigencies of fortune, so do naturalist texts
aspire to present examples of controlled turmoil, the outcome of which must
seem spontaneous, or *natural,* even as they are strictly determined by the
imagination of the author, by the limitations of society, and by whatever
other forces affect the production of artistic representations of human experience. A prizefight, for example, relies upon the apparent spontaneity of
a contest for physical and strategic domination between two people, a re-

enactment of an instinctive, primal struggle for survival. At the same time, the perceived authenticity of this event remains contingent upon the physical and social construction of the boxing ring, a distinct space separated by ropes and rules from the paying customers on the outside. In sporting events, the outcome is always uncertain, yet in a sense entirely predictable. In other words, the spectators' attention relies upon not only the knowledge that a victory will emerge, but also the faith that winners and losers are not predetermined, that the outcome remains "in play." Thus does the spectacle of athletic competition resemble the efforts of naturalist writers who seek to capture the complex determinism of real life in a work of the imagination. Like the reporter on the sidelines, the naturalist tries to interpret the infinite possibilities of human experience within the confines of a discrete event produced for the entertainment of a curious audience of consumers. The peculiar dynamics of spectator sports, therefore, reinscribe the relationship between author, audience, and text set forth in the fictional works of Frank Norris, Stephen Crane, and Jack London in particular, and in the ethos of American literary naturalism in general.

In this chapter, I will investigate the establishment of a masculinist ethos in the earliest examples of American literary naturalism and the transformation of this ethos into a code of artistic production that reveals key tensions informing the phenomenon of American authorship at the turn of the century. Amid the current critical preoccupation with the cultural contexts of these works, few have examined the role of a uniquely American sporting culture in shaping the attitudes of writers such as Crane, Norris, and London toward masculinity, professionalism, national identity, and the role of the artist. As writers with an active, documented interest in the rise of spectator sports, these men created texts that reflect the ideological concerns central to the athletic craze that began in the 1890s. Spectator sports became an important reflection of the issues of race, class, and gender that divided American society at the turn of the century, and the predominantly white, middle- and upper-class men who comprised the primary audience for such contests found in them a confirmation of their own manliness and position in society. Simultaneously, however, these spectacles served to reinforce the lines between participant and spectator, which contributed to white male anxieties about social change.

The problematic and unstable posture of the literary naturalist, yearning for participation in what Norris calls "life, not literature" and seeking to construct an aesthetic sensibility free from the feminizing grasp of both "art" and commerce, finds expression in the journalism and fiction of Norris, Crane, and London. Rather than explicitly demarcating the line between spectacle and audience, spectator sports—like naturalist texts—demand a level of identification with the figure of the brute, as a standard-bearer for racial integrity, which simultaneously blurs and reemphasizes the race and class boundaries between author and object. In *Form and History in American Literary Naturalism,* June Howard writes, "Defining the Other demarcates the boundary of the self and asserts power and privilege—but even better, portraying proletarianism could, quite literally, enable the naturalist to avoid it" (140). Although naturalist writers embrace brutality as a thematic concern, they conspicuously profit from their representations of it. The line that defines the boundary of "self" and "Other," however, remains elusive. Howard points out that the formal discontinuities and disruptions in naturalist texts reveal the tensions between warring "antinomies" of brute and spectator. I would suggest, however, that these tensions are far from hidden within the form of these novels; rather, they occupy a prominent role in the very conception of these texts. Although earlier definitions of authorship retained the genteel and dispassionate perspective of an artist who maintains a respectable distance from his subject, naturalism calls for seemingly incompatible viewpoints. On the one hand, the author adopts the attitude of a Kiplingesque man of action and, on the other, that of an impartial social scientist. The naturalist writer must simultaneously occupy a space inside *and* outside the ring—a difficult trick indeed. This tension between the roles of observer and participant informs the self-definition of the author and the emergence of an aesthetic program that is both unique to the naturalist movement of the late nineteenth century and significant within the larger context of American literary history. These contradictory impulses derive, in large part, from the paradoxical categories of race and nation that prevailed during the late nineteenth century. Anglo-Saxon males imagined themselves besieged by social forces beyond their control and sought a reconciliation of the primitive and the civilized in literature, as in sport. Naturalist fiction thus reflects the difficult balancing act required of an art that defined itself as "artless." Furthermore, it is through the discourse of gender that the aesthetic sensibility peculiar to literary naturalism emerges.

American naturalist writers saw themselves in direct opposition to the "artists"—both British and American—whose aesthetic principles helped define the "mauve decade" of the 1890s, and this opposition found expression in overtly masculinist discourse. The competing forces of effete aestheticism and masculinist ideology are perhaps most memorably personified in the confrontation between the most outspoken—and famous—literary aesthete, Oscar Wilde, and John Sholto Douglas, the ninth Marquess of Queensberry. Queensberry's son, Lord Alfred Douglas, gained notoriety as the object of Wilde's affection while a student at Oxford, and the scandal that ensued over the relationship between the famous author and the young aristocrat culminated with the legal battles that led to Wilde's conviction on charges of indecency and sodomy. Infuriated at his son's involvement with Wilde, Queensberry left his calling card at the writer's club with the words "To Oscar Wilde posing Somdomite [sic]," an act that prompted Wilde to initiate a libel suit against the Marquess. The suit failed, and the court's conclusion that Queensberry's accusation against Wilde was, in fact, true triggered the fateful criminal trial against Wilde himself. Although Queensberry gained some celebrity for his pivotal role in the downfall of Wilde and what newspapers called "the aesthetic cult, in its nasty form,"[1] his name is most often cited as the patron of the famous "Marquess of Queensberry rules," which revolutionized the sport of boxing by introducing timed rounds, weight classifications, and standards of scoring. He was himself a pugilist of some renown and the very embodiment of a nineteenth-century British "sportsman"—an aristocrat who combined an allegiance to the elite sensibility of his own class with a penchant for gambling, drinking, womanizing, and an emulation of the ruthlessness and violence associated with the working class. "The impression that has been given of Queensberry," writes Wilde biographer Richard Ellmann, "is that he was a simple brute. In fact he was a complex one. Insofar as he was brutal, he practiced a rule-bound brutality" (387). Just as Queensberry's rules imposed a sense of order on the seeming chaos and atavism of prizefighting, often referred to as the "manly art," so does the notion of masculinity that he represents walk a fine line between the constraints of "civilization" and the animalistic urges that define male desire.

Naturalist writers' interest in the "rule-bound brutality" of sporting culture was not purely metaphorical. In his essay "The True Reward of the Novelist," Norris extols the role that boxers play in American society and expresses his wish for an equally assertive, manly form of literature. For Norris, racial and artistic destiny are intertwined with the masculine impulse embodied not only by the spectacle occurring within the confines of the boxing ring but also by the particular male bodies involved. Norris writes, "We are all Anglo-Saxons enough to enjoy the sight of a fight, would go a block or two out of the way to see one, or be a dollar or so out of pocket. But let it not be these jointed manikins worked with a thread. At least let it be Mr. Robert Fitzsimmons or Mr. James Jeffries" (*Criticism* 85). That Norris should connect working-class Irish Americans such as Fitzsimmons and Jeffries with an ideology of Anglo-Saxon destiny reveals the extent to which sports, in general, and boxing, in particular, helped assimilate select immigrant groups into American culture, partly through contrast with those excluded by race—most commonly African Americans—from participation in these unifying rituals. In many ways, the boxing ring served as the proving ground for national identity.

Also relevant is Norris's emphasis on the sport of boxing as a money-making spectacle. As Christian Messenger notes in *Sport and the Spirit of Play in American Fiction*, "The decades between 1850 and 1890 produced perhaps the most far-reaching changes in American sport, moving from the days of little organization, scant codifying of rules, and a limited communication and transportation network to the time when boxing, baseball, and college football became American popular obsessions as spectatorial pastimes" (83). The transformation of sport from participatory exercise into popular entertainment coincides dramatically with the rise of professionalism in all fields and with the ongoing "crisis in masculinity" that preoccupied American society during this era. According to historian Stephen Riess, "The rising middle-class interest in sport reflected a desire by workers in sedentary jobs to demonstrate physical prowess and manliness and to gain recognition which bureaucratic occupations did not always supply" (*City Games* 61). In this context, the emergence of professional spectator sports in the United States provides important insight into the ways in which naturalist texts employ and adapt the masculinist ethos of the Progressive Era in the shaping of an aesthetic strategy that continues to influence the concept of the writer in American culture. With its interwoven notions of manliness, professionalism, national identity, and spectacle, the sporting culture of the late nineteenth century reflects and illuminates the formal characteristics of American literary naturalism. In order to understand the relevance of this sporting culture, one must first consider the metamorphosis of sport from amateur pastime to commercial enterprise in the period following the Civil War—a metamorphosis that paralleled a radical redefinition of manhood.

Critics have suggested that several factors contributed to the perceived crisis in American masculinity at the end of the nineteenth century. As economically secure Anglo-American males settled into white-collar jobs, far removed from the physical rigor of farming and frontier life, they felt their authority challenged, not only by the bureaucratization of the workplace but also by those gains made by women in the labor marketplace and by the burgeoning numbers of immigrant workers whose presence in blue-collar positions and in the emerging labor unions highlighted the sedentary, refined—and therefore, unmasculine—nature of most middle-class jobs. Anxieties over these perceived threats would inform the complex, and often contradictory, ideas about manhood that emerged in the 1890s.

E. Anthony Rotundo suggests the development of nineteenth century American masculinity in three broad phases. Out of the Puritan tradition in New England came an early "communal manhood," which emphasized a man's duty to his community and assumed that men, as the more reasonable sex, should guide and preserve the well-being of women, children, and others unable to provide for themselves. With the rise of republicanism, a market economy, and more diverse population, the ideal of "self-made manhood" began to dominate the American consciousness, marked by the independence, ambition, and aggression necessary for survival in a competitive environment. This period in American culture perceived women as more virtuous and therefore essential to restrain the exuberant individualism of self-made men. By the end of the nineteenth century, however, the more aggressive tendencies of manhood gained in value, with an even greater emphasis on physical strength and virility. Rotundo claims that "this new *passionate manhood* was in some respects an elaboration of existing beliefs about self-made manhood, but it stretched those beliefs in directions that would have shocked the old individualists of the early 1800s" (5). The era of "passionate manhood" no longer required the gentle guidance of feminine virtue, but rather called for aggression, ambition, and brutality—a celebration of the primitive to combat the various "feminizing" forces of an increasingly technical and bureaucratized society. It became increasingly important, in fact, to redefine the triumphs of an ordered society as essentially manly acts.

No one better demonstrates the unique and paradoxical definition of late nineteenth-century masculinity than Theodore Roosevelt, who transformed his public image from that of an asthmatic, privileged Easterner into the epitome of the rough-hewn Western entrepreneur. As a political figure, Roosevelt managed to institute the progressive reforms necessary for the successful growth of the American economy by differentiating these refinements from the feminine qualities heretofore associated with a civilized culture. According to Joe L. Dubbert, "Roosevelt was seen as the kind of virile male who was rescuing America from corruption without effeminizing American institutions in the process" (*A Man's Place* 131). The pursuit of mere money was vastly inferior to the adherence to a manly code of conduct, and Roosevelt likened the sort of "cheating" perpetuated by trusts and influence-peddlers to dishonorable actions on the playing field. This link between "playing by the rules" and masculinity helped bring the concept of civilization out of the domestic sphere dominated by women and into the manly realm of business, combat, and sport. In a sense, the progressivism espoused by Roosevelt involved a sort of "Marquess of Queensberry rules" for society at large, a "rule-bound brutality," not unlike that which Ellmann ascribes to Queensberry himself. The technological innovations and emphasis on "scientific" objectivity that spanned all areas of American life also played a significant role in the development of sports as organized, regulated, and profitable entities. The Progressive political reforms articulated and implemented at the turn of the century mirrored the growing institutionalizing of athletics, and both trends placed tremendous emphasis on the masculine impulse as their source.

Gail Bederman points out the essential links between the late nineteenth-century concept of civilization, the evolving definition of masculinity and the notion of race. "In a variety of ways," writes Bederman, "Americans who were trying to reformulate gender explained their ideas about manhood by drawing connections between male power and white supremacy" (20).[2] With the growing faith in medical science, Americans began to concern themselves with heretofore unrecognized "ailments" that afflicted upper- and middle-class white men, including "neurasthenia"—a nervous condition producing mental and physical weakness—and homosexuality, defined not as a behavior but as a sort of deficiency of masculine "force." One of the primary instigators of this theory, George M. Beard, in his book *Sexual Neurasthenia,* published in 1898, writes, "The strong, the phlegmatic, the healthy, the well-balanced temperaments—those who live out-doors and work with the muscle more than the mind—are not tormented with sexual desire to the same degree or in the same way as the hysterical, the sensitive, the nervous—those who live in-doors and use the mind much and the muscle very little" (qtd. in Mrozek 25). Men diagnosed with neurasthenia, including Roosevelt himself, were often prescribed outdoor activity, and Roosevelt's relocation to the Dakota Territory served as his own corrective to the ailments that were linked with inadequate masculinity. In *Manhood in America,* sociologist Michael Kimmel compares the rest cure prescribed to female neurasthenics with the antidote for men and its connection to the frontier ethos: "Riding the range, breathing the fresh country air, and exerting the body and resting the mind were curative for men, and in the two last decades of the century, large numbers of weak and puny city men—like Theodore Roosevelt, Owen Wister, Frederic Remington, and Thomas Eakins—all came west to find a cure for their insufficient manhood" (135). Figuratively, masculinity was expressed as a measurable commodity, held in adequate supply by some men, sorely lacking in others. In an era in which racial purity was altered by the presence of "one drop of blood," so too was gender imbalance defined in quantifiable terms.

With these worries came an obsessive interest in the white male body as a symbol for American civilization. In the late nineteenth century, as Rotundo notes, "The male body moved to the center of men's gender concerns" (222), and the physical prowess that had been seen as the province of the working class began to concern men whose class and occupation had far removed them from the strenuous labor involved in the development of a strong body. As Kimmel argues, "This preoccupation with physicality meant that men's bodies carried a different sort of weight than earlier. The body did not *contain* the man, expressing the man within; now, that body *was* the man" (127). Moral, intellectual, and physical strength became inextricably linked, and sophisticated, cultivated men embraced the primitive as a necessary corrective to their increasingly sedentary lives. Discussing Roosevelt's call for "the strenuous life" and Ernest Thompson Seton's establishment of the Woodcraft movement and the Boy Scouts of America, Mark Seltzer notes that "linking together anxieties about the male natural body and the body of the nation—linking together, that is, body-building and nation-building—Seton's or Roosevelt's programs for the making of men posit not merely that the individual is something that can be made but that the male natural body and national geography are surrogate terms" (149–50). Seeing athletics as part of their institutional mission, the nation's vanguard institutions of higher learning began to incorporate organized sports into their curricula, and the concept of "physical education" swept through such colleges as Harvard, Yale, and the University of Chicago at precisely the moment when other curricular reforms began to take hold as well.[3] Roosevelt and other reformers concerned themselves with the notion of racial suicide, perceiving a connection between the growing physical weakness of the white male and the influx of immigrants, the emergence of the "new woman," falling birth rates in "advanced" nations, and the closing of the western frontier.[4] Psychologists such as G. Stanley Hall saw sports not only as healthy diversions but as activities that reinforced the mental superiority of the Anglo-Saxon male by "rehearsing racial history" on the playing field (qtd. in Dubbert 173). In *The Leisure Ethic: Work and Play in American Literature, 1840–1940,* William Gleason describes the racial presumptions central to the development of the Progressive Era recreation movement: "When the recreation reformers imagined collective civic life in America, for example, many of them pictured an Anglo-Saxon nation nurtured on Anglo-Saxon team games" (17). In such an environment, there might occur the paradoxical elevation of uneducated, working-class professional athletes to the role of saviors of the "civilized" white race.

Central to the changes in American society at century's end is the emergence of so-called consumer culture; as the economy grew and diversified, so did the variety of products and entertainments for an increasingly urban, financially secure middle class. Like any other leisure commodity, sport flourished in the emerging marketplace of mass entertainment. Dubbert writes,

> The crucial question that aroused a storm of controversy well into the twentieth century was whether the physical-education movement in colleges and high schools initiated to promote manly bodies had been subverted into something quite different. What had started out to promote better physical development among young men, especially those in the city, had evolved into a spectator-sports boom by 1900. (176)

This tension between the masculinizing effect of sport on the effete male and the passivity and detachment of the spectator informs an understanding of the paradox of American sporting culture since the 1890s. As upper-class males emulated the physicality of the working class, they simultaneously sought to distance themselves from the undesirable characteristics of that identity. The act of appropriation, of "playing" primitive, helped to define and demarcate class distinctions, even as the spread of sports as entertainment extended across lines of class and ethnicity. Thorstein Veblen, a consistent critic of the spectator sports boom, discusses the importance of organized athletics among the so-called leisure class: "Addiction to athletic sports, not only in the way of direct participation, but also in the way of sentiment and moral support, is, in a more or less pronounced degree, a characteristic of the leisure class; and it is a trait which that class shares with the lower-class delinquents, and with such atavistic elements throughout the body of the community as are endowed with a dominant predacious trend" (272). For Veblen, the spread of athletic competition recapitulates the predatory nature of capitalism, and its appeal among the upper classes, as well as within the popular culture, serves as confirmation of its importance to the ideology that maintains economic inequalities within society. At the end of the nineteenth century, three sports in particular—boxing, football, and baseball—emerged as the dominant preoccupations of the American popular imagination, and the changes in these emerging pastimes resonate in the artistic sensibility of such admirers of sport as Crane, Norris, and London.

The sport of boxing underwent extraordinary upheaval in the final decades of the nineteenth century. From its origins in the British tradition of bare-knuckle prizefighting, boxing emerged, along with baseball and football, as an organized and regulated spectacle, with the widespread adoption of Queensberry's rules and the staging of fights under the auspices of respectable athletic clubs. Until the 1890s, prizefighters had operated as independent contractors, challenging opponents and agreeing to terms for their (usually illegal) bouts on a per-fight basis and competing before tiny crowds, often in publicly undisclosed locations, with contests fought entirely for the benefit of well-heeled gambling interests. With the adoption of gloves and uniform rounds, the disreputable sport of prizefighting became legitimate, respectable, and hugely popular. Elliot Gorn, in his study of prizefighting in America, documents the role played by the adoption of Queensberry rules in American boxing and by the rise of the last bare-knuckle champion, John L. Sullivan. "The Queensberry rules," writes Gorn, "redrew the arbitrary yet essential border separating acceptable deviance from unpardonable vice; they sanitized prize fighting just enough to make it a legal spectator sport, yet not so much that gentlemen at ringside would lose the taste of 'real life'" (223). Indeed, the most obvious manifestation of Queensberry rules, the wearing of padded leather gloves, demonstrates the paradoxical effect of the emerging respectability of boxing. Although padded gloves greatly diminished the amount of blood spilled during a fight, particularly from bruised and beaten hands, they allowed the fighters to hit opponents with much greater force, resulting in frequent internal and brain injuries. To spectators, boxing appeared more "civilized," but its effects were often more brutal.

The ascent of Sullivan exemplified and, to some degree, *enabled* the growing popular acceptance of boxing in the final decades of the nineteenth century. Like many successful prizefighters before him, Sullivan was an Irish American whose family formed part of the massive wave of immigration from Ireland and Eastern Europe during the nineteenth century. The illicit sport of prizefighting had thrived in the emerging urban landscape of saloons and tenements, and as concerns for the feminization of American culture arose during the 1880s, the stage was set for prizefighting's shift from the backrooms of saloons to a more public arena. One of the dominant centers of pugilism in this period, New Orleans, played host to the two final bouts of Sullivan's storied career, and a comparison of these events illustrates the shifting nature of the sport in the 1890s. Sullivan's 1889 bare-knuckle heavyweight title defense against Jake Kilrain took place on private land in the village of Richburg, Mississippi, before an audience of nearly 2,000 "sports" from across the United States, brought to the remote site by chartered railroad cars from New Orleans.[5] The bout was technically illegal under Mississippi and Louisiana laws, and its exact location remained a closely guarded secret from all but a few organizers. Reports of its preparation and scheduling, carried by newspapers nationwide for months before the event, were publicly denounced by the governors of both states, who threatened criminal prosecution for all organizers and participants.[6] Sullivan's victory after seventy-five rounds and more than two hours was reported with varying amounts of excitement and opprobrium by newspapers throughout the nation. Having violated Mississippi law, Sullivan, Kilrain, and the fight's sponsors were later indicted, but all were either acquitted, fined, or convicted of minor offenses. Mississippi's governor, Isenberg observes in *John L. Sullivan and His America*, "was face to face with the imperatives of the cult of masculinity" (278). Ultimately, the legislative obstacles to prizefighting proved unenforceable.

After his defeat of Kilrain, Sullivan starred in a theatrical melodrama, went on an extended overseas tour, and considered running for the U.S. Congress before entertaining further offers to defend his title. By the time Sullivan agreed to meet the leading contender, Jim Corbett, three years later, the boxing scene had changed dramatically. When Sullivan returned to New Orleans to fight Corbett in 1892, the circumstances differed significantly from those surrounding his last match. In 1890, the New Orleans City Council had legalized gloved boxing, and the city's blue-blooded men's clubs began to officially sponsor professional fights in public arenas.[7] No longer restricted to the "gentlemen of the fancy" and staged for the benefit of gambling interests, the new bouts were openly commercial in nature. By facilitating "the transformation of the ring into something approaching business," Gorn claims, "New Orleans athletic clubs did more than simply attract new talent; they helped systematize boxing" (242). This new system made referees pay employees, established strict weight classifications, and ended the selection of opponents by personal challenge—a remnant of the aristocratic duel. As the first heavyweight championship match under the Queensberry rules, Sullivan vs. Corbett signaled the arrival of boxing as commercial entertainment. Coming in the climactic bout of a three-event "Carnival of Champions," Corbett's dramatic knockout of Sullivan in the twenty-first round brought the bare-knuckle era to a close with a decisive blow.

Sullivan's transformation from working-class sports hero to theatrical star, public figure, and commercial icon occurred within the discourse of masculinity that occupied national attention across class lines during this era. According to Gorn, "Upper-class fascination with prowess was stimulated in part by fears that modern living rendered males intellectually and emotionally impotent; men emphasized the importance of vigor because, rather suddenly, they were terrified of losing it" (187). For the elite members of society, boxers represented manly force in its most basic form. Sullivan became the first mainstream "celebrity" of the sport, not only for the working-class immigrant culture he personified, but for white-collar upper- and middle-class culture at large. He was, argues Isenberg, "the first significant mass cultural hero in American life" (13). That it was a burly Irishman who would facilitate this metamorphosis is no coincidence.[8] The Irish represented, for the Anglo-Saxon elite, a perfect Other—marked by essential differences, primitive, uncivilized, yet at the same time familiar, reflective of certain primal forces long sublimated by the veneer of civilization among the privileged classes.[9] For the Irish immigrants themselves, boxing, and indeed other professional sports, offered an assimilation strategy into mainstream American culture, not only as participants, as in the case of Sullivan himself, who acquired significant wealth and status as a result of his pugilistic prowess, but as spectators, participants in the consumption of leisure and the display of nationalist fervor and pride.[10]

The status of the Irishman as a liminal figure between the racial Other and the dominant Anglo-Saxon highlights the simplified social Darwinism of the late nineteenth century, in which Anglo-Saxons figured as the pinnacle of human evolution. If, as racialist theories of the time maintained, Africans, Native Americans, and Asians were clearly inferior, subject to the domination of "civilized" whites, then those immigrants from Eastern Europe, the Mediterranean, and Ireland occupied a transitional evolutionary group who threatened to assimilate in ways not possible for those with more pronounced racial differences. The Irish, in particular, with their presumed animalistic behavior and crude customs, served as atavistic versions of middle- and upper-class whites and represented the primal essence lurking beneath Anglo-Saxon civilization. Although looking and sounding like Anglo-Saxons (unlike the multilingual immigrants from the European continent), the Irish ultimately possessed essential differences—of temperament, culture, and social status—which marked them as "other" within the dominant culture. Crane and Norris both rely heavily on popular understanding of this role for the Irish in their fictional explorations of brutality and degeneration.

In *Maggie: A Girl of the Streets*, the horror and depravity of Maggie Johnson's life in the slums of New York's Bowery remains at a distance from the reader, not only as a result of Crane's pervasive irony, but also because Maggie, her family, and her neighbors are Irish immigrants whose lives serve as cautionary reminders of the "*other* half" documented in Jacob Riis's widely read study *How the Other Half Lives*.[11] Although their notions of themselves mimic, in inept fashion, the superficiality and emptiness of middle-class virtues, their distance from the lives of Crane's readership allows Crane to illustrate the baseness of their values.[12] Similarly, Norris's *McTeague* relies on assumptions about Irish Americans to document the decline of a simple-minded dentist from the margins of respectability to brutality and squalor. Norris based his novel on a real murder case in San Francisco, the newspaper accounts of which emphasized the brutishness of the Irish killer.[13] Although McTeague himself is clearly identified as Other, he is just as clearly less foreign than Trina and her Swiss family; the hysterical Mexican charwoman Maria Macapa; the greedy, miserly Jew Zerkow; and the other exaggerated ethnic types that inhabit San Francisco's Polk Street. He is, after all, a forty-niner's son, a real Westerner, but his genetic background betrays him, as what were once minor vices—his drinking, his clumsiness, and his temper—transform McTeague into a murderous beast. For Crane and Norris, Irish characters function as funhouse mirrors for Anglo-Saxon civilization—at once revealing the potential for degeneration and yet remaining very much apart from the society they reflect.

In both style and content, Norris's description of McTeague's character shows the influence of contemporary social science, particularly the "positivist" school of criminal anthropology, led by Cesare Lombroso. Lombroso and his disciples believed in the identification, through empirical data, of "born criminals" whose ancestry and physical traits foretell the proclivity toward violent or antisocial behavior. Such ideas had gained widespread acceptance by the end of the nineteenth century and shaped a series of reforms in the American penal system, including parole and indeterminate sentencing, policies that relied on the distinction between born criminals and offenders who might be rehabilitated.[14] Evidence suggests that Norris's own understanding of Lombroso's ideas came from his exposure to Max Nordau's widely read book *Degeneration,* and his interest in the various "scientific" fields of evolutionary thought stemmed largely from his enthusiastic attendance in Professor Joseph LeConte's lectures in zoology and geology at the University of California. The subject matter and plots of "Lauth" and "A Case for Lombroso" make clear Norris's acceptance of the prevailing wisdom among criminal anthropologists.[15]

Beyond an enthusiastic, if limited, academic interest in social science is his writing style itself, which uneasily combines the cold, imperious language of contemporary sociology and anthropology with sensationalism and melodrama. In Norris's early novels, as William Dillingham notes in "Frank Norris and the Genteel Tradition," "His tone is a blend either of humor and contempt or of aloofness and condescension" (111). The narrative voice of *McTeague,* like that of Crane's *Maggie,* cultivates a fierce ironic detachment from the characters, in Norris's case through clinical, scientific language borrowed from contemporary anthropology. Introducing McTeague, for instance, Norris notes, "His head was square-cut, angular; the jaw salient, like that of the carnivora."[16] Many critics have identified as Norris's primary narrative technique the methodical accumulation of details, presented as objective documentary evidence for the fictional developments.[17] Simultaneously, however, Norris often undermines the narrator's role as objective observer. He indulges in subjective judgments, repeatedly describing the meager intellect of his protagonist, a "poor crude dentist of Polk Street, stupid, ignorant, vulgar, with his sham education and plebeian tastes" (282). Norris also reiterates the sensational rhetoric of contemporary journalism, such as the accounts of Patrick Collins's case, upon which Norris based the plot of his novel. When depicting McTeague's murder of Trina, however, Norris's penchant for documentary detail yields to more genteel standards. McTeague lunges at Trina with "his enormous fists, clenched till the knuckles whitened, raised in the air." "Then," the narrator declares, as though in hushed tones, "it became abominable" (525). This tension between objective observer and bitter moralist typifies the dialectic present in Norris's work, and within naturalist discourse. On one hand, the narrator represents the detached scientist of Zola's "experimental novel"—on the other, an outraged spectator, appalled by the degeneration and atavism of the characters. In both cases, however, the author remains an outsider, necessarily connected to the text, yet distinctly apart from it, separated by barriers of class, race, and—by inference—gender, as the formidable masculinity of characters such as McTeague remains an essential component of their identity.

Closely connected with the destructive or degenerative tendencies lurking beneath the surface of apparently civilized men is the equally formidable force of masculine sexuality. Crane and Norris both suggest that the appearance of sexual desire in a man inevitably awakens a violent beast, which, left unchecked, may completely dominate his personality. Certainly this is the case with McTeague, who, although physically powerful, remains morally and intellectually too weak to halt his slide into total atavistic abandon. It is Trina's physical allure that first inflames McTeague's animalistic proclivities. While Trina lies in the operating chair in his ramshackle "Dental Parlor," "unconscious and helpless and very pretty," McTeague struggles to subdue "the sudden panther leap of the animal, lips drawn, fangs aflash, hideous, monstrous, not to be resisted" that his sexual desire has aroused (27–28). As his dentistry career unravels and his ties with the semirespectable denizens of Polk Street disintegrate, McTeague becomes less and less able to control the animal within. His passion for Trina turns to violence, and he gains satisfaction not from a healthy sexuality, but from gnawing on Trina's fingers, "crunching and grinding them with his immense teeth" (239). McTeague's murder of his wife serves as the irrevocable culmination of his increasing brutality.

Although the simple, lowly McTeague serves as a stark example by Norris of the degeneration brought forth by unchecked masculine sexuality, such tendencies are not restricted to those marked by such ethnic and class differences from the Anglo-Saxon "norm" as defined by the dominant culture. In his novel *Vandover and the Brute,* Norris presents a similar descent into animalistic abandon, this time afflicting a gifted painter of his own class. A more potent combination of factors than those affecting McTeague prevent Vandover from halting his slide into degeneracy, but his brutal, uncontrollable carnality represents, for Norris, an unfortunate overextension of normal masculine sexual desire—which is always beastlike in even the most benign circumstances. The ideal heroic figure, therefore, is a man who can negotiate between the extremes of primitive and civilized behaviors. This negotiation may result from the initiation of an educated, feminized man into a violent hypermasculine world, such as Humphrey Van Weyden's rough education at the hands of Wolf Larsen in London's *The Sea-Wolf,* or it may involve the softening of a coarse bachelor by a strong-willed woman, as is the case with Buck Annixter in Norris's *The Octopus* or with Condy Rivers in Norris's autobiographical novel, *Blix.* In each case, the heroic figure is invariably an educated, upper-class Anglo-Saxon, who may adopt the manners and mores of working-class men, but who ultimately stands quite apart from them.

Norris's fascination with the force of human sexuality and its consequences extends to the other characters in *McTeague,* significantly subtitled "A Story of San Francisco." The book focuses considerable attention on the other figures that populate McTeague's neighborhood, carefully describing the habits and characteristics of "one of those cross streets peculiar to Western cities" (265) and the eccentric residents of McTeague's "flat." In "Among Cliff Dwellers," a brief sketch published in the *Wave* in 1897, Norris, in like fashion, describes the "queer, extraordinary mingling of peoples" living on San Francisco's Telegraph Hill (*Complete Edition* 9: 98). With its title suggesting contemporary anthropological studies of primitive societies, the article is part sociological treatise, part wide-eyed travelogue, and demonstrates Norris's interest in miscegenation, a topic of great interest to Joseph LeConte and other evolutionary theorists. LeConte believed that "judicious crossing" within what he called "primary races" would produce successful and desirable offspring.[18] Widespread intermixing between distinct racial groups, however, produced weaker hybrids that were often sterile; thus, unchecked miscegenation would lead inexorably to the destruction of those races involved. Norris's study of Telegraph Hill, in which racial hybridity forms the central theme, illustrates the effect of these theories. Norris describes with wonder children "of an origin so composite that not even the college of heralds could straighten the tangle" (98). Among the "queerer combinations," Norris writes with particular amazement of one in particular:

I have heard of—may I yet live to see him!—a man who washes glasses in a Portuguese wine shop on the other side of the hill, whose father was a Negro and whose mother a Chinese slave girl. As I say, I have not yet set eyes on this particular Cliff Dweller. I can form no guess as to what his appearance should be. Can you? Imagine the Mongolian and African types merged into one. He should have the flat nose, and yet the almond eye; the thick lip, and yet the high cheek bone; but how as to his hair? Should it be short and crinkly, or long and straight, or merely wavy? But the ideas of the man, his bias, his prejudices, his conception of things, his thoughts—what a jumble, what an amorphous, formless mist! (98–99)

In this passage Norris reveals not only the linkage between the physical and intellectual characteristics of race, but also the spectacle provided by the "queer" offspring of interracial couplings. Despite his protestations to the contrary, Norris conjures up a variety of visual images to describe the appearance of this wondrous creature and invites the reader to speculate on his equally incongruous psychology behind the "formless mist."

Reiterating the fears of theorists such as LeConte, Norris senses the weakening of Anglo-Saxon dominance not only with the growth of the immigrant population but with the miscegenation that has accompanied immigration. Suggesting the ominous fecundity of the "Cliff Dwellers," Norris claims, "The hill is swarming and boiling with the life of them" (101). He further warns the reader that "a great milling is going on, and a fusing of peoples, and in a few more generations the Celt and the Italian, the Mexican and the Chinaman, the Negro and the Portuguese, and the Levantines and the 'scatter-mouches' will be merged into one type. And a curious type it will be" (101). Like the aboriginal Cliff Dwellers of the American West, to which Norris's title refers, these people represent an evolutionary dead end; their miscegenation is nothing less than a blueprint for extinction. It is no coincidence, in this context, that the sexual unions presented by *McTeague* are fruitless, in both a literal and a figurative sense. The immigrant coupling of McTeague and Trina ends in murder and death, as does the marriage of Zerkow and Maria. McTeague and Trina remain childless, whereas Maria gives birth to "a wretched, sickly child with not even strength enough nor wits enough to cry, . . . a strange hybrid little being" who dies, unnamed, shortly after its birth (431). The only union that does not end in bloodshed is, at best, poignant and pathetic. Old Grannis, the English dog surgeon, and Miss Baker, the elderly spinster, who have lived next door to each other in silence for years, at last begin what Norris refers to as "the long-retarded romance of their commonplace and uneventful lives" (493). Too old to produce offspring, too meek and undistinguished to matter to anyone else, Grannis and Miss Baker, the only Anglo-Saxon characters in the novel, provide a sympathetic romantic subplot that suggests the sad decline of the old order in a turbulent and dangerous age. Standing "in a little Elysium of their own creating," they exit the story walking "hand in hand in a delicious garden where it was always autumn" (493).[19] In the context of the McTeagues' violent demise, the author and reader, along with the old couple, remain on the sidelines as spectators of the real action, a role that paradoxically reinforces cultural fears about crumbling Anglo-Saxon dominance, even as it establishes the power of the audience of paying consumers to control and direct the spectacle before it.

Although the lines separating the spectator from the participant in athletics are primarily defined by class and race, London, in his novel *The Game,* illustrates the complex and inconsistent role of gender in this distinction. The novel is a conventionally melodramatic romance, in which a girl, Genevieve, fails to understand the attraction of the boxing ring for her suitor, Joe. In what is to be the climactic bout of Joe's career, he is killed by a freak accident in the ring, while Genevieve, disguised as a man, watches from a "peep-hole" in the arena. London's interest in the so-called sweet science is not hard to fathom. Indeed, the boxing ring would seem an ideal proving ground for the social Darwinism so prevalent during the Progressive Era and so central to London's literary output. What better example of Spencerian "survival of the fittest" than the spectacle of two men squaring off on an enclosed arena until only one remains standing? But, aside from the compatibility of boxing and naturalist philosophy, the sport provides insight into the *form* that naturalistic fiction takes for London, as well as for his literary contemporaries.

Scott Derrick, in his essay "Making a Heterosexual Man: Gender, Sexuality, and Narrative in the Fiction of Jack London," sees Genevieve's observation of the fight scene as a reversal of the phenomenon described by feminist critics as the "male gaze," in which Joe is "feminized by her scrutiny"—an inversion of gender convention that proves fatal for the man (117). This inverted gaze is not unique to the boxing scene itself. Earlier in the story, London describes Genevieve's admiration of Joe in similar terms: "His words had drawn Genevieve's gaze to his face, and she had pleasured in the clear skin, the clear eyes, the cheek soft and smooth as a girl's" (*Game* 30). London repeatedly compares Joe's and Genevieve's "beauty"—a quality that is virtually synonymous with whiteness.[20] London writes:

> He was twenty, she eighteen, boy and girl, the pair of them, and made for progeny, healthy and normal, with steady blood pounding through their bodies; and wherever they went together, even on Sunday outings across the bay amongst people who did not know him, eyes were continually drawn to them. He matched her girl's beauty with his boy's beauty, her grace with his strength, her delicacy of line and fibre with the harsher vigor and muscle of the male. Frank-faced, fresh-colored, almost ingenuous in expression, eyes blue and wide apart, he drew and held the gaze of more than one woman far above him in the social scale." (79)

Genevieve and Joe are each the object of the other's loving gaze, but they are also, together and separately, on display for the world to see. Their robust Anglo-Saxon sexuality, "healthy and normal" and "made for progeny," draws the scrutiny and approval of their social superiors. The act of looking forms the central theme of the novel, and the spectacle of the romantic couple parallels the spectacle of two men in the ring. Just as his "boy's beauty" draws and holds the gaze of female admirers, Joe's stripped body also captures the attention of the male audience at the boxing match. The ringside audience longs to both inhabit and possess Joe's body, to claim it as its own.

If Genevieve attains the status of a ringside spectator by pretending to be a man, what is the nature of the "normal" spectator-participant relationship as it exists between men? The homoeroticism of this relationship suggests a desire on the part of the spectators to possess the primitive male body, a theme that recurs throughout London's fiction. Unlike conventional notions of the male gaze, however, all the masculine power belongs to the object: well-heeled spectators spend money to consume the spectacle of two men fighting for their amusement, a transaction that complicates the social and economic positions of the audience and the fighter. The fighter's masculinity attracts the audience's gaze, and the "unmanly" status of the spectators ironically inverts the usual subject-object relationship. Although superior by class, or at least by superficial appearance and the size of their pocketbooks, the paying customers willingly submit to the temporary dominance of the brute. What is being exchanged for their entertainment dollar is manliness, transferred to the spectators from those clearly marked, either by class or race, as less civilized. This discomfort that accompanies the role of spectator involves not only the audience gathered to watch Joe's boxing match, but the audience of London's novel as well. The book's narrative depicts the bout through Genevieve's eyes, staring at Joe, disrobed, through a peephole in the dressing room: "She sat alone, with none to see, but her face was burning with shame at sight of the beautiful nakedness of her lover" (*Game* 111). Genevieve observes that "his skin was fair as a woman's, far more satiny, and no rudimentary hair growth marred its white lustre" (113). She is not alone, however, in her admiration for the spectacle of Joe's body: "Cheers and hand-clapping stormed up, and she heard affectionate cries of 'Oh, you, Joe!' Men shouted it at him again and again" (114). Genevieve is disguised as a man because women had no place at a boxing match—not only is their presence unbecoming, but it poses a threat to the exclusively male ritual by making explicit the sexual nature of the interchange. Furthermore, London's novel, by presenting the match from Genevieve's point of view, implicates the reader in this relationship. As she walks, disguised, through the crowd, Genevieve sees reporters from the local papers; Mr. Silverstein, "his weazen features glowing with anticipation"; as well as an obsequious store manager, "austere, side-whiskered, pink and white," who has sold the couple carpeting earlier in the novel (107–08). The reporters, the Jew, and the white-collar merchant are all outsiders looking in, just as Genevieve is—just as author and reader are—at the action in the ring.

The inverted gaze between feminized spectator and masculine object is nowhere more explicitly demonstrated than in London's description of Humphrey Van Weyden's relationship with Wolf Larsen in *The Sea-Wolf*. Van Weyden's desire to possess Larsen's manliness takes the form of a very explicit admiration for Larsen's primitive male body. Consider the following passage:

> I had never before seen him stripped, and the sight of his body quite took my breath away. It has never been my weakness to exalt the flesh—far from it; but there is enough of the artist in me to appreciate its wonder.
>
> I must say that I was fascinated by the perfect lines of Wolf Larsen's figure, and by what I may term the terrible beauty of it. I had noticed the men in the forecastle. Powerfully muscled though some of them were, there had been something wrong with all of them. . . . Oofty-Oofty had been the only one whose lines were at all pleasing, while in so far as they pleased, that far had they been what I should call feminine.
>
> But Wolf Larsen was the man-type, the masculine, and almost a god in his perfectness. As he moved about or raised his arms the great muscles leapt and moved under the satiny skin. . . . His body, thanks to his Scandinavian stock, was fair as the fairest woman's. I remember his putting his hand up to feel of the wound on his head, and my watching the biceps move like a living thing under its white sheath. It was the biceps that had nearly crushed out my life once, that I had seen strike so many killing blows. I could not take my eyes from him. I stood motionless, a roll of antiseptic cotton in my hand unwinding and spilling itself down to the floor.
>
> He noticed me, and I became conscious that I was staring at him. (98–99)

London here distinguishes between the feminized aboriginal body of Oofty-Oofty, an Australian "Kanaka," and Larsen's Scandinavian "man-type"—atavistic, yet appropriately European in origin. With "enough of the artist" in him, Van Weyden finds himself marveling at this specimen before him, a figure that represents in the purest form the primitive masculinity that belongs to his own racial heritage, but which has been long buried beneath the trappings of civilization. The feminization of the artist and the audience, suggested by *The Game,* becomes nearly explicit with the first-person narration of *The Sea-Wolf.* The aesthetic anxieties merely suggested by third-person narratives are here brought to the fore. The obvious discomfort felt by Van Weyden, caught in his paralyzed admiration for the muscular captain, reflects the anxiety of the artist-as-spectator who describes the masculine world of action, yet remains quite separate from it. According to Howard, "The spectator must try out the role of the brute in order to control it" (152). Van Weyden's transcendence of his feminized status occurs only when he emulates Larsen and, in effect, consumes the Scandinavian's atavistic manliness.

As does Norris's *McTeague,* London's fiction highlights the connection between sexuality and violence, and the homoerotics of Van Weyden's relationship to Larsen occur in the context of the imminent threat of physical injury. The thought of the "killing blows" administered by Larsen's muscular arms invites Van Weyden's devoted gaze. Violence is also an integral part of Joe's attraction to Genevieve in *The Game:*

> Nor did Joe escape the prick of curious desires, chiefest among which, perhaps was the desire to hurt Genevieve. When, after long and tortuous degrees, he had achieved the bliss of putting his arm around her waist, he felt spasmodic impulses to make the embrace crushing, till she should cry out with the hurt. It was not his nature to wish to hurt any living thing. Even in the ring, to hurt was never the intention of any blow he struck. In such case he played the Game, and the goal of the Game was to down an antagonist and keep that antagonist down for a space of ten seconds. So he never struck merely to hurt; the hurt was incidental to the end, and the end was quite another matter. And yet here, with this girl he loved, came the desire to hurt. . . . He could not understand, and felt that he was discovering depths of brutality in his nature of which he had never dreamed. (69–70)

London, like Norris, reflects the widespread understanding of human sexuality as a natural reversion to brutal, animal instincts, analogous to the relationship of hunter to prey. Genevieve, for her part, trembles "with a vague and nameless delight" when Joe accidentally causes her pain with one of his embraces (70). Such is the pattern for "normal" male-female sexuality, the dynamics of which London compares to the action in the boxing ring. The point of a match, after all, is to establish dominance, to withstand painful blows and "down an antagonist," thereby confirming one's superiority as a competitor and as a man.

Along with the increased interest in athletics as entertainment came the phenomenon known as "spectatoritis"—a by-product of spectator sports that produced, in the words of Seton, "flat-chested cigarette smokers with shaky nerves and doubtful vitality" (*Boy Scouts of America* xi). The founder of the Boy Scouts of America, Seton worked tirelessly to counteract what he understood to be the debilitating feminization of young men, capitalizing on long-standing American anti-intellectualism, as well as fears of racial degeneration. Metaphorically linked with such "diseases" as neurasthenia and homosexuality, "spectatoritis" resulted from the act of gawking at the sight of almost naked working-class men engaged in mortal combat. Upper- and middle-class members of the sporting audience, therefore, felt driven to combat the uneasy suggestion of feminization in this interchange. The need to participate in the spectacle of organized athletics found its most significant consequence in the rise of football, a sport that, unlike boxing, drew from among the upper classes for its participants.

Indeed, no phenomenon better demonstrates the appropriation of primitive masculinity by upper-class males at the turn of the century than does the emergent popularity of intercollegiate football. By the 1890s, the other major spectator sports of the time, boxing and baseball, had become large-scale commercial enterprises performed by professionals—primarily working-class and immigrant men for whom athletics provided an escape from the urban ghetto or the coal mine. Early heroes of professional sports were largely sons of immigrants, either Irish (e.g., heavyweight boxing champions John L. Sullivan and Jim Corbett and early baseball stars "King" Kelly and John McGraw) or German (e.g., later baseball legends Honus Wagner and Babe Ruth). The most popular football games, however, were played by undergraduates of the nation's elite colleges—young men of education and privilege. Whereas boxing had developed with upper-class "gentlemen of the fancy" observing and wagering on the exploits of working-class men, occasionally donning gloves for a few rounds of sparring, the participatory impulse in football resulted in the complete immersion of the upper-class male in the spectacle itself. Riess, in his book *City Games: The Evolution of American Urban Society and the Rise of Sports*, emphasizes the role that football played in shaping a generation of privileged young men: "Football, more than any other intercollegiate sport, fit in with the needs of upper- and upper-middle-class urban youth at a time when America was ripe for a violent and virile sport that stood for honorable values in stark contrast to the corruption, greed, and materialism of the Gilded Age" (55–56). It is significant that the essential character of intercollegiate football depended on its difference from "professional" athletics, such as the patently commercial realm of prizefighting.[21]

The increasingly visible stage of the gridiron allowed for public display of upper-class manliness without the taint of vulgar commercialism. The evolution of professional journalism and the changing coverage of sporting events in major newspapers at the end of the nineteenth century made possible this increased attention on intercollegiate football. The period after the Civil War had seen the rise of a number of journals devoted exclusively to the sporting subculture that had developed in large cities. Journals such as the *New York Clipper* and the *Police Gazette* helped spread the visibility and allure of athletics as popular entertainment, and by the 1890s, daily newspapers created the "sports page," thereby further legitimizing sport as a suitable subject for journalistic treatment.[22] Taking part in this process were Crane and Norris, whose journalistic work included articles on football.[23] Norris, whom Christian Messenger identifies as an "early popularizer of the social philosophy of American college sport" (146), wrote a regular column on football for the *Wave* in 1896, reporting on the University of California and Stanford teams, as well as those of local amateur clubs.[24] In the same year, Crane wrote an article for the New York *Journal* on the hugely popular football game between Harvard University and the Carlisle Indians.

The football team of the American Indian School in Carlisle, Pennsylvania, offers one of the more remarkable examples of the curious impulses driving Americans' fascination with football, and Crane's article crystallizes several issues central to the phenomenon. Michael Oriard, in *Reading Football*, a study of the relationship between the popular press and the growth of early intercollegiate football, remarks upon the bizarre juxtaposition in newspaper reports between the photographs of partially or totally nude Indians and the relatively restrained prose describing the game. The *Journal's* depiction explicitly emphasizes the connection between the Indians' physiognomy and their credibility as a worthy gridiron opponent. Eventually, writes Oriard of the rivalry, "the novelty wore off, and Carlisle left the warpath to become more simply a football team" (243). During this period, however, the reporting on Carlisle's talented team consistently focused on the primitive character of the Indians and their ability to translate their innate racial characteristics into success on the field of play. According to Oriard, "Crane's account was not racist but racialist: a narrative of attempted Indian revenge for 'four centuries of oppression and humiliation'" (239). "How old Geronimo would have enjoyed it!" Crane exclaims. "The point of view of the warriors was terse but plain: 'They have stolen a continent from us. . . . Let us, then, brother, be revenged'" (*Works* 8: 669). Describing the "aborigines" as "impassive" foes who "were like children, mightily well-behaved and docile children" before the game, Crane remarks on the obstinacy and effectiveness of the Indians' "systematic and rather primitive mass playing" (*Works* 8: 671). After withstanding the "savage charges" of the Carlisle team, however, "The Harvard men played like fiends" and duplicated the narrative of Western conquest on the football field (*Works* 8: 671–72). Crane's words, combined with the images of the Indians' manly physiques, serve to highlight the connection between athletic prowess, manliness, and racial survival. Although white men would normally seek to distinguish themselves from racial Others in most situations, the football field provided a setting in which the masculine representatives of each race could—in fact, should—meet on equal terms. Not only were Harvard's men cultured and sophisticated off the field, they could, when necessary, stand toe to toe with the most cunning and powerful "savages." In the context of the discourse surrounding games and "play," white men could successfully appropriate those primitive characteristics of the Carlisle Indians deemed necessary for racial survival. In this sense, football amounted to a sort of minstrel performance, in which college teams embraced a ritualized form of savagery for both the entertainment of leisure-hungry audiences and the restoration of the crucial atavistic essence of the Anglo-Saxon race.[25]

If the emergence of intercollegiate football reflected the need for young men of education and privilege to emulate the homosocial physicality personified by men of another class—or race—even while maintaining a clear distance from these manly Others, it also required a careful negotiation of the boundary between the homosocial and the homosexual.[26] Indeed, the glorification of the male body so central to the definition of masculinity during this period often ventured into the realm of the homoerotic (as it does in the previous passage from London's *Sea-Wolf*).[27] Sporting discourse sublimated the sexual component of the homosocial by simultaneously emphasizing the warlike violence of sport and its relationship to the games of young boys. The interplay of these elements certainly informs Crane's fiction. His famous insistence on his knowledge of football as the source for the "realistic" depictions of battle scenes in *The Red Badge of Courage*, for instance, would be an acceptable premise for Crane's contemporaries.[28] The rhetoric employed by coaches such as Yale's legendary Walter Camp and the value placed by Roosevelt on athletics as one of the key components of "the strenuous life" made explicit the connection between military effectiveness and training on the football field. Indeed, during the 1890s, the branches of the U.S. armed forces, like the vanguard universities, installed athletics and exercise as formal components of a soldier's training.[29] Simultaneously, sports were touted as promoting a youthful spirit of play that counteracted the increasingly refined and sedentary comforts of domesticity.

Crane, particularly in his collection of Whilomville stories, invokes the connection between the play of children and the violence of war. "His New Mittens," for example, opens with a scene in which a group of boys "snowballing gleefully in a field" declare to a young playmate, "We're having a battle" (*Works* 3: 83). The boys, taking the parts of "soldiers" and "Indians," enact an "altercation" of grand proportions, in which "it was proper for the soldiers always to thrash the Indians" (*Works* 3: 85). Crane's irony captures both the delusions of grandeur essential to young boys' games and the predominant narrative by which the stronger boys affirm their power over their weaker "comrades." When the smaller boys tire of being pelted with snow and refuse to play Indians, one "formidable lad" shouts, "Well, alright then. I'll be an Indian myself," and all the others quickly change sides, until there are no soldiers left (*Works* 3: 85). Soon enough, however, the stronger boys reassert their status as soldiers and administer a proper thrashing to the "real" Indians. As with the Carlisle-Harvard football games, the temporary appearance of equality belies the true narrative of conquest and domination that must eventually take precedence.

For Crane, the homosocial world of battle and comradeship is always in direct conflict with the "civilized" world of the home and the mother. The snowball battle in Crane's story occurs within the context of a boy's struggle between his mother's concern for a new pair of mittens and his companions' taunting at his unwillingness to join the battle. The episode, with its clear racial distinctions, provides striking parallels with Joseph Kett's discussion of the emergence of the "playground movement" in the Progressive Era under the forceful leadership of Joseph Lee, who was "not only an aristocrat, but also an uncompromising racist, convinced that weaker races were straining the purity of the Anglo-Saxon strain" (226). For Lee, Kett writes, "play was neither a preparation for life nor a release from work, but life itself; all work should be so suffused by play instincts that any distinctions between work and play would become purely verbal. The trouble was that modern conditions frustrated play instincts, not because boys had no place to play but because a bureaucratic and specialized society run by experts provided few outlets for instinctive drives" (225).

The tension between a mother's domesticity and the "manly" world of instinct is as real to the young protagonist of this story as it is to Henry Fleming in *The Red Badge of Courage,* who ignores his mother's worries and enlists with the Union army. In fact, the "dangers" posed by an overly strong relationship between mother and son contributed to the perceived feminization of middle- and upper-class men and led to the creation of boys' clubs in the military/chivalric mold throughout the United States at the turn of the century, a phenomenon that culminated in the establishment of the Boy Scouts of America in 1910. An emphasis on militarism and chivalry for young boys' organizations not only reinforced "male superordination in gender relations," as Jeffery Hantover notes in the essay "The Boy Scouts and the Validation of Masculinity," but also underlined the allegiance of American manhood to a notion of Anglo-Saxon tradition and destiny.[30]

The cult of amateurism that enveloped the reporting on intercollegiate football stands in stark contrast to the growing professionalism in other areas, including journalism and the organization of athletics. Coaches such as Walter Camp at Yale and Amos Alonzo Stagg at the University of Chicago oversaw the introduction of a myriad of rules governing the sport of football and participated in the regimentation of the game, even as they perpetuated the rhetoric of amateurism.[31] According to Camp, "A gentleman does not sell himself" (qtd. in Ronald A. Smith 66). Unlike football, baseball had been largely a professional enterprise at least since the 1870s, and the trend toward professionalization would continue throughout the Progressive Era. Benjamin Rader is not unique among critics in claiming that "the 1890s may have been the most important decade in baseball history" (*Baseball* 63), with the institution of the National League monopoly in 1892 and the standardization, in 1893, of such fundamental rules as the distance of sixty feet, six inches between the pitcher's mound and home plate. This period also saw the dominance, under the leadership of hard-nosed managers such as the celebrated John McGraw, of the "scientific" or "inside" game, which involved careful calculation of percentages and the innovation of strategies, such as the sacrifice bunt and the hit-and-run, intended to advance base runners methodically. The old days of upper-class participation in the "sporting fraternity" were long past, and the newer players—largely drawn from the community of recent German and Irish immigrants—combined a serious intensity in the ballpark with a reputation for drinking, fighting, and rowdy public display off the field. It is no coincidental irony, however, that collegiate football, a sport dominated by upper-class participants, remained the more brutal contest. In some ways, major league baseball's codification of rules of conduct, both on and off the playing field, arose as a form of social control over the working-class participants who had taken over the game. The middle-class reporters who presented the game to the public served as both custodians for baseball's now-faded gentlemanly image and middlemen for the team owners' product.

Stephen Crane was no stranger to the baseball diamond, and his contributions as a catcher during his years at both Lafayette and Syracuse Universities made him something of an athletic hero for a time, a legacy emphasized, and even exaggerated, by several biographers. "They used to say at Syracuse University," Crane wrote in an 1896 letter, "that I was cut out to be a professional base-ball player. And the truth of the matter is that I went there more to play base-ball than to study" (*Letters* 78). In his biography of Crane, R. W. Stallman repeats the apocryphal story that Crane "declined a post on a major baseball team after deciding to risk his future as a writer" (28–29). Whether or not the physically slight Crane could have succeeded as an athlete is uncertain, but it is not surprising that he should choose a different vocation. As one critic notes, "While middle-class youths were attracted to professional baseball by high salaries, among other factors, the evidence suggests that they were less likely to view the sport as a career" than were working-class and immigrant men (Adelman 180). The life of a sportsman held great attraction for Crane, as it must have for Norris, London, and others, but like the worlds of the Bowery and the battlefield, it was a life from which he would maintain his distance in his role as a writer, who serves as an intermediary between the spectacle and the consumers who read his work. The game of fiction, much like baseball, operated under a set of rules that reflected the anxieties of professionalism, manhood, and national identity. How Crane and his contemporaries negotiated the rules of *this* game would help establish the notion of the naturalist author as a kind of journalistic mediator, rather than an aesthetically sophisticated instigator, of the fictional world of the novel.

Of course, journalism retained an allure not only as a defense against potential accusations of effete artistry, but for practical economic reasons as well. Like Crane, London parlayed his successful career as a novelist into a number of journalistic assignments, and, as with Crane, these assignments included stints as both war correspondent and sports reporter. Of particular relevance to London's interest in race and masculinity are his dispatches concerning the most celebrated prizefight of the era—Jack Johnson's 1910 bout with Jim Jeffries. Like Joe Louis's boxing match with Max Schmeling in 1938, or Jackie Robinson's entry into Major League Baseball in 1947, Johnson's decisive victory over the white former champion, held in Reno, Nevada, on the fourth of July, would have profound consequences throughout American society far beyond its apparent significance within the world of athletic competition.[32] So-called race riots erupted throughout the United States, as mobs of angry white citizens terrorized African Americans in several major cities. The first African American to hold the title of heavyweight champion, Johnson would have occupied a precarious position in the American consciousness under any circumstances, but his brash character, his physical and psychological domination of his opponents, and—perhaps, most importantly—his open fondness for the company of white women only served to compound the anxiety, fear, and rage that his bout with Jeffries produced in white America.[33]

Johnson had won the title in 1908 by defeating an inauspicious Canadian champion named Tommy Burns in a much-publicized and controversial bout held in Australia.[34] Burns was the first boxer to break the unofficial "color line" established by John L. Sullivan, the last bare-knuckle champion, who claimed, in 1892, "I will not fight a negro. I never have and never shall" (qtd. in Gilmore 26). Sullivan's decree, which made explicit a long-standing policy to effectively prohibit black fighters from competing for the heavyweight championship, occurred in the same year that Homer Plessy was denied access to a segregated railroad car in Louisiana—the event that precipitated the infamous *Plessy v. Ferguson* decision of 1896 and the codification of so-called Jim Crow laws in the United States.[35] Sullivan's American successors, James "Gentleman Jim" Corbett, Robert Fitzsimmons, and Jim Jeffries, adhered to a "whites-only" policy in choosing opponents, overlooking several prominent black contenders, most notably the impressive Australian fighter Peter Jackson. Burns's willingness to challenge this convention and fight Jack Johnson has been viewed primarily as a business decision. The absence of strong white contenders and an Australian promoter's guarantee of $30,000 overcame Burns's reluctance to accept the challenge issued by Johnson and his manager, Sam Fitzpatrick (Roberts 56). It is also significant that Burns, a Canadian, fought Johnson in Australia. Although racism figured prominently in boxing within the British commonwealth, a more abstract and aristocratic notion of "fair play" may have mitigated the impulse to maintain racial segregation. Furthermore, Australia was then experiencing a particularly strong wave of xenophobia and racist sentiment, as pessimistic white Australians saw themselves as besieged on all sides by "the darker races." In this context, a defeat of Johnson by Burns would offer white Australians a welcome respite from perceived losses in other arenas, an ideological problem quite unlike that faced by whites in the United States, where challenges to Jim Crow could only weaken the confident partnership of racism and American exceptionalism. Johnson's victory over Burns, although troubling to whites in Australia and throughout the waning British empire, did not carry the same catastrophic impact there that it did for an ascendant white American ideology. Upon hearing of Burns's decision to fight Johnson and allow a black man a chance at the heavyweight crown, Sullivan exclaimed, "Shame on the money-mad Champion! Shame on the man who upsets good American precedents because there are Dollars, Dollars, Dollars in it" (qtd. in Gilmore 27–28). This antinomy of commerce and sportsmanship mirrors the concept of fair play that informed the antitrust economic policies of the Progressive Era. According to Roosevelt and his contemporaries, manly virtue and the rule-bound principles found on the football field and baseball diamond offered a model for the capitalist marketplace that placed national identity, honor, and fairness above mere profits. London, by then at his commercial pinnacle as a novelist, became the first to call for the return of the last "true" white champion in his dispatch for the New York *Herald:* "Jim Jeffries must emerge from his alfalfa farm and remove the golden smile from Jack Johnson's face" (*Jack London Reports* 264). For London and others, Johnson's perceived arrogance, embodied by his "golden smile," proved more troublesome than even his athletic prowess as a symbol of white impotence and black resistance.

After several years of searching for a white contender, the boxing establishment convinced Jeffries, America's "Great White Hope," to return, amid tremendous fanfare and high expectations. A crowd of more than 20,000 gathered in Reno, and a virtual army of reporters filed daily dispatches to a curious nation for weeks before the fight. London, who describes the extensive preparations for the championship match in several installments, joined most of his colleagues in predicting an easy victory for Jeffries. Furthermore, his dispatches helped fan the flames of the national uproar that preceded the Johnson-Jeffries match, claiming, "Viewed from every possible angle, there has never been anything like it in the history of the ring, and there is no chance for anything like it to occur in the future—at least in the lifetime of those alive today" (*Jack London Reports* 285). For London, along with most of his contemporaries, national and racial identities were intricately intertwined, and as David Theo Goldberg notes, "Racist discourse has to be grounded in the relations of bodies to each other, and in ways of seeing (other) bodies" (305). London praises Johnson's "cool brain" and "instinct for a blow that is positive genius," but, he writes, "Against this man will stand Jeffries, an even more remarkable man, a grizzly giant, huge and rugged, of a type we are prone to believe was more common in other days when the world was young" (*Jack London Reports* 265). Reflecting the paradoxical embrace of the primitive that is emblematic of turn-of-the-century white masculinity, London seemingly inverts the more predictable depictions of the "civilized" white man and the "primitive" black man. In the boxing ring, London assumes, the brute can and *should* be the winner. Like Wolf Larsen, Jeffries seemed to possess the primitive essence of Teutonic manhood—a quality that made him unfit for the literary salon, perhaps, but necessary for the maintenance of white civilization.

In his characterization of Johnson before the fight, London attempts to contain the potential dangers of the black boxer through the racial concept of recapitulation, which holds that adults of less developed races share certain qualities with children of more advanced races.[36] London writes, "Under all his large garniture of fighting strength, Johnson is happy-go-lucky in temperament, as light and carefree as a child. He is easily amused. He lives more in the moment, and joy and sorrow are swift passing moods with him" (*Jack London Reports* 266). The threat of Johnson's hypermasculine physicality is mitigated by his childish disposition, and he lacks the necessary brutishness of Jeffries, who is "more a Germanic tribesman and warrior of two thousand years ago than a civilized man of the twentieth century" (267). Here the writer reveals the thorny paradox of Anglo-Saxon racial ideology: How can the "civilized" world celebrate the atavistic essence of manhood while maintaining legal and cultural authority over those "primitive" races that represent atavism itself? "Another thing," London writes, "despite Jeff's primitiveness, he is more disciplined than the other man, vastly more disciplined" (267). In Jeffries, London finds the ideal combination of the primitive and the civilized—a "disciplined" brute who will inevitably defeat the apish Johnson's "cleverness."

In fact, Johnson was, by all accounts, a boxer of extraordinary technical skill—in London's own comparison, a "boxer" to Jeffries's "fighter" (*Jack London Reports* 267). As Gerald Early notes, Johnson's extraordinary technique and his unapologetic attitude had a powerful impact on the future prospects of African American boxers. Not only would black contenders be denied chances at the title for several years, but those who eventually built successful careers often felt it necessary to project a more benign image than Johnson's—both in their role as public figures and in the ring itself. According to Early, "Because Jack Johnson was such a technically accomplished fighter and because of the bitter taste he left on the collective palette of the American male sporting public, black fighters may have found it advantageous to adopt a more clumsy, less schooled appearance of fighting" ("Three Notes" 141).[37] As objects for public consumption, black fighters learned the dangers of being too "clever."

From his role as reporter, London described the extensive preparations for the championship match and, along with nearly all observers, predicted an easy victory for Jeffries. Crowds throughout the country—black and white—gathered in arenas, saloons, and public streets to listen to wire service reports of the match. The fight itself was hardly a contest. After entering the ring to the strains of a popular tune entitled "All Coons Look Alike to Me," Johnson permitted the bout to last until the fifteenth round only so that he might better taunt Jeffries. Johnson reportedly announced, "Package for Mister Jeff," before each bone-crushing blow. When the knockout punch finally, and mercifully, arrived, Jeffries had been utterly humiliated.[38]

A letter to the *New York Times,* reflecting the frantic tone across white America, called the match "A calamity to this country worse than the San Francisco earthquake" (qtd. in Farr 127). Throughout the United States, mobs of angry whites attacked those black citizens who dared celebrate

Johnson's victory, or in some cases any black citizen who dared appear in public at all. Hundreds were injured, and at least eight were killed in the immediate aftermath of the fight.[39] Other, less immediate consequences of the upset included the passage by the U.S. Congress of two notorious pieces of legislation. One, a ban on the interstate transport of boxing films, arose from the widespread fear that footage of Jeffries's defeat would shock and horrify the general public and would incite further civil unrest. The other, known as the "White Slave Traffic Act" and often referred to by the name of its sponsor as the "Mann Act," prohibited the transportation of women across state lines for "immoral purposes" and had been debated with Johnson and his numerous white girlfriends in mind. In his own written response to the bout, London reluctantly admits Johnson's superiority over Jeffries:

> Jeff today disposed of one question. He could not come back. Johnson in turn answered another question. He has not the yellow streak. But he only answered that question for to-day. The ferocity of the hairy-chested caveman and grizzly giant combined did not intimidate the cool-headed negro. . . .
>
> But the question of the yellow streak is not answered for all time. Just as Johnson has never been extended, so has he never shown the yellow streak. Just as a man may rise up, heaven alone knows where, who will extend Johnson, just so may that man bring out the yellow streak, and then again, he may not. So far the burden of proof all rests on the conclusion that Johnson has no yellow streak. (*Jack London Reports* 294–95)

Here, London reiterates a common apprehension directed toward any boxer, but toward Johnson in particular throughout his career—the "yellow streak." Once exposed, this mark of cowardice can never be removed from a boxer's reputation. In the language of the day, the word *yellow* carried with it a number of connotations, primarily negative, and particularly so for London and his ideological comrades. In addition to its usage for "cowardice," the word had long been associated with anti-Asian race baiting (especially in the American West),[40] as well as with aestheticism, notably after the appearance of *The Yellow Book*.[41] Indeed, the term "yellow journalism," applied to the muckraking tactics and inflammatory rhetoric of newspapers, such as William Randolph Hearst's New York *Journal* and Joseph Pulitzer's New

York *World,* had its origins in a widely read comic character, "The Yellow Kid," a waiflike child of slums wearing a yellow nightgown who delivered satirical commentary on the topics of the day, including the highbrow aesthetic pretensions of the upper classes.[42]

In many ways, the phenomenon of commercial prizefighting reinscribes the problematic definition of naturalism described by Zola in "The Experimental Novel," in which representative "types" are allowed to interact in the pages of the text without apparent interference from the author. Like the "observations" that Zola stages in his fiction, a boxing match provides an ideal crucible in which to test the true character of the participants, and the quality in question is neither skill nor strength, but manliness—the lack of a "yellow streak." In his account, London almost obsessively repeats the "question of the yellow streak," as if rephrasing this question will somehow lead to a different answer. The possibility that such a clear and "scientific" contest between these two men should result in such a verdict was, to London, unthinkable. Before his own defeat at the hands of Johnson, Burns confidently had declared, "All coons are yellow" (qtd. in Roberts 53). With his victory over Burns and a succession of undistinguished white challengers, Johnson proved troublesome to accepted notions of white superiority, but with his domination of Jeffries, a proven champion and "hairy-chested caveman" who embodied the atavistic core of late nineteenth-century manhood, Johnson caused deep and irreparable damage to the ideology of masculinity that had developed during the Progressive Era.

Clinging optimistically to his notions of white superiority, London suggests that "a man may rise up" to defeat Johnson and "bring out the yellow streak" (*Jack London Reports* 294). In fact, it is in defeat that a boxer most clearly answers the question. Johnson did eventually lose to Jess Willard in a highly controversial match in 1915, but his defeat was hardly as ignominious as London may have wished. After this fight, in a sort of eulogy for Johnson's career in the ring, another sometime journalist, James Weldon Johnson, revisits the same issue:

> However much we may cultivate the finer sensibilities, however much we may decry the exercise of brute force, still there is something in a great fight and a clean and fearless fighter that stirs every man with red blood in his veins. Johnson fought a great fight. He showed no signs

of the yellow streak, and it must be remembered, too, that it was the fight of one lone black man against the world. (*Selected Writings* 1: 125)

James Weldon Johnson, who gained notoriety as the first African American secretary of the National Association for the Advancement of Colored People (NAACP) and as the author of the novel *The Autobiography of an Ex-Colored Man,* employs rhetoric much like that of London and his Anglo-Saxon compatriots. He not only reiterates London's language—"the yellow streak"—and the concept of the boxing ring as crucible, but he also emphasizes his investment of racial identity in Jack Johnson's *and the spectators'* "red-blooded" masculinity. Of course, the connotations of the word *yellow* for African Americans would include the implication of mixed blood, "red" or otherwise.[43] The presence of "Gentleman Jim" Corbett and John L. Sullivan in Jeffries's corner during the fight served to underscore the perception that Johnson was fighting not just one man, but an entire system that had been entrenched for nearly two decades. The very manhood of his race had been placed squarely on Jack Johnson's broad shoulders. In the context of what W. E. B. Du Bois refers to in *The Souls of Black Folk* as the "manhood rights of the Negro" (35), Johnson's presence and legacy would reverberate strongly.

The obvious disagreement between London and James Weldon Johnson on the racial ideologies and policies of Jim Crow America should not obscure the similarity of the position they occupy. As literary reporters, they serve as intermediaries between the spectators and the spectacle, between the detached, cultivated, "feminized" realm of literature and culture and the brutal, masculine world of the boxing ring. Such is the problematic and unstable posture of the literary naturalist, and the anxiety inherent in this position manifests itself through the figure of the artist within naturalist fiction. The writer seeks a meaningful link to the brutal world inside the ring, even while retaining the privileged perspective of the outsider.

As one of the few African American intellectuals to publicly praise Jack Johnson, James Weldon Johnson claims in a newspaper article that "the white race, in spite of its vaunted civilization, pays more respect to the argument of force than any other race in the world." Thus, he insists, "[Johnson's] pugilistic record is something of a racial asset" (*Selected Writings* 1: 126).[44] Johnson's support for the boxer stands in contrast to the public discomfort expressed by both Du Bois and Booker T. Washington—for quite different reasons—about the rise of such a problematic cultural hero. In his own *real* autobiography, James Weldon Johnson claims that Frederick Douglass kept, on the wall of his study, a picture of Peter Jackson, a renowned black Australian heavyweight who was repeatedly denied a title shot by Sullivan and his successors. Johnson writes, "He used to point to it and say 'Peter is doing a great deal with his fists to solve the Negro question.' I think that Jack, even after the reckoning of his big and little failings has been made, may be said to have done his share" (*Along This Way* 208). Indeed, Douglass's own representation of the "argument of force," his fistfight with the brutal overseer Mr. Covey in the *Narrative of the Life of Frederick Douglass, An American Slave,* provides a powerful, if problematic, template for African American manhood.[45] Johnson's esteem for his namesake's career in the ring and his interest in boxing as a cultural battleground reveal a paradoxical connection with the aesthetic sensibility of race-conscious, white Progressive Era writers and the ideologies of masculinity that permeated American intellectual life at the turn of the century. In the end, the naturalist writer must contend with the questions "Is writing a form of action or not? Does the transformation of 'life' into 'literature' merely recapitulate the passivity of the spectator, or does it, in the hands of the naturalist, break free from the emasculating intimations of 'art?'" These same questions haunt the naturalistic narratives of writers with contradictory interests in the social change at the turn of the century, and James Weldon Johnson's efforts to define and sustain a culture in opposition to the Anglo-Saxon nationalism of Norris and London seem to reiterate, or perhaps recontextualize, their discourse, even as he challenges their cultural authority. Emerging as it does during a particularly volatile period for issues of race and gender in the United States, American literary naturalism simultaneously reflects the cultural tensions of the age and proposes a problematic solution to the dilemma of authorship that would raise as many questions as it allegedly solved.

2 / "Subtle Brotherhood" in Stephen Crane's Tales of Adventure

Alienation, Anxiety, and the Rites of Manhood

We have arranged our life contrary to the moral and the physical nature of man, and we strain all the forces of our mind in order to assure man that this is the true life. Everything which we call culture, our sciences and our arts, these improvements of the comforts of life, are attempts to deceive man's moral, natural needs.

—Leo Tolstoy

If, as Edwin Cady suggests, "the trope basic to Crane's vision was that of the game" (103), then the stories collected in volume 5 of the University of Virginia edition of Stephen Crane's works offer the most comprehensive view of the author's foremost artistic device. The recurrence of games and the rules of sportsmanship throughout these stories helps link them thematically and indicates the importance of turn-of-the-century sporting culture discussed in chapter 1 to Crane's understanding of human nature and artistic expression.[1] Although Crane's interest in games and the discourse of play has long been the subject of study, its significance within the specific cultural context of the rise of spectator sports suggests an important aesthetic link with other naturalists and calls for a reconsideration of traditional understandings of Crane's recurring trope. More than a mere rhetorical device, the game offers Crane the discursive instrument with which to probe the aesthetic challenge of naturalism—namely, how to maintain the distance of the scientific observer while avoiding the passive disengagement of the spectator. In a society increasingly fascinated with the consumption of entertainment, Crane's interest in the workings of games of chance and athletic contests reveals his awareness of the uses of amusement in a consumer marketplace and the potential fate of his own fiction in this setting.

Card games, footraces, dice throwing, and boxing matches provide the backdrop that allows Crane to examine the interaction of men in the exclusively masculine world of the "sporting life." In this context, life-or-death struggles such as that following the shipwreck in "The Open Boat," become elaborate games themselves, in which terrible hazards seemingly replicate a meaningless throw of the dice. The blurred lines between staged contests and "real" battles offer insight into Crane's view of life—and art. As both the creator and reporter of the fictional encounters, Crane must stand apart from them, even as he argues for action and involvement. Such is the paradoxical nature of the artist as naturalist, and the uneasy definition of this role in Crane's stories, located within the discourse of masculinity, remains central to our understanding of American literary naturalism.

In the Virginia edition, editor Fredson Bowers places a number of Crane's Western stories alongside those works chosen by Crane for the American publication of *The Open Boat and Other Tales of Adventure,* the title story of which is often regarded by critics as Crane's most mature and complex creation—the pinnacle of the writer's brief but important career. Although published over several years in a variety of settings, most of these stories derived from Crane's own journey to the West and Mexico during 1895. After the remarkable commercial success of *The Red Badge of Courage,* Crane enjoyed a period of personal and artistic freedom, during which he concentrated on travel, war correspondence, and the composition of these stories. In his role as war correspondent, Crane booked passage to cover the revolt in Cuba and nearly lost his life in a shipwreck off the coast of Florida in January 1897, an event that forms the basis for "The Open Boat." During the final years of his life, much of Crane's time and energy would be spent writing hackwork and potboilers agreed by most to be unworthy of his talents, a fact that has contributed to the stature of those short stories written during the period of Crane's greatest artistic independence and has allowed critics to view these works as the most representative of Crane's literary aspirations. Frank Bergon points out the particular significance of the Western stories in a consideration of Crane's overall career: "The drama of the real West and Mexico so aptly coincided with the essential question pervading Crane's fiction—when can a man trust his own perceptions?—that not only are these tales among the best of his work, but they offer the truest account of the fading Wild West to be found in nineteenth-century American fiction" (102).

The artistic success of these stories, and their focus on Crane's central epistemological themes, suggest the importance of this volume in understanding the aesthetic goals that Crane established for his fiction. Also, as products of the epoch that marked the supposed "closing" of the American frontier—that area defined by Frederick Jackson Turner as "the meeting point between savagery and civilization"—the *Tales of Adventure* reflect Crane's investment in the cultural ideas of his time.

Bowers's edition presents this group of stories chronologically, in order of composition, a method that reveals a sort of narrative arc to Crane's aesthetic program over this period. These stories often feature protagonists who are quite clearly outsiders in this world of adventure and whose actions and anxieties reveal difficult truths about the human capacity for self-knowledge. The earliest examples, written soon after Crane's tour of the West and Mexico, are steeped in the stark irony so characteristic of Crane's previous fiction. Stories such as "A Man and Some Others" and "The Five White Mice" establish strict ironic distance from the behavior of a group of Americans in Mexico—a perspective shared, to some degree, by the outsider figures in the texts. The epiphanies reached by these figures consistently reveal hard facts about the ephemeral nature of human life and about our primal responses to this reality. Despite their autobiographical origins, Crane maintains a level of ironic detachment in these texts not unlike the point of view demonstrated in his earlier slum-based fiction, most notably *Maggie: A Girl of the Streets.* In "The Open Boat," however, Crane employs a more complex and fluid narrative voice—one that fluctuates between extreme ironic detachment and profound sympathy. It is, in part, this complexity that has ensured the prominence of "The Open Boat" in Crane's oeuvre. Like Crane's most widely read work, *The Red Badge of Courage,* "The Open Boat" leaves open many of its central questions and concerns. Through its protagonist, the correspondent, the text provides what might be Crane's least ironic characterization, as well as his most positive and emphatic ending, in which the role of the successful artist as an "interpreter" of human events is explicitly stated. In the wake of this apparent breakthrough, the subsequent Western stories mark a significant qualification of this aesthetic affirmation and a return to consistent irony, albeit of a darker and more ambiguous variety than that exhibited in the Mexican tales. From the somewhat playful debunking of Western myth in "The Bride Comes to Yellow Sky" to the unrelenting bitterness and gallows humor of "Twelve O'Clock" and "Moonlight on the Snow," these texts reveal Crane's growing ambivalence about the human potential for self-knowledge and artistic expression. The most resonant of these Western stories, "The Blue Hotel," seems to deliver a curious rejoinder to the optimism that concludes "The Open Boat." The interpreter of "The Blue Hotel" fails where the correspondent succeeds. As Crane complicates and confounds the optimistic view of artistic expression given in "The Open Boat," he simultaneously discloses the prominence of a code of manly conduct in the establishment of his blueprint for the successful artist. The instability of this blueprint reflects both the difficult negotiation between insider and outsider required of Crane's ideal artist and the problematic notion of masculinity on which this negotiation metaphorically relies.

Much of Crane's short fiction depicts a journey from ignorance to wisdom, an epistemological struggle consistently mediated by the degree of irony in Crane's narrative. In perhaps the most celebrated example of this journey, the first sentence in "The Open Boat," "None of them knew the color of the sky,"[2] gives way in the end to the statement "they felt that they could then be interpreters" (92). In the course of the story, one character—the correspondent—emerges as the principal "interpreter" of the event, and it is through his consciousness that Crane explores not only the development of wisdom but the means through which to convey this wisdom—the awakening of an artist. The correspondent's enlightenment at the conclusion of "The Open Boat" closely parallels the awareness achieved by the Easterner in "The Blue Hotel." Upon realizing his complicity, through inaction, in the death of the Swede, the Easterner reaches an epiphany about his own abilities to decipher meaning, as well as about ethical truths. What the correspondent and the Easterner realize, then, is their capacity to "interpret," to translate experience into narrative, to be artists. The paradigm of interpretation provides a model for understanding Crane's aesthetic principles, as does the fact that these characters' transformations coincide with their immersion into exclusively masculine rites and situations. It is this connection between Crane's notion of masculinity and the role of the artist that I wish to explore in these texts.

In *The Color of the Sky: A Study of Stephen Crane*, David Halliburton draws a significant parallel between Crane's artistic sensibility and late nineteenth-century aestheticism. Crane's strategies of satire and irony, Halliburton maintains, create a narrative distance not unlike that of British aesthetes such as Walter Pater.[3] Likewise, Michael Davitt Bell notes, "While Crane's subject [in *The Red Badge of Courage*] tied him to a writer like Rudyard

Kipling, he *wrote*, it seemed, like an aesthete" (143). Within Crane's short stories lies a growing unease about the nature of authorship, an anxiety about the inevitable isolation of the artist from the subject, which occurs in spite of Crane's avowed commitment to the actualities of experience. In describing what he calls Crane's "cinematic" style, Bergon claims, "One effect of Crane's fiction is that it often compels the reader to become, like Henry Fleming, 'deeply absorbed as a spectator.' But in a sense, Crane tried to eliminate the camera that separated the spectator from experience" (13–14). This balancing act—maintaining the distance necessary for a critical view of the characters' actions, yet placing the startling, and often shocking, facts of experience before the reader—has resulted in a consistent problem for critics. How does one reconcile Crane's impressionism and irony with the presumed goals and assumptions of naturalism?

Halliburton's association of Crane's impressionistic and self-conscious "artistic" style with the British "decadents" contrasts sharply with the long-established acknowledgment of Leo Tolstoy's influence on Crane. Ellen Moers, for example, carefully traces the impact of Tolstoy's ideas on American writers of the late nineteenth century, particularly William Dean Howells, Theodore Dreiser, and Crane.[4] Moers claims that "wherever the pictorial realism of the period went below surfaces and telling 'the truth' had more than journalistic implications, there the force of Tolstoy's example is marked" (54). Tolstoy, in his essays on writing, invokes the ethical responsibilities of the novelist to accurately represent reality and work for the improvement of society and rejects the adulation of beauty, most ardently typified by the aestheticism of Pater and the doctrine of "art for art's sake." Donald Pizer, in a discussion of Crane's later short story "The Monster," establishes a textual link between Tolstoy's moral self-inquiry "What to Do?" and the question desperately repeated by Dr. Trescott, the protagonist of "The Monster": "What am I to do?"[5] Pizer claims that Crane, as "an ironic and satiric moralist" ("Neglected Allusion" 129), reinscribes Tolstoy's Christian viewpoint in a specific moral context: "For Tolstoy's moral polemic, Crane substitutes the obliqueness of symbolic fiction" ("Neglected Allusion" 128). Dr. Trescott's question about "what to do" is an ethical one, but for Tolstoy (and Crane) it is an aesthetic concern as well. In "What Shall We Do?" Tolstoy asks himself "What to do?" and directly confronts the problem of detached authorship:

I used to put that question to myself, but in reality answered it by determining in advance the kind of agreeable activity with which I was called to serve man. What I really asked myself was this: "How can I, such a fine author, who have acquired so much knowledge and so many talents, use them for the benefit of man?" . . . If the question had stood before me as it now stands before me, after I have repented, namely, what I, such a corrupt man, must do, the answer would have been easy: I must first of all try to earn an honest living, that is, to learn how not to live by sitting on the backs of others and, while learning it and having learned it, upon every occasion to be useful to people with my hands, and feet, and brain, and heart, and with all that to which the masses lay any claim. (*Complete Works* 9: 293–94)

In Tolstoy's view, then, the vocation of an author—educated, sedentary, removed from the rigors of physical labor—stands in fundamental opposition to the moral obligation to seek "an honest living." Tolstoy's profound influence on Crane manifests itself not only in the ethical concerns central to his fiction, but in this highly ambivalent attitude toward the very idea of authorship itself. Bell argues that this tension between the pull of "reality" and the demands of art is central to the American realists and naturalists:

To many of their American proponents, the ideas of realism and naturalism have mattered far less as theories of literature than as means for neutralizing anxieties about the writer's status in a culture still intensely suspicious or contemptuous of 'art' and the 'artistic.' To proclaim oneself a realist or naturalist in this context was most fundamentally to claim for literature the status of a 'real'—that is, socially normal—activity, to define literature not in its own terms but in the terms sanctioned by an abidingly anti-'literary' cultural orthodoxy. (7–8)

The challenge for Crane as an artist lies in the seeming incompatibility of Tolstoy's ethical imperative—and the endemic distrust of the "artistic" that has always existed within American anti-intellectualism—with the narrative detachment required in translating the facts of experience into art.

Our understanding of Crane's aesthetic sensibility depends largely on the relationship between journalism and fiction, as it existed for Crane and his contemporaries and as it reverberates throughout his own writing. Traditionally critics have maintained that the emergence of professional reporters within the broad literary marketplace influenced the development of realistic and naturalistic fiction by expanding literary subject matter and by emphasizing an objective and distinctively unliterary style. As Christopher Wilson asserts in *The Labor of Words,* however, far from having a "democratizing" effect on authorship, the rise of the popular press created an elite class of writer who occupied a "unique cultural position among modern professions" that transgressed, if not transcended, various class and economic distinctions (16). If market changes brought about the demise of the reporter as a bohemian dilettante with literary pretensions, Crane, in some ways, represents a throwback to an earlier era. His fiction shows little influence of the reportorial style of his journalistic colleagues; rather, his journalism reflects the irony and impressionism of his "literary" work. Michael Robertson, in *Stephen Crane, Journalism, and the Making of Modern American Literature,* claims that the common critical view on the naturalist symbiosis between journalism and fiction, which sees journalism as a stepping-stone to serious fiction, misrepresents the approach taken by Crane and his contemporaries. Although Howells and Henry James remained hostile to journalism based on their own limited and unsuccessful stints as reporters, Crane moved easily between journalism and fiction.[6] Robertson discusses what he calls the "fact-fiction discourse" of the 1890s, predating the modern notion of journalistic "objectivity." Newspapers at the turn of the century made little distinction between fictional narratives, "straight" reporting on events, and "sketches" that may or may not have been based on true events. Indeed, Crane published examples of each of these kinds of writing in newspapers throughout his career. By looking at examples of Crane's journalistic writing that have been dismissed by critics as nonliterary, Robertson seeks both to discover their "literariness" and to refine our understanding of the central role of journalism in shaping modern American literature. If Crane sought the role of reporter in his career, it stemmed in large part from the popular perception of journalism as a manly vocation, and Crane may have cloaked his literary technique in journalistic discourse in order to camouflage his own artistry. In considering Crane's short stories, therefore, it is crucial to distinguish them from Crane's journalistic dispatches. Although his efforts at journalism and fiction share certain formal characteristics, the stories reveal an awareness of the problem of the artist within a cultural climate distinctly hostile to the very notion of artistry. The ironic distance of Crane's narrative voice, in certain ways, reflects the anxiety inherent in his own position.

Nowhere is Crane's detached irony more pervasive than in the four stories that depict the life of Americans in Mexico: "One Dash—Horses," "The Wise Men: A Detail of American Life in Mexico," "The Five White Mice," and "A Man and Some Others."[7] In these tales, Crane translates autobiographical details into a particularly stylized brand of fiction. These stories also contain a theme that persists throughout Crane's work—the struggle of a small group of men cast into an alien, forbidding environment and put to the test. Such microcosms of the human struggle reappear throughout his fiction in the form of Henry Fleming's army unit, the saloons of *George's Mother*, the small town inhabited by Dr. Trescott and his neighbors in "The Monster," and, quintessentially, the dinghy in "The Open Boat." The Americans in "The Wise Men" and "The Five White Mice" are members of a small expatriate community in Mexico City, single men, artists, writers, ne'er-do-wells, and "men of leisure" whose lives revolve around the ritualized homosocial amusements of the saloon, the sporting life, and the theatre. Success or failure in the performance of these rituals serves either to buttress or undermine their embattled sense of identity as men and as Anglo-Saxons in an explicitly "foreign" climate. Crane's ironic tone consistently nullifies the self-aggrandizing esprit de corps that defines the existence of these displaced and marginal men, the "well-informed and the great talkers of the American colony" (*Works* 5: 26), a "cosmopolitan crowd" who "ate, drank, played billiards, gossiped, or read in the glaring yellow light" of the city's English-speaking cafés (*Works* 5: 33).

The differences of race, culture, and language that set apart the expatriates in Mexico from their surroundings offer a literal representation of the sense of alienation and uncertainty that runs through Crane's work. Critics have offered conflicting opinions on Crane's decidedly unflattering depictions of Mexicans in these stories.[8] Much of the difficulty in knowing what to make of these characterizations stems from the uncertain status of the narrative voice, as either overtly sympathetic to the clearly ethnocentric, if not racist, perceptions of the Anglo-American characters or, conversely, as ironically critical of the simplistic prejudices of figures such as Richardson, the protagonist of "One Dash—Horses." In this regard, it is useful to consider Crane's purely journalistic writing on his Mexican sojourn. In a sketch entitled "Above All Things," submitted to the Bacheller syndicate but left unpublished in Crane's lifetime, he expresses the impossibility of understanding people of a different culture. In typical Crane fashion, this brief sketch offers both an offhand study of the poverty and apparent despair in the lives of "the lower classes of Indians" in Mexico and a statement of aesthetic purpose. In a frequently quoted passage, Crane describes the arrogance of a visitor such as himself who presumes to comprehend those of a foreign culture: "It might perhaps be said—if anyone dared—that the most worthless literature of the world has been that which has been written by the men of one nation concerning the men of another" (*Stephen Crane in the West and Mexico* 74). An author, Crane asserts, "can be sure of two things, form and color" (74). Without question, Crane's affinity for impressionistic visual descriptions—for instance, the "worm of yellow convicts" seen on the distant shore of Blackwell's Island at the opening of *Maggie*—reinforces this broad aesthetic claim. Also significant, however, is the hesitation with which he offers his theories, beginning with "It might perhaps be said. . . ." Indeed, throughout "Above All Things," Crane maintains his reluctance to offer definitive statements about the Mexicans he describes. A glance at the opening sentences of several paragraphs reveals the following pattern of uncertainty: "At first it seemed to me," "I am venturing to say," and "As far as I can perceive him" (74–75). As a writer, Crane remains skeptical of his own ability to understand the people and events he observes. In this context, the indeterminate nature of Crane's portrayal of Mexicans—as either self-consciously or unconsciously racist—only highlights the real object of his study in the Mexican short stories: the individual expatriates themselves. Just as the landscape stretching out before Richardson in "One Dash—Horses" is "a vast, pointless ocean of black" (*Works* 5: 13), so does Mexico serve as a fearsome void into which Crane casts his Anglo characters. The "Otherness" of the Mexican frontier serves to unite the Americans in a common struggle to *understand*, in a literal sense, the alien language that surrounds them, but also to understand the true nature of their tenuous existence. And it is their status as Americans and as men that defines this existence.

For Crane and his contemporaries, the activities that defined American manhood emerged from the "sporting life" surrounding urban bachelor culture in the late nineteenth century. The culture found its locus among the saloons, gambling halls, and grandstands that served the growing community of middle-class men with the time, money, and inclination to seek diversions that assuaged their embattled sense of masculinity. Crane's Mexican stories reveal the importance of such manly rites as drinking, dice throwing, card playing, and athletic contests to a group of men who are, quite literally, alienated from the society around them.[9] What makes the expatriates feel like men, and like Americans, is their ability to participate in the rituals of the bachelor culture. For the characters in "The Wise Men" and "The Five White Mice," the urban bustle of Mexico City exists only as a backdrop for the insular world of a few saloons that cater to the American expatriates. The former story involves a risky gambit on the part of two young members of this fraternity, "the New York Kid" and "the San Francisco Kid," who wager an exorbitant sum of money on the ability of "Pop," a middle-aged bartender, to defeat a younger and seemingly more agile bartender in a footrace. Many of the same characters reappear in "The Five White Mice," which opens with the New York Kid winning, through a game of poker dice, a box at that evening's circus and some money, then betting everything on one final "dash." He recites a "gambler's slogan" before throwing the dice:

> Oh, five white mice of chance,
> Shirts of wool and corduroy pants,
> Gold and wine, women and sin,
> All for you if you let me come in—
> Into this house of chance. (*Works* 5: 42)

The Kid, however, loses the bet and must take the winners to the circus, thereby foregoing an evening of debauchery with the "Frisco Kid" and another friend, Benson. Because of this turn of events, the New York Kid is sober, "his face . . . luminous with virtue" upon meeting his comrades later that evening (45). When Benson drunkenly provokes a fight with a group of three Mexicans, the Kid's sobriety proves invaluable. After the others, too inebriated to understand the gravity of the situation, allow the confrontation to escalate, the Kid pulls his gun out and drives away the ominous strangers. Despite, or perhaps because of, his fear, the New York Kid behaves properly: "A combination of honorable manhood and inability prevented him from running away" (49). Because of his apparent bad luck at dice, the Kid remains sober and is clearheaded enough to face this dangerous situation with poise, bluffing the Mexicans as he would an opponent at a hand of poker.

In the end, Crane writes with characteristic irony, "nothing had happened" (52).[10]

Crane's narrative voice recapitulates the same understatement with which his characters greet the vagaries of "the house of chance." When Pop wins the footrace in "The Wise Men," much to the surprise of all spectators, including the two "Kids," the victors collect their winnings with the self-assured restraint and humility required by the manly code of behavior:

> The Kids, grinning, said: "How much did you lose, Benson?"
> Benson said defiantly: "Oh, not so much. How much did you win?"
> "Oh, not so much." (38)

As Chester Wolford points out, Crane's emphasis on the importance of self-control, of "behaving well" when confronted with a stroke of either good luck or misfortune, suggests a model for Ernest Hemingway's notion of "grace under pressure" (35ff.).[11] The story also reveals the role of language in establishing a code of conduct. Not only are they masters of understatement, the "Kids" and their comrades struggle to avoid needless communication entirely. Their resistance to language is part of what binds the members of the group together. The "female voices . . . giggling and chattering" that Richardson hears from the next room in "One Dash—Horses" embody the emptiness and superficiality of verbal communication when contrasted with the manly world of action.[12] To be a man is to remain silent, and language itself is not only unnecessary but essentially meaningless.

The plot of "A Man and Some Others" also calls attention to the gap between words and action. In this story, Bill, a rugged sheepherder—"a tattered individual with a tangle of hair and beard, and with a complexion turned brick color from the sun and whisky" (*Works* 5: 59)—stands up to a group of deceitful Mexicans (the description of whom parallels that of the threatening pedestrians in "The Five White Mice" or the drunken desperados of "One Dash—Horses") who admonish him in broken English to "geet off range. We no like. Un'erstan'? We no like" (54). In contrast to Bill's rough-hewn persona, the appearance of a stranger in his camp illustrates the recurring conflict in Crane's Western stories between the Eastern and Western, fictional and factual, false and authentic: "Bill saw a type which did not belong in the mesquit. The young fellow had invested in some Mexican trappings of an expensive kind. Bill's eyes searched the outfit for some sign of craft, but there was none. Even with his local regalia, it was clear that the young man was of a far, black Northern city" (58).

Like Richardson and the New York Kid, the "stranger" is an Easterner who has embarked on a romantic adventure but, in the act of playing a fanciful role, discovers frightening truths. As he is drawn into Bill's conflict with the Mexicans, the stranger asks, "Well, why in the name of wonder don't you go get the sheriff?" To this question, Bill can only offer a wordless response: "'Oh h—!' said Bill" (*Works* 5: 60). The stranger's appeal to "civilization" demonstrates his own naiveté about the West, and Bill's reaction again underscores the inadequacy of language and its inability to convey reality through mere words. During the subsequent gunfight, the stranger, panicked by the sight of a man Bill has killed, says, "He makes me feel like a murderer":

> "But," said Bill, puzzling, "you didn't shoot him, mister; I shot him."
> "I know; but I feel that way, somehow. I can't get rid of it."
> Bill considered for a time; then he said diffidently: "Mister, you're a eddycated man, ain't you?"
> "What?"
> "You're what they call a'—a' eddycated man, ain't you?" (64)

Their conversation is interrupted by gunfire, and the stranger's horse is shot: "'This comes from discussin' things,' cried Bill, angrily" (64). According to the code by which Bill leads his life, only trouble can follow from idle conversation. The stranger, too, eventually accepts his role in the battle:

> The lightning action of the next few moments was of the fabric of dreams to the stranger. The muscular struggle may not be real to the drowning man. His mind may be fixed on the far, straight shadows back of the stars, and the terror of them. And so the fight, and his part in it, had to the stranger only the quality of a picture half-drawn. The rush of feet, the spatter of shots, the cries, the swollen faces seen like masks on the smoke, resembled a happening of the night.
> And yet afterward certain lines, forms, lived out so strongly from the incoherence that they were always in his memory.
> He killed a man, and the thought went swiftly by him, like the fear on the gale, that it was easy to kill a man. (66)

Crane's description of the melee, in its striking combination of impression-istic sensory details and introspective reverie, recalls Henry Fleming's expe-riences in the battle scenes of *The Red Badge of Courage*. Apprehensive about his performance of the role of "murderer," the stranger loses his fear and anxiety in the act itself. Once he actually does kill a man, he realizes how easy it is. Bill and the stranger fight off the attackers, but only after Bill has been mortally wounded. Left alive to tell Bill's story, the stranger feels inadequate to the task; though "certain lines, forms" remain vivid to him after the battle, the hallucinatory picture that endures is incomplete, its meaning hazy.

The phantasmal depictions of violent or dangerous scenes that occur in Crane's writing share a common preoccupation with the convergence of the extraordinary and the mundane in such moments. After illustrating the fierce climax of Bill's fight with the Mexicans, for instance, Crane describes the jarring intrusion of trivial images in the mind of the stranger: "He wore the gentle idiot smile of an aged beggar as he watched three Mexicans limp-ing and staggering in the distance. He noted at this time that one who still possessed a serape had from it none of the grandeur of the cloaked Spaniard, but that against the sky the silhouette resembled a cornucopia of childhood's Christmas" (*Works* 5: 67). Not only is the deadly "game" played out in the desert far removed from the joys of childhood, but the stranger's experience replaces the romantic "grandeur" typical of Western adventure tales with incongruous imagery from his youth. The inability of the reasoning mind to make sense of sudden, powerful actions contributes to Crane's sense of the difficulties inherent in literary reconstruction of past events. In "The Five White Mice," the Kid melodramatically imagines his own death and its devastating impact on his family and friends even as he stares down the ominous Mexicans, juxtaposing the fanciful pictures in his mind with the decidedly less romantic reality before him: "These views were perfectly stereopticon, flashing in and away from his thought with an inconceivable rapidity until after all they were simply one quick dismal impression. And now here is the unreal real: into this Kid's nostrils, at the expectant moment of slaughter, had come the scent of new-mown hay, a fragrance from a field of prostrate grass, a fragrance which contained the sunshine, the bees, the peace of meadows and the wonder of a distant crooning stream" (49). In this passage, one sees a self-conscious synopsis of Crane's own impression-istic style—a stream of seemingly unconnected images merging into a single impression that is greater than the sum of its parts. The overt reference to photography—an art form of great interest to Crane—and the ruminations on the nature of the Kid's thoughts are followed by an example of discordant thinking, triggered by sensory impressions. Here too is what Crane calls the "unreal real"—the improbable perceptions of the human mind in extraordinary circumstances. Moments of crisis present the individual with a paradoxical combination of heightened awareness of and peculiar dissociation from one's immediate surroundings. The ability to *act* in such situations is what determines a man's courage; the ability to analyze or interpret these situations requires a distance from the events that, for instance, the stranger in "A Man and Some Others" no longer possesses. Cast into the role of actor, yet by nature driven to understand and articulate meaning, the stranger can do neither effectively, instead standing "motionless, his mouth just agape and the same stupid glance in his eyes" (67).

The stranger feels for Bill "some deep form of idolatry." Crane writes, "Bill was dying, and the dignity of last defeat, the superiority of him who stands in his grave, was in the pose of the lost sheep-herder" (*Works* 5: 66–67). At that moment, the stranger believes he understands the meaning of Bill's fate and is left with the lesser role of survivor, one who lives to tell others of his brush with death. If Bill is the "man" of the story's title, the stranger can only be one of the Others. The outsider briefly becomes a participant, but once the action ends, he returns to the status of spectator, left to ponder "the superiority of him who stands in his grave" (67) and to imperfectly interpret Bill's life and actions for future audiences.

Given the "manly" distrust of language and its inability to fully capture the truths of life, Crane's chosen profession as a writer of fiction becomes a challenge to his status as a full and active participant in the rituals of American masculinity. Crane effectively identifies the challenge of his specific literary project in "The Open Boat" at the beginning of the story's third section, in which he states: "It would be difficult to describe the subtle brotherhood of men that was here established on the seas" (*Works* 5: 73). This "difficult description" is, of course, what the story is all about. In this passage, Crane emphasizes the problems with expressing this "subtle brotherhood" through language, particularly through the language of the participants themselves. Of their camaraderie, Crane claims, "No one said that it was so. No one mentioned it. But it dwelt in the boat, and each man felt it warm him" (73). In this distinctly masculine context, the mere telling of the story seems to violate the subtle brotherhood that has been established on the sea.[13] Crane must, therefore, establish a role for the artist that does not violate this sacred fraternity and throw into question the manliness of the speaker.[14] The role that Crane assigns for this purpose is what he calls, by the end of the story, an "interpreter." Halliburton defines the correspondent role as that of "a particular type of mediator, a combination of the spokesperson and the interlocutor," who actively interprets the experiences of the four men and constructs meaning from the experience (246–47). It is telling that Crane chooses to identify the protagonist, a character drawn from his own experience during the shipwreck of the *Commodore,* as a "correspondent" rather than "author," "writer," "novelist" (all of which would be more accurate self-descriptions, in terms of popular perception), or even "reporter." The chosen term represents a less feminized occupation, but it also highlights the role of the audience—the writer must have readers with whom to "correspond." The aim of the writer, thus, is not beauty or self-expression, but rather accurate transmission of the facts of experience to the reader.

For Crane, the metaphorical gendering that develops in "The Open Boat" is essential for constructing a naturalistic aesthetic perspective. Crane chooses to construct a narrative universe wherein individual men, particular to the social context of turn-of-the-century America, symbolize the struggle of "Man," and this gendered maneuver does not merely reveal Crane's investment in the "cult of masculinity" of the 1890s, but it also establishes Crane's use of gender as a metaphorical tool with which to argue his aesthetic claims. Traits associated with manhood become, for Crane, attributes of the artist in a naturalistic setting. In transforming his own experience into a narrative of survival on the ocean, he participates in the established discourse of sea adventure, whose best-known practitioners include Kipling and Robert Louis Stevenson, as well as Crane's friend, Joseph Conrad. Bert Bender identifies the central struggle in American sea fiction: "Traditionally, the chief problem has been how to resolve the conflict between the ideal of brotherhood and the reality of discord necessitated by the Darwinian view of warring nature and the Spencerian idea of the survival of the fittest" (10). In his own contribution to the genre, Crane emphasizes the unity and masculinity of this "ideal of brotherhood," in part by placing the individual's struggle against natural forces in strictly gendered terms. The consistent gendering of human experience emerges dramatically from the text of "The Open Boat."

Crane sets up the gendered dualism of epistemology when the inhabitants of the open boat confront the possibility of drowning. Crane writes,

> They then briefly exchanged some addresses and admonitions. As for the reflections of the men, there was a great deal of rage in them. Perchance they might be formulated thus: "If I am going to be drowned— if I am going to be drowned—if I am going to be drowned, why, in the name of the seven mad gods who rule the sea, was I allowed to come thus far and contemplate sand and trees? . . . It is preposterous. If this old ninny-woman, Fate, cannot do better than this, she should be deprived of the management of men's fortunes. She is an old hen who knows not her intention." (*Works* 5: 77)

Several important themes emerge from this passage. As in "Above All Things," Crane expresses hesitation over the power of his own language and the form he gives to the men's thoughts, cautioning "*perchance* they *might* be formulated thus." Further, he grants to the men an eloquence in their consciousness that is without complement in the dialogue of the narrative. The paragraphs immediately preceding this section contain unimaginative and terse statements attributed to the men as a whole: " 'Funny they don't see us,' said the men" and " 'We'll swamp sure,' said everybody" (*Works* 5: 76). Indeed, it is implicit that the consciousness bemoaning the frivolity of Fate, although representative of all the men, is that of the correspondent, the professional manipulator of language.[15] In spite of his command of language, however, the correspondent chooses to be "one of the men"—eschewing frivolous and inconclusive conversation as much as possible. Not coincidentally, the most talkative man on the boat proves to be the cook, who occupied a distinctly "feminine" role aboard the *Commodore* and contributes least to the survival of the group.

Perhaps most striking about the previous passage is its critical, even obsessive, feminization of natural forces. There is certainly nothing unusual about the linguistic convention of a feminine Nature, but Crane's decision to address "Fate," an extension of the notion of "Mother Nature"—rather than a traditional male "God"—is striking, particularly in light of his frequent invocation of the Christian deity elsewhere in his writing. Fate is a "ninny-woman," an "old hen who knows not her intention." Crane thus casts the quest for meaning in strictly gendered terms. The desire for knowledge and understanding stems from masculine "rage," a desperate insistence on reason, whereas the vagaries of a deterministic universe are depicted through the feminine qualities of indecisiveness and intellectual frailty. Invoking a pagan pantheon—"the seven mad gods who rule the sea"—allows Crane to circumvent the paternalistic order of Christianity and place the blame where he feels it belongs—on a feminized Nature.

Crane reinforces the feminization of Nature at the beginning of the seventh section, when he repeats the question "If I am going to be drowned . . . why . . . was I allowed to come thus far?" (*Works* 5: 84). Crane specifically refers to nature as female and perceives in Nature a response to his prayers: "A high cold star on a winter's night is the word he *feels* that she says to him. Thereafter he knows the pathos of his situation" (85) [italics added]. Crane suggests that the communication between Nature and the individual is constructed entirely out of the individual's perceptions. The power of language rests with the interpreter, not the speaker. The shifting definitions of Crane's "Nature"—as "Fate," an "old hen," a "ninny woman"—suggest the creation of an all-inclusive feminine Other, useful primarily for the definition, through opposition, of the brotherhood in the boat. Bram Dijkstra, in a study of misogyny in fin-de-siècle art, connects the demonization of the feminine in nature with the rise of scientific discourse: "Woman, as the embodiment of nature, was therefore continuously at war with man, whose very purpose was to go against or beyond nature" (237).[16] Crane, in "The Open Boat," exaggerates and belabors female Nature in order to gender as male the struggle of the correspondent to interpret, to find meaning—or create meaning—amid the Darwinian tumult of the natural world.

When a forgotten snippet of sentimental poetry enters the correspondent's head, his reaction offers insight into Crane's notion of the artist as interpreter. The poem in question, Caroline Norton's "Bingen on the Rhine," though not credited in the story, would be familiar to many of Crane's contemporary readers. Frequently anthologized in textbooks and recited by schoolchildren, Norton's poem represents precisely the kind of mawkish, middlebrow diversion that aroused the hostility of the literary naturalists. The correspondent recalls the following lines of the poem:

A soldier of the Legion lay dying in Algiers,
There was lack of woman's nursing, there was dearth of woman's tears;
But a comrade stood beside him, and he took that comrade's hand,

And he said: "I never more shall see my own, my native land."
(*Works* 5: 85)

In one sense, Crane's insertion of the poem into the narrative serves to high-light the obvious disparity between the heavy-handed sentimentality of the verse and the harsh realism of his own writing—two perspectives as differ-ent as the North African desert and the Atlantic Ocean.[17] Crane's irony, how-ever, is mitigated somewhat; in spite of the distinctly pedestrian attitudes and ideas associated with Norton's poem, the correspondent's *use* of the verse as a catalyst for his own understanding is quite genuine. The story within the poem itself reiterates the exclusively male world of the open boat, where there is likewise a "lack of woman's nursing." It is from a male comrade that the dying soldier takes comfort. Indeed, the poem attempts to depict the "subtle brotherhood of men" to which Crane's work refers, and the awk-wardness of the verse supports Crane's contention about the difficulty of such an attempt.

Once again, in the correspondent's recollection of the poem, the power to control language emerges from the act of interpretation. As a schoolboy, the correspondent felt no affinity for the popular verse and no sympathy for the dying soldier. According to Crane, "It was less to him than the breaking of a pencil's point" (*Works* 5: 85). Only as a result of his current predicament and the perspective granted him by this experience does the correspondent come to understand the meaning of the poem. "It was," Crane writes, "no longer merely a picture of a few throes in the breast of a poet, meanwhile drinking tea and warming his feet at the grate: it was an actuality—stern, mournful, and fine" (85). Crane clearly distinguishes between the masculine interpreter and the poet—here depicted as male, but lacking any masculine qualities. This image of the poet, in fact, matches that of a stereotypical aesthete, physically weak and removed from experience. It is the interpreter, engaged in rowing, who creates an "actuality" from these lines of poetry. Crane summarizes the correspondent's newly discovered appreciation for the poem: "He was sorry for the soldier of the Legion who lay dying in Algiers" (86). The importance of the work of art, ultimately, is the evocation of sympathy—feeling sorry for the soldier. The correspondent is thus able to conceive of the "pathos" of his own condition in terms of a broader, human-istic realization. Such a realization is consistent with Tolstoy's idea of the purpose of art: "It is a means of union among men, joining them together in the same feelings, and indispensable for the life and progress towards well-being of individuals and of humanity" (*"What Is Art"* 123).[18] The sort of comprehension and communion to which art aspires, then, resembles nothing so much as the rapport shared between male comrades, whether in a military unit, on board a ship, on a playing field, or in a saloon. As interpreter, the correspondent transcends the limitations of the specific text, as well as his specific circumstance, and achieves true understanding by becoming a member of a selective fraternity and a full participant in the actions required by the manly code. The dynamics of this interpretive relationship reveal Crane's anxiety over the traditional role of artist in the equation. In essence, the correspondent becomes his own story, rather than a mere bystander, but this successful transgression of the boundaries between observer and participant is not always so easily crossed.

If "The Open Boat" shows a correspondent who becomes the protagonist of a life-or-death adventure, "Death and the Child" shows the failure of a similar character to achieve such involvement. In this story, drawn to some extent from Crane's experiences reporting on the Greco-Turkish war, Peza, a war correspondent, finds himself an unprepared, if not unwilling, participant in a battle. Motivated by sympathy for the plight of his fellow Greeks, Peza declares, "Now I want to fight" (*Works* 5: 123) and asks a soldier for a weapon and directions to the battle. "I came as a correspondent," he says, ". . . but now wish to help" (133). Throughout the tale, Crane calls attention to Peza's exaggerated and unreal notion of war as a grand spectacle, referring to the battle as a "carnival of woe" that suggests the "pageants of carnage that had marched through the dreams of his childhood" (124–25). For Peza, meaning is bestowed on action by the presence of an appreciative audience, and he is disconcerted by the prospect of an unspectacular death among the exploding shells: "This theatre of slaughter, built by the inscrutable needs of the earth, was an enormous affair, and he reflected that the accidental death of an individual, Peza by name, would perhaps be nothing at all" (126). Here, Crane revisits themes explored in earlier stories. When confronted with the knife-wielding Mexican in "The Five White Mice," the New York Kid contemplates both the imminence and the insignificance of his own death, as well as the imperfect translation of his demise into narrative form: "The Eastern lad suddenly decided that he was going to be killed. His mind leaped forward and studied the aftermath. The story would be a marvel of brevity when it reached the far New York home, written in a careful hand

on a bit of cheap paper topped and footed and backed by the printed for-
tifications of the cable company" (*Works* 5: 48). Out of these bleak thoughts,
however, the Kid manages to find the "combination of honorable manhood
and inability [which] prevented him from running away" (49). Crane employs the same dark and bitter voice when the correspondent considers the
probability of his own death in "The Open Boat": "When it occurs to a man
that nature does not regard him as important, and that she feels she would
not maim the universe by disposing of him, he at first wishes to throw bricks
at the temple, and he hates deeply the fact that there are no bricks and no
temples. Any visible expression of nature would surely be pelleted with his
jeers" (*Works* 5: 84–85). Here, as with Peza's rancor at the "inscrutable needs
of the earth," Crane invokes "nature" in its most abstract, hostile, and feminine form as the inevitable enemy of the individual man. It is in response to
this moment of despair that the correspondent achieves a sort of human-
ist epiphany, turning first to the words of the half-forgotten poem, and
finally to his comrades. Peza, however, has no comrades. Rather, he wanders
through the outskirts of the battlefield like "a corpse walking on the bottom
of the sea" (129). He lacks the "vanity of experience" held by the real soldiers.

What "Death and the Child" reveals most explicitly is the mechanism
that regulates those spectacular rituals—including warfare—that defined
masculinity for turn-of-the-century American culture. In a particularly relevant discussion of historical adventure novels of the 1890s, Amy Kaplan
identifies and elucidates the impulse to stage violent scenes for the benefit of
female spectators, thereby establishing the virility and dominance of the romantic male hero in the context of imperial aggression. "On this fictional
new frontier," writes Kaplan, "physical rejuvenation does not emerge from
bloody contests with a native other; the novels instead offer regeneration
through a spectacle before the female gaze" ("Romancing the Empire" 675).
In Crane's case, however, the author "splits the fighting male subject in
two—the actor and the spectator, who takes the form of the journalist, as
panderer in the arousal of spectatorial lust" (678). The female role in the
usual formula is thus subsumed by the reporter, who documents and interprets the spectacle for the audience, safe in their far-off homes.[19] This feminization of the spectator recapitulates the uneasy observation of Joe and Wolf
Larsen by the literary audience in London's *The Game* and *The Sea-Wolf*,
respectively, discussed in Chapter 1.

In "The Open Boat," Crane allows the correspondent full participation in the life-and-death struggle—in part because, although the men are briefly observed by distant figures on the beach, any meaningful activities take place away from the public's gaze. Nonetheless, Crane calls attention to the potentially spectacular nature of the survivors' struggle: "Viewed from a balcony, the whole thing would, doubtless, have been weirdly picturesque. But the men in the boat had no time to see it, and if they had had leisure, there were other things to occupy their minds" (*Works* 5: 70). The image of a theater balcony, site of the leisurely consumption of entertainment, provides a harsh contrast with the reality of their situation, but the absence of a theatrical audience provides Crane the opportunity to remind the *reading* audience of the dramatic tableau he describes. Crane compares the tossing of the boat to a "bucking broncho" (71), suggesting a feature of the popular "wild West shows" that toured the United States during the 1890s.[20] Observing the turbulent sea around them—"probably splendid" in other circumstances—the men debate their chances of survival:

> "Bully good thing it's an on-shore wind," said the cook. "If not, where would we be? Wouldn't have a show."
> "That's right," said the correspondent.
> The busy oiler nodded his assent.
> Then the captain, in the bow, chuckled in a way that expressed humor, contempt, tragedy, all in one. "Do you think we've got much of a show now, boys?" said he. (70–71)

Crane's use of the idiomatic *show,* meaning "chance," inevitably resonates with another meaning of the word, suggesting the "humor, contempt, tragedy" in the performance of the four men. The fact that the men are engaged in the actions necessary to save their own lives and therefore too "busy" to ponder the drama of their own situation not only gives them the chance to succeed, but it paradoxically contributes to the "splendid" heroics that make Crane's story successful. Unlike the historical romances discussed by Kaplan, Crane's tale retains the fact-fiction discourse of realism, as defined by Robertson, in which "true" journalistic accounts adopt the narrative techniques of fiction, and vice versa. Like the correspondent's understanding of the sentimental poem, life on the boat is "an actuality—stern, mournful, and fine," providing meaning in contrast to the frivolous artificiality that defines the civilized world on shore. While on the boat, the correspondent remains very much an "actor" in the events, becoming an interpreter only after reaching the shore and thus returning to the world of society, leisure, and artifice. His immersion in the "unreal real" of the open boat allows the correspondent to correct the misreadings of society. When a tourist on the beach waves his coat at the shipwrecked men, they slowly realize that "he don't mean anything; he's just playing" (80). Like the tourist, readers of fiction loiter in the complacency of misunderstanding, unable to interpret the facts before them. The optimism at the end of "The Open Boat" lies in Crane's hope that the artist's involvement in the struggles of life will enable him to transcend the romantic misreadings that have heretofore defined literary production.

Peza in "Death and the Child" cannot so seamlessly move between the roles of spectator and actor. War, unlike the struggle on the life raft, cannot exist apart from the self-consciousness of public spectacle. Despite his desire to become one of the soldiers, Peza inevitably remains an outsider amidst the "motley line of privates in the trench" (*Works* 5: 134). When he leaves an inactive location in search of the heat of battle, he encounters resistance from the soldiers: "The officers all tried to dissuade him from departing. It was really not worth the trouble. The battery would begin again directly. Then it would be amusing for him" (134). Peza repeatedly pronounces his patriotic intention to fight rather than be "amused," but "these officers gave no heed to his exalted declarations. They seemed too jaded. They were fighting the men who were fighting them. Palaver of the particular kind had subsided before their intense preoccupation in war as a craft. Moreover, many men had talked in that manner, and only talked" (134–35). The professional soldiers resist Peza's attempts at jovial camaraderie; their own "brotherhood," like those of all manly comrades (whether shiftless gamblers in Mexico City, authentic frontiersmen, or shipwrecked sailors), is defined by deeds, not words. Peza, a correspondent and by definition a professional talker, refuses to perform his assigned role as observer and outsider. Ignoring the soldiers' objections, Peza continues toward the front. "However," Crane writes, "when he reflected upon their ways afterward, he saw dimly that they were actuated principally by some universal childish desire for a spectator of their fine things. They were going into action, and they wished to be seen at war, precise and fearless" (135). By denying his spectatorial position, Peza has taken from the soldiers the very meaning behind their actions. War, the ultimate masculine performance, cannot proceed without an audience. The reporter's refusal to serve as mediator between the spectacle and the audience at home undermines not only the manliness of the individual soldiers but the masculine authority of the nation itself.

By emphasizing the "childish desire" that propels the soldiers' performative manhood, Crane calls attention to the metonymic relationship between the play of children and the violence of men that figures prominently throughout his published work. Beginning with the "howling urchins" who challenge "the honor of Rum Alley" in the pitched battle for a scrap heap at the opening of *Maggie,* Crane repeatedly explores the connections between child's play and man's combat (*Works* 1: 1). Although Crane's accounts of the violent games of young boys illustrate the grandiose pretensions of children, it also suggests the artificiality and playfulness at work in the deadly games of adults. If the rise of violent sports, such as football and boxing, invoked the spirit of boyhood in the construction of revitalized manhood, it also provided the link between the playing fields of schoolboys and the battlefields of men. The domestic world of women had no place in the continuum from boy's games through men's sports to the "real" contests of war. Reporters, as intermediaries to the feminized domestic realm, were likewise forced to watch from the sidelines, no matter their pretense of direct involvement.[21] The actual "child" in "Death and the Child," a young boy abandoned by his refugee parents, watches in confusion as the battle transpires in the valley below. When confronted by the strange figure of Peza, by now dirty, wounded, and stripped of his illusions about the romance of battle, the child simply asks, "Are you a man?" (141). Crane leaves the question unanswered. The moment is unavoidably reminiscent of the end of *The Red Badge of Courage,* when Crane says of Henry Fleming, "He had been to touch the great death, and found that, after all, it was but the great death. He was a man" (*Works* 2:135). Crane's irony carries with it a double-edged meaning— Henry both is and is not the courageous example of manhood that exists in his imagination. But Peza cannot even achieve the dubious comfort of self-delusion; his experiences deny him the ability to construct a heroic version of his actions. He remains silent. Peza's failure to achieve the synthesis of action and understanding that is the correspondent's ultimate accomplishment in "The Open Boat" reveals Crane's apprehensions about his own status, and the final Western stories reflect a paradoxical concern for the impossibility of accurate artistic interpretation and the dangerous power that interpretive narratives possess. The rituals of men, whether a game of dice, a gunfight on the frontier, or a bloody battle of war, may simply be games, as those of children, and may lack coherent meaning, but they are undeniably *real* in ways that art is not. When artists attempt to construct meaning, their efforts, far from reflecting the facts, distort and undermine the codes that maintain human society.

One difference between Crane's earlier Western stories and those which conclude the *Tales of Adventure* is that, in the early stories, the manly codes of behavior, however groundless or absurd, essentially *work*. The homosocial world of the Americans in the Mexican frontier provides a framework that allows the Kid and Richardson to survive their encounters with the shadowy Mexicans and that gives Bill's death meaning for the stranger. The later Western stories more aggressively deconstruct the mythology of the West and call into question the value of such manly codes altogether. The job of the artist, therefore, becomes more complicated. If the codes that restrain society are themselves merely fictions, what role does the writer of "realist" fiction have?

Although the playful camaraderie of men in dangerous situations creates a constructive fraternal bond in "The Five White Mice" and "The Open Boat," the later Western tales reveal the hollow center of this brotherhood. The "wild West" of "Moonlight on the Snow," "Twelve O'Clock," and "The Bride Comes to Yellow Sky" unmasks a world that is both absurd and destructive. In "The Bride Comes to Yellow Sky," Crane inverts the more common formula established by the earlier Western stories, in which violence appears in the midst of seemingly innocuous and mundane matters. Here, the patrons of a saloon warn a visiting "drummer" about the dangerous exploits of the town villain, Scratchy Wilson, and the intrepid bravery of the town marshal, Jack Potter. The showdown at the end of the story is a comic deflation of the saloon patrons' talk. Faced down by an unarmed Potter, returning from San Antonio with his new bride, Scratchy grudgingly drops his weapon and concedes, "I s'pose it's all off now" (*Works* 5: 120). The masculine ritual that has been played out by Scratchy and the marshal over and over in the streets of Yellow Sky is forever ruined by the encroaching domesticity of the East, embodied quite literally by Mrs. Jack Potter herself. Like young boys whose game has been interrupted by a scolding mother, the two men reluctantly end their pointless cycle of conflict. The harsh light of civilization has revealed the emptiness and childishness of the manly spectacles replayed throughout the mythical West.

In the earlier Western stories, the line between East and West, between inexperience and experience, is explicit—a wide gulf that separates the observer from the observed. Here, however, the line becomes blurred. In "A Man and Some Others," Bill offers the paradigm of the onetime Eastern "tenderfoot" who remakes himself into an authentic frontiersman through a series of hard-fought challenges and accomplishments. Scratchy Wilson, on the other hand, merely plays the role of the desperado, clad in "a maroon-colored flannel shirt, which had been purchased for purposes of decoration, and made principally by some Jewish women on the East Side of New York" (*Works* 5: 116). "And," Crane adds, "his boots had red tops with gilded imprints, of the kind beloved in winter by little sledding boys on the hillsides of New England" (117). Although Crane's depictions of young boys at play in *Maggie,* "His New Mittens," and elsewhere highlights the heroic pretensions of children, he achieves the reverse effect here, deflating the "play" of grown men into a childish spectacle, cut from the whole cloth of Eastern mythology about the frontier. Scratchy's drunken tirade provides a perverse restatement of the correspondent's and Peza's tragic protestations to Nature: "There was no offer of fight—no offer of fight. The man called to the sky. There were no attractions. He bellowed and fumed and swayed his revolvers here and everywhere" (117). The "attractions" provided by a gunfight, like those of a carnival sideshow, are the real objective of the manly rituals undertaken by Scratchy and the marshal. The watchful eyes of encroaching civilization do not really alter, or tame, the savagery and bravado of the frontier; rather, their presence simply reveals the senseless and futile nature of this violence.

Whereas "The Bride Comes to Yellow Sky" offers a lighthearted reproach to the cult of masculinity and the quest "to touch the great death," subsequent stories, including "The Blue Hotel," expose a much darker vision of the idealized, silent brotherhood celebrated elsewhere in Crane's fiction.[22] The dramatic focus of "The Blue Hotel" is the fate of a hapless Swede, whose paranoia and mythical misconceptions about the American West eventually bring about his own demise. Ultimately, however, the motivations and thoughts of the Swede remain as mysterious to the reader as to the other characters in the story. Throughout "The Blue Hotel," the perspective of the character identified only as "the Easterner" emerges as that most nearly linked with the authorial voice, and it is the epistemological journey of the Easterner that forms the most striking evolution in the text.

The Easterner, the cowboy, and the Swede offer broad "types" representative of various forms of manhood in a curious setting that is every bit as isolated from civilization as the "open boat" of the correspondent, oiler, captain, and cook. When Scully, the Irish innkeeper, heralds the arrival of a snowstorm, Crane emphasizes this parallel: "The guests of the blue hotel, lighting their pipes, assented with grunts of lazy masculine contentment. No island of the sea could be exempt in the degree of this little room with its humming stove" (*Works* 5: 144). The only women in the story, Scully's wife and daughters, are nameless and voiceless and appear only to serve food to the guests. The game of cards undertaken by the men represents a typically masculine ritual and prefigures the actual violence that erupts when the Swede claims that Scully's son, Johnnie, is cheating. In all, the situation in "The Blue Hotel" exemplifies a trivialization and corruption of the "subtle brotherhood" in "The Open Boat." Even the bitter irony in the town's name, "Fort Romper," highlights the perversion of the gamesmanship that binds men together in other stories, as the amusements of five men thrown together by fate and a storm turn deadly. For the camaraderie and bravery of the seamen in the earlier story Crane substitutes selfishness and cowardice, and it is the Easterner, as the potential interpreter, who fails most profoundly.

The Easterner's initial failure to interpret occurs after the Swede says to Johnnie, "I suppose there have been a good many men killed in this room" (*Works* 5: 145–46). The other men react with somewhat artificial innocence to the Swede's notions of the wild West, and he turns to the other outsider, the Easterner, for support. "After prolonged and cautious reflection," the Easterner responds, "I don't understand you" (146). The Easterner's willful ignorance precludes any sympathy such as that which the correspondent feels for the soldier in Algiers, or even that which motivates Peza to take up arms against the Turks. The Easterner has failed in that he has not converted the knowledge that he clearly *does* possess into a meaningful response.

The Easterner, in many ways, typifies the aesthete, "warming his feet at the grate," in his reactions to the events of the story, and his lack of involvement is expressed metaphorically through his failed masculinity. During the card game and the fistfight, the Easterner participates only as a bystander, and his reactions indicate an effete sensibility. When the Swede and Johnnie prepare to fight under the guidance of Scully, "the Easterner's mind, like a film, took lasting impressions of three men" (*Works* 5: 159). The Easterner's mild protests—"Oh, wait a moment, can't you" (157)—disappear amid the arguments and accusations of the other men. His commentary on the events fails to make any impact. The Easterner's guilty revelation, at the end of the story, that Johnnie *had* been cheating, and that he had failed to support the Swede, highlights the significance of the Easterner's ineffectiveness during the fight. Even when his feeble voice can be heard, it offers no real insight into the conflict but poses only vague philosophical questions.

The Easterner's impotence as an interpreter mirrors his essential lack of masculine qualities.[23] "Pallid" (*Works* 5: 156) and "nervous" (158), the Easterner proves ineffectual as a member of the fraternity that forms in the blue hotel. Venturing outside into the blizzard for a fight, the men "lowered their heads and plunged into the tempest as into a sea" (158), and Crane highlights the differences between the spectators: "The Easterner's teeth were chattering, and he was hopping up and down like a mechanical toy. The cowboy stood rock-like" (159). The other men form a circle around Johnnie and the Swede, and under the guidance of Scully "the arrangements were swiftly made" (159). In the heat of battle, the men revert to broad "types" and reveal their essential differences of class, ethnicity, and education. During the fight, Scully's speech begins to lose its typical Western twang ("eddycation," "Git over, there") and revert to a heavy Irish brogue ("Kape back," "Johnnie, me boy!") (160). The cowboy, an archetypal male spectator at a boxing match, is gripped by "a holocaust of warlike desire" and cries out, "Go it, Johnnie! Go it! Kill him! Kill him!" (160). "To the Easterner," however, "there was a monotony of unchangeable fighting that was an abomination" (160). He refuses to fully participate in the atavistic ritual of watching men fight, a ceremony that defines Western, and indeed American, notions of manhood. When, in the conclusion, the Easterner confesses his failure to act on the Swede's behalf, he himself articulates this flaw in strictly gendered terms: "Johnnie was cheating. I saw him. I know it. I saw him. And I refused to stand up and be a man" (170). For the Easterner, the failure to take interpretive action represents a failure of masculinity, of individual power and authority. He lacks not knowledge but the will to communicate it.

The story's denouement, in which the Easterner finally reveals this knowledge both to the cowboy and to the reader, firmly establishes the emergence of the Easterner as an interpreter, in the artistic sense.[24] The Easterner, in the concluding section, effectively revokes his former detachment. "As a matter of fact," Cady writes, "the perspective of the Easterner is that of Christianity as interpreted by Tolstoi and no doubt mediated to Crane through Howells" (*Works* 5: 157). In this section, Crane clearly aligns the Easterner with his own complicity as an artist, as the author too has withheld this important information about Johnnie's cheating. In his reunion with the cowboy, the Easterner is transformed from the "little silent man from the East" (143) into an aggressive and eloquent speaker. After the Easterner begins to defend the Swede, Crane writes, the cowboy "browbeat the Easterner and reduced him to rage" (170). Crane's use of "rage," as in "The Open Boat," indicates a masculine response to the cowboy's folly. Such scenes of an individual cursing his fate are common in Crane's fiction, and the effect of each varies considerably. If this moment in "The Blue Hotel" parallels that in "The Open Boat," it contrasts significantly with the deleted chapter 12 in Crane's manuscript for *The Red Badge of Courage,* in which Henry's childish exaggeration of his sufferings clearly demonstrates his selfish inability to sympathize with his comrades and a shallow illogic typical of Crane's more self-deluded characters. Here, however, the Easterner's outburst reveals a concern for the Swede and a sense of communal responsibility that mitigates any temptation to read this passage ironically and transforms the Easterner from an ineffectual, even comic, character into a more complex, tormented spokesman for Crane's humanistic values. In this rage, the Easterner articulates his insights into the death of the Swede: "We are all in it! . . . Every sin is the result of a collaboration" (170). The Easterner's transformation from the meek outsider who responded to the Swede, "I don't understand you," to the impassioned orator who berates the simple-minded cowboy illustrates the development of the Easterner as an interpreter, but this development, of course, comes too late to help the Swede. The Easterner believes he has learned from experience, but at what cost?

Recurring in these later Western stories is the notion that the West, far from being a primitive antidote to the civilized East, is in fact a plainly artificial construction of Eastern myths and a reflection of the capitalist expansionism at the heart of American ideology. No longer a mythical landscape of manly conquest, the West has become a vast real estate development. The violent mythos that encouraged and sustained its conquest must now give way to encroaching civilization. Trading exaggerated stories of their town's sordid reputation as a watering hole for outlaws and rowdies, the townspeople at the opening of "Twelve O'Clock" worry about their ability to sell their property to wealthy financiers. One man says, " 'That don't do a town no good. Now, how would an eastern capiterlist'—(it was the town's humor to be always gassing of phantom investors who were likely to come any moment and pay a thousand prices for everything)—'how would an eastern capiterlist like that? Why, you couldn't see 'im fer th' dust on his trail" (*Works* 5: 171).[25] Similarly, "Moonlight on the Snow" opens with a discussion of the dubious notoriety of the grimly named town of "War Post" and the need to improve the town's image: "But ultimately it became known to War Post that the serene-browed angel of peace was in the vicinity. The angel was full of projects for taking comparatively useless bits of prairie and sawing them up into town lots, and making chaste and beautiful maps of his handiwork which shook the souls of people who had never been in the West. . . . And high in the air was the serene-browed angel of peace, with his endless gabble and his pretty maps" (179). In the interest of appealing to these unnamed and unseen Eastern developers, the town leaders, under the direction of Tom Larpent, a gambler and entrepreneur who "had been educated somewhere" (180), decide to adopt stricter laws to control the unruly cowpunchers and miscreants for whom the town is infamous. Crane writes that "since the main stipulation was virtue, War Post resolved to be virtuous. A great meeting was held, at which it was decreed that no man should kill another man under penalty of being hanged at once by the populace" (181). Of course, the town's response to its uncivilized reputation—a policy of lynching—is itself equally uncivilized. The dominant narrative of the West, that of violent conquest and rugged individualism, is under attack by the competing narrative of Eastern capitalism, and both fictions contribute to the brutal facts that dominate these stories.

If "authentic" Westerners usually remain suspicious of "eddycated" men from the East, the character of Tom Larpent demonstrates why this suspicion might be well placed. Whereas the Easterner in "The Blue Hotel" fails to speak up and prevent violence, Larpent, a transplanted Easterner, not only acts violently but uses his gift for language to prevent the town from acting against him.[26] He murders a man who, like the Swede does to Johnnie in "The Blue Hotel," accuses him of cheating, and he sits quietly, waiting for the town leaders to take him away to be hanged. Larpent's apparent complaisance and obliging willingness to be hanged confuses the townspeople, and his eloquent cynicism angers them: "'Tom,' quavered Bob Hether, 'for Gawd's sake, keep your mout' shut'" (*Works* 5: 184). As the men build a scaffold for Larpent's hanging, he continues to chide their sense of purpose: "Larpent's cold ironical survey drove them mad, and it entered the minds of some that it would be felicitous to hang him before he could talk more. But he occupied the time in pleasant discourse" (184–85). Larpent uses his interpretive powers to confuse and dissemble the town's resolution to "be virtuous." Unlike the ineffectual Easterner in "The Blue Hotel," Larpent not only acts violently himself but also speaks up to prevent a violent death—in this case, his own. The fictional narratives that govern the manly rituals of the West are, in Larpent's hands, dangerous weapons that undermine the very community they are meant to define and defend.

The essential "literariness" of Western myths, and the subsequent ability of certain interpreters to manipulate or misread these myths, threatens the fragile integrity offered by the masculine games so central to Crane's characters. When, in "The Blue Hotel," the cowboy and Johnnie speculate about the source of the Swede's paranoia, the Easterner offers an answer:

> "Oh, I don't know, but it seems to me that this man has been reading dime-novels, and he thinks he's right out in the middle of it—the shootin' and stabbin' and all."
>
> "But," said the cowboy, deeply scandalized, "this ain't Wyoming, ner none of them places. This is Nebrasker."
>
> "Yes," added Johnnie, "an' why don't he wait till he gits *out West?*"
>
> The travelled Easterner laughed. "It isn't different there even—not in these days. But he thinks he's right in the middle of hell."
>
> Johnnie and the cowboy mused long.
>
> "It's awful funny," remarked Johnnie at last.
>
> "Yes," said the cowboy. "This is a queer game." (*Works* 5: 152)

The Easterner, presumably as well read as he is well traveled, places the blame on the dime novels that have contributed to the mystification of the West, a mystification shared, it seems, by such authentic Westerners as Johnnie and the cowboy. They simply locate this myth in some remote place further west. The Swede—"queer"-ly—refuses to play by the rules of their "game" by insisting that Johnnie adhere to the rules of the actual card game they are playing. The Swede mistakenly locates the fictional narrative of the dime-novel "true West" in the "real" site of Fort Romper, Nebraska. Moreover, the Swede's fatal misapprehension of real and fictional narratives is further complicated by Crane's location of these interpretive "truths" within his fiction.

The contrasting experiences of successful interpreters, such as the correspondent of "The Open Boat," and failed interpreters, such as the Easterner of "The Blue Hotel" (as well as duplicitous interpreters, such as Tom Larpent of "Moonlight on the Snow"), raise questions about the direct involvement of the artist in the useful activities of life. Crane certainly accepts Tolstoy's claim that "man's first and most unquestionable duty is to participate in the struggle with nature to support his own life and that of others" (*I Cannot Be Silent* 96–97). It is precisely this "struggle with nature" that Crane proposes in "The Open Boat," using the metaphorical language of masculinity to resolve the problem of the passive artist as mere spectator. Crane's narrative calls for involvement, but, in "The Blue Hotel," this involvement would have erased, or at least altered, the story. The Easterner comes to believe that, had he acted properly and intervened on the Swede's behalf, there would have been no death of the Swede (and therefore no story). "The Swede might not have been killed," the Easterner later muses, "if everything had been square" (*Works* 5: 170)—that is, if there had been no cheating *or* if the Easterner had told the truth. Although the sacrifice of Billie in "The Open Boat" occurs *in spite of* the artist's involvement, the sacrifice of the Swede occurs precisely *because* the Easterner fails to "stand up and be a man."[27] In "The Five White Mice," the Kid and his friends avoid death through a combination of chance and the Kid's instinctive reactions to his own fear. In the end, "nothing had happened" because the Kid acts according to the manly codes that form the necessary artifice of his society. Conversely, the Easterner causes something bad to happen by failing to act or to interpret events and by allowing falsehoods to persist. The same Western myths that saved Richardson and the Kid destroy the Swede. The Swede believes he is in danger, and eventually, he is proven right. The Easterner's recognition of his own interpretive failure therefore complicates the aesthetic position established by Tolstoy and suggested by "The Open Boat." If experience enables some men to "then be interpreters," "what to do" with this newfound knowledge? By translating insight into text, the author inevitably establishes a spectatorial distance from the solid grounding of experience. If the strength of Crane's writing develops, as James Nagel claims, from the "constant interplay be-tween experience and comprehension" (22), the figure of the artist serves as an important location for the mediation of this interplay. For Crane, the struggle to become a *professional* interpreter, to create meaning from the chaos of nature—and to profit from it—is a "queer game" indeed.

3 / "Beauty Unmans Me"

Diminished Manhood and the Leisure Class in Norris and Wharton

The physical vigour acquired in the training for athletic games—so far as the training may be said to have this effect—is of advantage both to the individual and to the collectivity, in that, other things being equal, it conduces to economic serviceability. . . . Ferocity and cunning are of no use to the community except in its hostile dealings with other communities; and they are useful to the individual only because there is so large a proportion of the same traits actively present in the human environment to which he is exposed. Any individual who enters the competitive struggle without the due endowment of these traits is at a disadvantage, somewhat as a hornless steer would find himself at a disadvantage in a drove of horned cattle.
—Thorstein Veblen, *The Theory of the Leisure Class*

In a 1927 essay entitled "The Great American Novel," published during the height of her fame and fortune as an author, Edith Wharton elevates Frank Norris's *McTeague,* David Graham Phillips's *Susan Lenox,* and Robert Grant's *Unleavened Bread* to the status of "not only 'great American novels,' but great novels" (*Uncollected Critical Writings* 152–53). Notoriously stingy in her praise of literary contemporaries and forbears alike, Wharton selects a list of works that might surprise readers, not only because of the subsequent obscurity of Philips's and Grant's books but also because Norris's quintessentially naturalistic exploration of the seedy netherworld of San Francisco's underclass seems so unlike Wharton's own novels. In order for a novel to be truly "American," Wharton contends, "it must tell of persons so limited in education and opportunity that they live cut off from all the varied sources of culture which used to be considered the common heritage of English-speaking people. The great American novel must always be about Main Street, geographically, socially, and intellectually" (152).[1]

Always modest about her talents, Wharton produces a definition of greatness that apparently excludes any consideration of much of her own oeuvre, which deals largely with manners and mores of upper-class New Yorkers. Her novels seem to be "geographically, socially, and intellectually" about Fifth Avenue, not Main Street. More than milieu, however, her stated objectives for great literature focus primarily on artistic presentation and reception. Of these "great American novels," Wharton claims that "they came before their time, their bitter taste frightened a public long nurtured on ice-cream sodas and marshmallows" (*Uncollected Critical Writings* 153). Here Wharton defines a relationship between artist and audience bound by the materialist model of production and consumption: the public's desire to consume frivolous trifles has corrupted the literary marketplace and undermined her own efforts to produce meaningful art.

In his own bid to define his role in the arena of literature, Norris declares his intentions for his new "Epic of the Wheat" in an 1899 letter: "Now I think I know where I am at and what game I play the best. The Wheat series will be straight naturalism with all the guts I can get into it" (*Collected Letters* 93). Norris saw his planned "trilogy of the wheat" as a return to the tough-minded naturalism of *McTeague* and a rejection of the demands of the marketplace that had motivated him—at least in part—to publish an intervening set of books, often critically dismissed as his "popular novels." With his trilogy, *Moran of the Lady Letty, A Man's Woman,* and *Blix,* Norris sought to establish himself as a versatile and successful writer within the boundaries of adventure fiction (*Moran* and *A Man's Woman*) and of Howellsian realism (*Blix*). In this context, his statement of purpose in undertaking *The Octopus* inevitably raises formal questions about what exactly "straight naturalism" is. *The Octopus,* with its multiple plots and subplots, invocation of the classical epic, and frequent descents into vague mysticism and melodrama, hardly presents a unified, coherent formal pattern. Just what sort of "game" is Norris talking about? *The Octopus* not only constitutes an example of Norris's dialectical view of naturalism as the convergence of realism and romance, but it also offers vital information about Norris's aesthetics and his conception of the novelist in the modern era.

Wharton and Norris, despite the tremendous differences among their written works, share a common contempt for the middlebrow consumer culture of their time—an attitude that reflects, to some degree, their shared upper-class sensibilities. Wharton, whose mother's maiden name, Rhinelander, reflects her lineage as a scion of Old New York, and Norris, the son of a wealthy industrialist, both embarked on writing careers that benefited tremendously from the rise of professionalism in the literary sphere, even as they shared unease about the impact of this professionalism and the growing demands of their readership. The three novels that constitute the focus of this chapter, Norris's *The Octopus* and Wharton's *The House of Mirth* and *The Age of Innocence*, stand as examples of these writers' most successful, and most naturalistic, works and reveal their common concerns about the role of the novelist as a purveyor of "bitter taste" to a fickle and unreliable public. Their ambivalence about the limitations of professional authorship manifests itself in the formal characteristics of their writing, and specifically through the presence of weak male characters, whose actions—or, more often, episodes of costly *in*action—drive the books' narratives to their tragic conclusions.

The characterizations of the male protagonists in each of these books— Presley in *The Octopus*, Laurence Selden in *The House of Mirth*, and Newland Archer in *The Age of Innocence*—reveal the extent to which Norris and Wharton depend on the discourse of masculinity in shaping an aesthetic argument in these novels. Presley's inability to shape an artistic representation of his experience reflects a reluctance to fully engage in the actualities of experience, and, more specifically, to fulfill Norris's conception of manhood. With *The Octopus*, Norris proposes a narrative form meant to depict the emerging American empire of the late nineteenth century, and Presley's conflicting roles, as unreliable artist and insightful observer, represent Norris's repudiation of a misguided aesthetic approach as well as the anxieties present in Norris's own work. Similarly, in novels that chronicle the evolution of New York City from provincial capital to international seat of commercial power, Wharton endows Selden and Archer with some ability to perceive the injustices and hypocrisies of their societies, but denies them the power to fully interpret their perceptions and act upon them. Like Presley, Selden and Archer fail to construct a meaningful response to an unjust system, and this failure is one imbued with the rhetoric of masculinity and aesthetics—domains irrevocably connected in Wharton's mind.

Candace Waid, in *Edith Wharton's Letters from the Underworld*, explores Wharton's well-documented aversion to being linked with her female predecessors, including Sarah Orne Jewett and Mary Wilkins Freeman. She largely agreed with Nathaniel Hawthorne's famous characterization of the writers of "sentimental fiction" as "scribbling women" and sought to identify herself outside the confines of regionalism, "local-color," or domesticity. In so doing, Wharton recapitulates the strictly gendered formula of her era. "To Wharton," Waid writes, "reading and writing represented the masculine and adult province of knowledge and power" (11). Likewise, Elsa Nettels observes, "In that Wharton found her literary companionship among men and sought her place in the ranks of the male novelists, she regarded literature as a man's vocation" (86). In finding her place, of course, Wharton challenges this narrow definition of the novelist. In her study of Wharton's attempt at fusing local color with naturalism, most successfully in *Ethan Frome,* Donna Campbell claims that Wharton "provides a test case, an example of how the literary alliances of a strongly feminine, gender-linked tradition gave way before the imperatives of a predominantly masculine and generation-based rebellion against established forms" (148).[2] Although Wharton clearly believed that, as a woman, she might produce works of aesthetic value, she could do so only by adhering to the conventions of "masculine" writing—by writing, as it were, "like a man." This tension between her novels' feminist critique and masculinist aesthetics manifests itself in her texts in the association of ornamentation and superficial appearance with weakness, as well as in the inadequate "manliness" of those men who, by appreciating the novels' heroines as mere ornaments, fail to act appropriately.

The "problem" men of these novels form a peculiar and distinct male type within naturalist fiction. Unlike victims of degeneration, such as George Hurstwood in Theodore Dreiser's *Sister Carrie,* George Kelcey in Stephen Crane's *George's Mother,* or other Norris protagonists, including McTeague or Vandover, these characters ultimately exist outside the tragic cycle of the novel—they are left intact, if not unscathed, by novel's end. Their perspective provides the frame narrative through which the reader understands the downfall of other characters. Nor do they emerge triumphant from the maelstrom of the novel's strife, as do Frank Cowperwood in Dreiser's *The Financier* or Curtis Jadwin in Norris's *The Pit.* Rather, Presley, Selden, and Archer merely survive in a largely comfortable, if somewhat diminished, capacity. In each of these novels, success and failure occur explicitly within the Darwinian arena of capitalism, and the fate of the male characters, in particular, is tied to their ability to control their own economic fortunes. These three men, caught between abject failure and glorious success, are merely quietly subsumed and emasculated by the system against which they have briefly struggled. Whereas degenerated males such as McTeague or Hurstwood revert to atavism and brutality, and thriving entrepreneurs such as Cowperwood or Jadwin exhibit virility and physical strength, Presley, Selden, and Archer experience a lack of "manliness" that corresponds to the narrowing of their horizons. In essence, such characters serve as surrogates for Norris's and Wharton's upper- and middle-class audience—those spectators whose consumption of entertainment fuels the literary marketplace.

The widening journalistic coverage of athletics at the turn of the century offers insight into both Norris's and Wharton's use of these problematic spectator figures in their novels. Michael Oriard, in *Sporting with the Gods: The Rhetoric of Play and Game in American Culture,* explores the recurrence of "sporting metaphors" within the context of *The Octopus,* "a novel of epic contest," defined by a competition for financial supremacy between the railroad and the ranchers (210–13). Indeed, as Norris's comments about the "game" of writing naturalism demonstrates, authors in this period, like many Americans since then, could scarcely avoid sporting metaphors when defining success in any field. As in the boxing ring, football field, or baseball diamond, there are evident winners and losers in the divergent, yet equally naturalistic worlds of Norris's San Joaquin Valley ranches and Wharton's New York drawing rooms. More than mere spectators, however, Presley, Selden, and Archer represent and serve as the mediators of the various "games" played out within the narratives. Not simply innocent bystanders, they must live with their complicity in the downfall of others. Ultimately, Norris and Wharton have quite different stakes in the Progressive Era battles over gender and identity, yet these novels all explicitly suggest distinctly masculinist responses to the rise of the "new woman" and the demands of a "manly" notion of artistry. As participants in the treacherous arena of literature, Norris and Wharton took their places in the evolving field of professional authorship during a period in which ideologies of masculinity, national identity, and cultural authority converged. Norris's composition of *The Octopus* occurred in the aftermath of his work on the "popular novels," but also after his participation, as a journalist, in the Spanish-American War. Norris's work from the time provides considerable insight into the author's omnipresent ideas about Anglo-Saxon destiny and manhood. Furthermore, the infusion of journalistic narrative strategies into naturalistic prose would help shape Wharton's own response to the challenges of authorship.

The brief, intense conflict with Spain in 1898 has earned the title the "Correspondents' War"—not only for the role played by the press in fomenting and encouraging prowar sentiment but for the remarkable number of journalists who issued daily dispatches from Cuba. Indeed, the mythology of Theodore Roosevelt's "Rough Riders" was facilitated by the close relationships that Roosevelt sought and maintained with reporters and publishers.[3] By the time the fighting had begun, more than 150 reporters had registered as official war correspondents, and many others had informally joined the rush to document the United States' first war of the modern era. William Randolph Hearst, the outspoken publisher of the New York *Journal*—from whose editorial pages much of the anti-Spanish propaganda emerged—set up residence himself in Havana shortly after U.S. troops arrived, the better to oversee the work of his correspondents.[4] The newspaper accounts of the Spanish-American War, including those by prominent literary figures Crane, Norris, and Richard Harding Davis, reinforced popular notions of race and national identity in justifying American intervention.[5] These authors actively sought the role of war correspondent, without question a more "manly" pursuit to their way of thinking than that of novelist. Their reports, like other American accounts of the war, consistently reinforce the stereotype of the "Spaniard" as racial Other, a feminized, "old world" figure who lacks the manly resolve necessary to combat the "manifest destiny" of the United States.[6] This popular image, enflamed by the "yellow" newspaper syndicates, presented a perfect foil for the athletic American hero embodied by Roosevelt and his men. As a white Californian, Norris holds a predictably unflattering view of "the Spanish race," based on his experiences in San Francisco with Mexicans, Spanish Americans, and Portuguese immigrants. His newspaper sketch "Among Cliff Dwellers" depicts the inhabitants of Telegraph Hill—at that time, a melting pot for what Norris calls a "queer, extraordinary mingling of peoples" (*Collected Works* 98). Norris tells the story of "a very, very old Spaniard, and rather feeble" and marvels that this man spends all his time in this ghetto on the hill. Norris incredulously describes the old man's isolation: "For eight years this old man has never been down into the city. Old age has trapped him on the top of that sheer hill, and lays siege to him there. . . . This old man will never come down but feet first. The world rolls by beneath him, under his eyes and in reach of his ears. . . . He sees it all and hears it all and is yet as out of it, as exiled from it as if marooned on a South Pacific atoll" (99). For Norris, the old man symbolizes the place of the Spaniard in the American West—feeble, irrelevant, out of date. In his fiction, Norris presents those racially categorized as Spaniards as either frail old men, such as the hermit on Telegraph Hill, or as mad, unpredictable females, such as Maria Macapa, the Mexican charwoman in Norris's *McTeague,* who repeatedly tells the incoherent story of her once-noble family's lost wealth and status, describing over and over the gold-plated china that lies buried somewhere in the jungles of Central America. Throughout his writing, Norris reiterates Roosevelt's claim that "the trouble with Spain is that they are 200 years behind the times. It is impossible to get ahead of Yankees" (qtd. in Samuels and Samuels 22).

The fate of the Spaniard in Cuba—corrupt, dangerous, degenerate, or archaic—warned of the dangers in a debased and ineffectual aristocracy to an anxious American upper class, the members of which feared the effects of social change and the so-called feminization of American culture in the industrial age. Observers saw an innate connection between moral, intellectual, and physical strength, and upper-class men, through sports such as football, baseball, and boxing, embraced those rigorous activities deemed "primitive" as a necessary corrective to their lives of desk work and prosperous leisure. Roosevelt and other prominent reformers, including his friend Leonard Wood, the physician who held de jure command of the Rough Riders, publicly worried that the white male was becoming, quite literally, a weakling. Ivy Leaguers such as Roosevelt emphasized the role of football in "the strenuous life."[7] The upper-class males known as the Rough Riders' "Fifth Avenue Boys"—as newspapers dubbed the well-to-do friends and associates of Roosevelt's who joined the authentic Western roughnecks in the First Volunteer Cavalry—viewed *professional* athletics as the province of the working class. These young men, however, remained committed to the value of athletic discipline and performance, largely through their participation in intercollegiate football. Eager to avoid the affliction of "spectatoritis," upper-class young men sought any opportunity to prove their virility, including that offered by the war with Spain, and, according to Roosevelt and other like-minded "jingoes," it was experience in athletics—especially football—that would ensure the Americans' inevitable triumph. Like Roosevelt's brand of Progressivism in politics, football combined an aggressive, martial spirit with a keen sense of order and "fair play."[8]

Norris, Crane, and Davis had each gained footholds in the field of journalism through their work as sports reporters before becoming war correspondents.[9] The role of the reporter in presenting the brutality of sports to the newspaper's readership offered a rare opportunity to the writer to share, however vicariously, in the manliness of the participants. Similarly, the role of war correspondent offered these privileged artists the chance to participate in what Hearst called "journalism that acts," often quite literally. Reporters accompanied American forces throughout the brief Cuban campaign, sometimes carrying weapons, acting as confidants to military leaders, and blurring the lines between observer and participant. Despite these attempts to become part of the action, like those ringside at the prizefight, the correspondents were ultimately bystanders, facilitating the transfer of masculine authority from the spectacle—those men in combat—to the spectators at home.

Perhaps because of his own status as something of an outsider amid the Ivy League milieu of reporters such as Davis and Norris, Crane remains skeptical of the role of journalists as participants. In an article entitled "Regulars Get No Glory," Crane writes, "The society reporter, invaluable as he may be in times of peace, has no function during the blood and smoke of battle" (*Works* 9: 163). Furthermore, although volunteers such as the Rough Riders are "in the game honestly and sincerely" (163), they are, in the end, amateurs whose inexperience and arrogance erases the contributions of the professional soldiers. As Crane surely realized, the same could be said of celebrated authors whose success in the literary arena has allowed them to fulfill the more manly role of war correspondent. Less circumspect is Norris, who demonstrates his willingness to include all Anglo-Saxons, whether soldier, reporter, or reader, in the exploits of the military forces: "Santiago was ours . . . and the Anglo-Saxon blood of us, the blood of the race that has fought its way out of a swamp in Friesland, conquering and conquering and conquering, on to the westward, the race whose blood instinct is the acquiring of land, went galloping through our veins to the beat of our horses' hoofs" (*Surrender of Santiago* 19–20). Norris slips easily into first-person plural when discussing the triumph of the American forces in Santiago, and his rhetoric—with a characteristic absence of subtlety—invokes the role of Anglo-Saxon destiny in determining the outcome of the war. Admitting his role as a mere reporter, Norris claims: "Even though not a soldier, it was impossible not to know their feeling, glorying, arrogant, the fine, brutal arrogance of the Anglo-Saxon" (*Surrender of Santiago* 20).

Norris's understanding of the duty of the war correspondent derives in large part from the influence of Rudyard Kipling. In particular, the attitudes of Crane, Davis, and Norris invite comparison with Kipling's artist-hero, Dick Heldar, who fights alongside British colonial forces in the Sudan in *The*

Light That Failed: "With the soldiers sweated and toiled the correspondents of the newspapers, and they were almost as ignorant as their companions. But it was above all things necessary that England at breakfast should be amused and thrilled and interested" (19). Here Kipling's irony resembles Crane's bemused detachment more closely than Norris's "fine, brutal arrogance." Although underscoring the active role that Dick and the other correspondents take in the battle, Kipling remains mindful of the journalists' purpose—to "amuse" the readership back home. Although imperial conquest and a sense of racial destiny might motivate writers such as Norris in their journalistic duties, the selling of newspapers to a public with a voracious appetite for leisure and entertainment ultimately pays the bills.

This collision between a vague, racialized notion of duty and the demands of commerce contributed to the unease with which Progressive Era writers embraced a vocation in which one attempts to assert his manliness through words rather than deeds. Wharton claims, in *The Writing of Fiction:* "Verisimilitude is the truth of art, and any convention which hinders the illusion is obviously in the wrong place. Few hinder it more than the slovenly habit of some artists of tumbling in and out of their characters' minds, and suddenly drawing back to scrutinize them from the outside as the avowed Showman holding his puppets' strings" (65). In calling for the accuracy of a work of fiction, Wharton highlights the conflicting roles of showman and social scientist for the naturalistic author. The danger of remaining an outsider is the creation of an unconvincing text, yet exerting too much control over the characters' actions undermines the "naturalness" of the fictional events. The writer therefore must negotiate between involvement and equanimity, and this struggle, as is so common in Progressive Era America, asserts itself in gendered terms. The tension between "male" action and "female" observation has its roots in the volatile and highly charged cultural climate that witnessed the emergence of a modern sporting culture and launched the past century of American empire building. In an essay exploring Wharton's "imperialist aesthetics," Frederick Wegener refers to a passage from Wharton's late novel *The Gods Arrive:* "Describing the creative act through what many will consider a perennially male trope of mastery and compulsion, Wharton appropriates such a trope in a way that replenishes and strengthens, rather than undermines, its authority" (805).[10] For Wharton, as for other writers, race and gender serve to authenticate the identity of the reporter who "has no function during the blood and smoke of battle."

In the case of *The Octopus,* the "battle" in question is based quite specifically on a real event: the Mussel Slough Massacre, a one-sided fight between wheat ranchers in California's San Joaquin Valley and agents of the Southern Pacific Railroad.[11] The spectator charged with a duty to report this tragic event is Presley, a sometime writer living as a sort of benign freeloader—offering companionship and conversation in exchange for the opportunity to recover from a bout of consumption "in the dry, even climate of the San Joaquin for an indefinite amount of time" (584) and observe his host, Magnus Derrick, and his fellow ranchers as they carve their empires out of the fertile California soil. Norris notes that Presley "had graduated and post-graduated with high honours from an Eastern college, where he had devoted himself to a passionate study of literature, and more especially of poetry" (584). In his background and temperament, Presley seems to exhibit text-book symptoms of "neurasthenia," as it was then defined by George Beard and others in this era. In *American Nervousness, 1903,* Tom Lutz explores Norris's composition notes for *The Octopus* to identify Presley's neurasthenic characteristics: "Presley is an eastern dude who rides [a] bicycle instead of a horse, a brain-worker who writes rather than works, and an amateur occultist with a morbid interest in the cosmic musings of the mystic Vanamee. Presley has a neurasthenic relation to emotion (melancholic), to nerve force (refined, excitable, thus depleting), to psychology (morbid, unbalanced mind), to politics (anarchist, the political equivalent of 'excitable and un-balanced'), and to the supernatural (obsessive, almost prophetic)" (136). Presley's unhealthy body matches his unhealthy mind, corrupted by book learning, theory, and poetry. Presley occupies a problematic position as a protagonist because he is a failed writer himself. Norris typically includes artists in his novels, from the debauched painter of *Vandover and the Brute* to the resurrected hack journalist Condy Rivers of *Blix,* and he invariably draws upon his own experiences for certain details of their lives. Various factors, however, mitigate the critical temptation to read autobiography into such characters, including ironic distance of the narrative voice, the moral code established within the text, and the relevance of the biographical details themselves.

In this case, the ambiguous characterization of Presley forces readers to challenge the reliability, authority, and value of Presley's insights. Nowhere is this challenge greater than in the novel's controversial ending, in which Presley achieves a sort of philosophical epiphany. After all the ranchers have been killed, demoralized, driven out by the "octopus" that is the Pacific and Southwestern Railroad, Presley boards a ship, the *Swanhilda,* full of wheat bound for the starving masses of India, and reflects bitterly upon the devastation caused by the struggle over the San Joaquin Valley farmland. In his despair, however, Presley arrives at a remarkably optimistic conclusion:

> *But the* WHEAT *remained.* Untouched, unassailable, undefiled, that mighty world-force, that nourisher of nations, wrapped in Nirvanic calm, indifferent to the human swarm, gigantic, resistless, moved onward in its appointed grooves. . . . Falseness dies; injustice and oppression in the end of everything fade and vanish away. Greed, cruelty, selfishness, and inhumanity are short-lived; the individual suffers, but the race goes on. . . . The larger view always and through all shams, all wickedness, discovers the Truth that will, in the end, prevail, and all things, surely, inevitably, resistlessly work together for the good. (*The Octopus* 1097–98)

Presley's insight transforms the narrative landscape of *The Octopus,* and the various critical interpretations of this pivotal passage reveal its significance in achieving a full understanding of the novel. Harold Kaplan, for example, claims that Norris's assertion that "FORCE only existed" (*The Octopus* 1084) demonstrates "his naturalist theme as the conclusion of all narrative events" (115). "However," Kaplan continues, "the intellectual unity of the novel does not rest on this narrow, despairing principle but rather on the effort to conquer its implications" (115). Presley's dawning comprehension, then, recognizes the eventual good that will result from the dialectical clash between the Wheat and the Railroad. Ronald Martin, in *American Literature and the Universe of Force,* interprets the conclusion in a similar fashion, as "a double-voiced peroration, the last word of both Presley and the narrator" (171).[12] Indeed, the tragic events that occupy the bulk of Norris's narrative seem in stark contrast to Presley's heartening philosophy.[13] It is only within the context of Norris's ideological investment in Anglo-Saxon destiny that Presley's musings about "the world-force" of the wheat seem consistent with the adversity and failure that pervade the novel's conclusion. Presley may be speaking of the human "race" in this passage, but he is almost certainly speaking more specifically of the Anglo-Saxon race, and the westward voyage of the wheat represents the inevitable, "resistless" conquest of the Orient that is the destiny of America's Anglo-Saxon ruling class. Of course, the conflict in Cuba on which Norris so fervently reported served as the Caribbean theater of the campaign to establish an American empire. The occupation of the Philippines by American forces provided a clear example of the sort of inexorable westward Anglo-Saxon journey that Norris celebrates at the conclusion of *The Octopus.*

The interpretive dilemma encountered by critics derives largely from Norris's use of a flawed character to communicate what Norris clearly saw as philosophical truths. As a failed writer, Presley seems an unlikely character to articulate the thematic underpinnings of the novel in this closing section. Don Graham alludes to this problem: "Despite his artistic inadequacies, Presley is granted the major role of reflecting the last viewpoint presented in the novel" (119). What, then, is the nature of Presley's "artistic inadequacies"? Graham claims that "Presley the human being qua philosopher is kept quite distinct from Presley the artist, who remains tainted with the lavender tarbrush of elite aestheticism" (122). In assessing Presley's artistic shortcomings, Donald Pizer points out, "Both Presley's early and later failures stem from the same cause—his intellectuality" (*Novels* 135). Norris, therefore, finally distances himself from Presley not philosophically, but aesthetically: Presley, the nervous and consumptive poet, eventually understands the philosophical "truths" depicted in the narrative, but he remains unable to express these truths through art. The artistic failings in Presley's approach—elitism, aestheticism, intellectualism—represent recognized handicaps in Norris's conception of the artist, and an examination of Presley's artistic inadequacy illuminates the naturalist aesthetic that Norris's novel itself promotes.

The distaste for Victorian aestheticism that Norris expresses in his essays also emerges within *The Octopus.* Norris's complex, though primarily antagonistic, views on aestheticism can be traced to his own flirtation with the movement early in his career, his subsequent emulation of Kipling's adventure stories, and his often strained relationships with those San Francisco artists and writers known as "Les Jeunes," whose involvement with Victorian aestheticism remains documented in their publication, *The Lark.*[14] Norris felt that the work of Les Jeunes, by emulating the detached elitism of the British aesthetes, developed precisely the wrong approach to creating an appropriate literature of the Western American experience. In an essay written for the *Wave* in which he spells out his hopes for literary representations of life and culture in San Francisco, Norris expresses his attitude toward the aesthetics of Les Jeunes in explicitly gendered terms: "Les Jeunes. Yes, there are Les Jeunes, and the *Lark* was delightful—delightful fooling, but here's a graver note and a more virile to be sounded [*sic*]. Les Jeunes can do better than the *Lark*. Give us stories now, give us men, strong, brutal men, with red-hot blood in 'em, with unleashed passions rampant in 'em, blood and bones and viscera in 'em, and women, too, that move and have their being" (*Criticism* 30). Presley's outward opposition to aestheticism aligns him with Norris and distinguishes him from other artist figures in the novel, even as his affinity with the "strong, brutal men" of the San Joaquin Valley remains tenuous at best.

As a writer living among the wheat ranchers of the San Joaquin Valley, Presley deals primarily with pragmatic, unpretentious men and women. Among those few who share Presley's artistic interests, however, is Magnus Derrick's wife Annie. Norris introduces her "stirring her coffee with one hand, held open with the other the pages of Walter Pater's 'Marius'" (*The Octopus* 623). A former teacher, Annie Derrick embodies the values of the late nineteenth-century aestheticism for which Norris does not conceal his contempt: "Her taste was the delicacy of point lace. . . . 'Marius the Epicurean,' 'The Essays of Elia,' 'Sesame and Lillies,' 'The Stones of Venice,' and the little toy magazines, full of the flaccid banalities of the 'Minor Poets,' were continually in her hands" (625). This figurative emasculation hints at the withdrawal from life that these works represent. In the midst of the "direct brutality of ten thousand acres of wheat" (624), Annie Derrick has "retired within herself" (625). For her, the enormity and abundance of nature seems almost obscene: "There was something vaguely indecent in the sight, this food of the people . . . weltering here under the sun in all the unconscious nakedness of a sprawling primordial Titan" (624). In the grand design of the natural world, Mrs. Derrick sees only concupiscence. Her very concept of Nature represents, for Norris, something "unnatural," and in this context, the implied homoeroticism and decadence of aestheticism appears as deviant rather than merely effeminate. In his essay "Frank Norris and the Genteel Tradition," William Dillingham claims that Norris is "as much a product of polite society" (203) as William Dean Howells, Henry James, and the restrained realists against whom he rebelled. The "Puritan view of sex" (201) that Dillingham identifies in Norris's novels, however, springs not from an aversion to sexuality, but to non-normative sexuality that serves no apparent procreative function. Presley echoes Norris's values by seeing in the natural landscape a "purposeful" regenerative power, whereas Annie Derrick can perceive only hedonistic sensuality.

Annie Derrick expects Presley, as a writer, to share her literary and aesthetic views, but "his indifference to 'style,' to elegant English, was a positive affront" (*The Octopus* 625).[15] Presley's ridicule of the "neatly phrased rondeaux" of her "little magazines" offends Mrs. Derrick's sensibilities, as does his description of his unwritten poem on the West:

> His "Song of the West," which only once, incoherent and fierce, he had tried to explain to her, its swift, tumultuous life, its truth, its nobility and savagery, its heroism and obscenity, had revolted her.
>
> "But, Presley," she had murmured, "that is not literature."
>
> "No," he had cried between his teeth, "no, thank God, it is not."
> (625)

Presley's aversion to traditional notions of "style" and "literature" echoes Norris's own ideas, in which these attributes denote an elite sensibility and dubious masculinity.[16] "Truth," for Norris and Presley alike, necessarily involves brutality and savagery—what Norris describes in his essays as "blood and bones and viscera." Also significant is Presley's (presumably unsuccessful) attempt to communicate his vision, which, although "fierce," remains "incoherent." The alternative to effete aestheticism, to "literature," though desperately needed, remains unclear to Presley.

Perhaps the most obvious manifestation of Norris's views on aestheticism appears in his characterization of Hartrath, the painter whom Presley encounters in San Francisco while accompanying the Derricks during their legal battle with the railroad. Intruding upon Lyman Derrick's gentlemen's club, Hartrath is described as "a certain middle-aged man, flamboyantly dressed, who wore his hair long, who was afflicted with sore eyes, and the collar of whose velvet coat was sprinkled with dandruff" (*The Octopus* 814). A mean-spirited caricature of Les Jeunes, Hartrath also serves as further contrast to Presley's artistic intentions—an uneasy reflection of his own anxieties. Hartrath's painting "A Study of the Contra Costa Foothills" is admired by the fashionable patrons of a benefit auction for its technical attributes, in which "the reddish brown cows in the picture were reminiscent of Daubigny, and . . . the handling of the masses was altogether Millet, but . . .

not quite Corot" (824). Hartrath's talent, if any, is purely derivative. As part of the stylish circle of aesthetes surrounding Mrs. Cedarquist, Presley's dilettantish aunt, Hartrath not only exemplifies a lack of creativity but an essential lack of virility. After shaking Hartrath's "flaccid hand," Presley endures Mrs. Cedarquist's comparison of the two artists' work: "In Mr. Presley's sonnet . . . there is the same note as in your picture" (827). Hartrath responds to Mrs. Cedarquist's compliments with a disingenuous but dramatic reply: "'I am *too* sensitive. It is my cross. Beauty,' he closed his sore eyes with a little expression of pain, 'beauty unmans me'" (827). The originality lacking in Hartrath's painting corresponds to the masculine force lacking in his character. Hartrath's distinct lack of both masculinity and creative power indicates the importance that Norris attaches to a masculine impulse, and Norris further explores this relationship in the subsequent development of Presley's own artistry.

The auction that includes Hartrath's painting benefits the "Million-Dollar Fair," described by Norris as a "gala for the entire Fake" (*The Octopus* 826). Among the prominent sponsors of the Fair is Shelgrim, the head of the Pacific and Southwestern Railroad.[17] Hartrath and his fellow aesthetes serve largely for the amusement of Mrs. Cedarquist, "a relative of Shelgrim himself" (827).[18] The unnatural relationship between patron and artist is consummated in the text by Mrs. Cedarquist's purchase of Hartrath's painting at the auction. Norris intensifies the connection between the aesthete's commodified "art" and the corrupt society it serves when, during the auction, Magnus Derrick receives a letter informing him of a court ruling in favor of Shelgrim and the Railroad. The many arms of the octopus that seeks to destroy the ranchers also manipulate the cultural productions of Hartrath and his colleagues. Hartrath stands as Presley's uneasy mirror image; in him, Presley sees a cautionary example of the "decayed professors, virtuosi, litterateurs, and artists," "fakirs" who "worked the community as shell-game tricksters work a county fair, departing with bursting pocketbooks" (826). The aestheticism they propound operates in consort with the degenerative power of the trusts and serves to support a corrupt and destructive system. Norris also associates the "Million-Dollar Fair" with a motley assortment of ideologies, nationalities, and ethnic types, from whom the "irrepressible Sham" derives its threatening decadence. Among the "fakirs," Norris mentions "a widow of some Mohammedan of Bengal or Rajputana, . . . a decayed musician who had been ejected from a young ladies' musical conservatory of Europe because of certain surprising pamphlets on free love, . . . a Japanese youth who wore spectacles and a grey flannel shirt, . . . a university professor, with the bristling beard of an anarchist chief-of-section, . . . a high caste Chinaman" (825). The deterioration of Anglo-American artistic sensibility is explicitly linked with the threat of foreign influence from both Europe and the Far East, and the perverse mélange of cultures troubles Norris as deeply as the "extraordinary mingling of peoples" of Telegraph Hill.

If Hartrath and Mrs. Cedarquist's circle, as well as Annie Derrick, present a strongly negative portrait of aestheticism and its influence, the characterization of Vanamee, the shepherd, complicates this picture to some extent. Norris derived much of the character of Vanamee from his friend Bruce Porter, a San Francisco aesthete and contributor to *The Lark*.[19] Norris describes Vanamee as "a poet by instinct" who possesses "a great sensitiveness to beauty and an almost abnormal capacity for great happiness and great sorrow; he felt things intensely, deeply" (*The Octopus* 605). Here Norris's language allows Vanamee a more sympathetic rewording of Hartrath's swooning declaration "Beauty unmans me." Norris's physical description of Vanamee likewise suggests a more agreeable version of Hartrath: "His long, black hair, such as one sees in the saints and evangelists of the pre-Raphaelite artists, hung over his ears" (747). Not simply another Hartrath without the dandruff, Vanamee retains a dignity of purpose never accorded the satellites of Mrs. Cedarquist. Much of Presley's (and Norris's) respect for Vanamee stems from his decision to live in Nature, "like a half-inspired shepherd of the Hebraic legends, a dweller in the wilderness, gifted with strange powers" (747). This appeal of Vanamee's retreat into nature, however, belies the withdrawal from human contact that his life entails, a withdrawal reflected in Vanamee's alluring, but ultimately misleading, aesthetics.

Throughout *The Octopus,* Presley follows the aesthetic advice provided by Vanamee, despite the obvious distinctions between the two men's chosen artistic paths. Like Norris himself, Vanamee values "life" over "literature." When Presley informs Vanamee of his projected "poem of the West," Vanamee recognizes his intentions: "Yes, it is there. It is Life, the primitive, simple, direct Life, passionate, tumultuous. Yes, there is an epic there." Presley responds, "Epic, yes, that's it. It is the epic I'm searching for" (609). Soon after suggesting the epic form, however, Vanamee implies that Presley should abandon poetry altogether: " 'Well, yes, it is there—your epic,' observed Vanamee, as they went along. 'But why write? Why not *live* in it?' "

(609).[20] Presley, however, cannot abandon writing: "'I must find expression. I could not lose myself like that in your desert'" (610). By embracing Nature, Vanamee ultimately "loses himself" as an artist, a retreat not unlike that of Annie Derrick. Whether or not "a poet by instinct," Vanamee has withdrawn from the social role of the artist. The ironic flaw in Vanamee's embrace of "the primitive, simple, direct Life" (609) is its isolation from society, and it is this isolation that Presley rejects. Barbara Hochman effectively summarizes Norris's own attitude toward such a choice: "For Norris, in life, the antidote to fear or despondency, isolation and uncertainty, was not philosophical distance or scientific knowledge, but human contact and artistic production" (*Art of Frank Norris* 13–14). The philosophical distance that Vanamee creates for himself undermines any direct, *artistic* involvement in life. Presley seeks to embrace artistic production, but in doing so, he nonetheless falls prey to the lure of Vanamee's inadequate aestheticism.

After accepting Vanamee's suggestion of the epic form, Presley climbs atop a hill and engages in a sort of Romantic daydream, during which he begins to feel the inspiration for his epic: "A delightful numbness invaded his mind and his body. He was not asleep, he was not awake, stupefied merely, lapsing back to the state of the faun, the satyr" (*The Octopus* 612).[21] In this state, "the beauty of his poem, its idyl, came to him like a caress" (615). Presley's Romantic "idyl" is soon disturbed, however, by a train, "the galloping monster, the terror of steel and steam," which strikes and destroys Vanamee's ill-tended flock of sheep. This intrusion of brutal reality proves incompatible with Presley's idyllic vision and destroys his creative energy: "The hideous ruin in the engine's path drove all thought of the poem from his mind. The inspiration vanished like a mist" (617). It is just such painful reality, of course, that Presley hopes to evoke with his epic, but his idyllic reverie, influenced by the careless shepherd Vanamee, proves inadequate to the task. The synthesis of Romance and Realism, as articulated by Norris, eludes Presley.

The composition and publication of Presley's poem "The Toilers" further highlights the failure of his aesthetic vision, as well as the injurious influence of Vanamee upon this vision. Graham fully explains Norris's source for Presley's "The Toilers" as Edwin Markham's "The Man with the Hoe," published in *The Lark* and based on a painting by Millet.[22] This information clearly establishes the connection between Presley's effort and the San Francisco aesthetes, personified in *The Octopus* by Hartrath. Despite his outspoken aversion to Hartrath and his approach, Presley ultimately produces a work that parallels the aesthetic "weakness" of Hartrath's painting. An examination of Presley's composition of the poem confirms what is, for Norris, a dangerous association.

After having "flung aside" the notes for his epic "Song of the West" (*The Octopus* 871), Presley begins writing poetry "inspired by the sight of a painting he had seen in Cedarquist's art gallery" (872). Driven to complete his poem by the emotional rhetoric of Caraher and Dyke, two men who are planning violent action against the railroad, Presley writes the final lines of his poem in a fury of poetic insight, "the phrases building themselves up to great, forcible sentences, full of eloquence, of fire, of passion" (872). Contemplating the oppression of the railroad and thinking that "the plain story of it set down in truthful statement of fact would not be believed by the outside world" (872), Presley opts for a romanticized approach, in which "his earnestness was almost a frenzy" (873). At Vanamee's insistence, Presley publishes the poem in newspapers, rather than the derided "little magazines," and "The Toilers" enjoys tremendous commercial success, in the process becoming commodified and incorporated into the popular culture.[23] Presley senses that his message has somehow been lost. In his climactic meeting with Shelgrim, the very target of his poem's wrath correctly dismisses "The Toilers" as derivative of a superior painting and proclaims, "You might just as well have kept quiet" (1035), and Presley realizes the futility of his efforts. The "message" of Presley's poem, however valid and deeply felt, is ultimately undermined by the form it takes. In *The Fiction of Frank Norris: The Aesthetic Context,* Graham describes the publication of Markham's "The Man with the Hoe," which appeared in an ornate volume, "a very fine piece of fin-de-siècle printing," after its initial appearance in the newspaper: "However handsome, this book was a bit of aestheticism that signaled the complete acceptance of the 'radical' poem in genteel circles. The same thing happens to Presley's poem" (97). Although both poems, real and fictional, are a success in conventional terms, their acceptance within the refined drawing rooms of the very industrialists who inspired their critique signals their inadequacies as works of socially engaged art.

Presley's ongoing failure to communicate his artistic vision, and his repeated backsliding into aestheticism, might be attributed in part to what Pizer terms "his incapacitating intellectuality" (*Novels* 136). Norris's anti-intellectualism is well documented in his essays, and his writing consistently eschews obscurity and intricate wordplay. Presley, however, values lyricism over clarity, and his inability to recognize the superiority of prose over poetry, of "plain story" over eloquent verse, proves to be his aesthetic downfall. Norris includes in the text of *The Octopus* excerpts from Presley's journal, but none of "The Toilers." This choice itself reveals Norris's privileging of "journalistic" rather than poetic language and indicates the effectiveness of Presley's direct rhetorical expression. Why, then, is Presley unable to acknowledge the problem with his poetry, despite his burning desire to communicate directly with the people? Pizer suggests one approach to this question with his elaboration on the "poet by training" and his intellectuality: "[Presley's] temperament has been overrefined by years of study, and he is either too withdrawn or too sensitive to participate successfully in the concrete actualities of life which are the artist's true matrix. . . . There is a hint, toward the close of the novel, in Presley's response to Hilma, that with the aid of a strong woman he might, like Condy Rivers, reinforce his temperament and prove himself as an artist" (*Novels* 135–36).

Significantly, Pizer locates the necessary participation in the "actualities of life" in sexuality and the relationship between a man and a woman. Condy Rivers, the autobiographical protagonist of Norris's *Blix,* achieves success as a writer only through the development of a romantic relationship with the strong-willed, yet distinctly feminine, Travis Bessemer. In his examination of Norris's "popular" novels, Pizer has established a "masculine-feminine ethic . . . in which men achieve a correct masculinity with the aid of women who themselves move from masculinity to femininity" (*Novels* 110–11).[24]

In *The Octopus,* the clearest example of the possibilities offered by a successful male-female union is the relationship between the hard-driving rancher Buck Annixter and Hilma Tree, the simple, hard-working milkmaid whom Annixter eventually marries. From his introduction into the text, Annixter appears as an often comical exemplar of masculine competitiveness: "His world was hard, crude, a world of men only—men who were to be combated, opposed—his hand was against nearly every one of them. Women he distrusted with the instinctive distrust of the overgrown schoolboy" (757). Annixter's boyish ferocity, although a negative characteristic, serves as an essential component of his ambition and accomplishment, a distasteful but necessary phase on the path to maturity. As Dillingham explains, "Almost overnight, Annixter changes from a selfish and sometimes

cruel eccentric, a hater of women and most men, to a selfless, loving husband" (200). Hilma's taming of *"Buck"* Annixter mirrors his control over his
prized "buckskin" horse—a successful harnessing of manly force, rather
than an emasculating conquest. This analogy brings into sharp contrast the
shortcomings of Presley, who himself rides no horse, but a bicycle, on his
sojourns through the valley. "From beginning to end," June Howard notes,
"Presley is a spectator" (117), and his attempts at action, from the political
(bombing railroad agent S. Behrman's house) to the literary ("The Toilers"),
are doomed to failure. Indeed, Presley's lack of engagement in the masculine-
feminine matrix reveals a problem not only of ethics, but of aesthetics
as well.

Certainly, Norris is not the first author to link creative and sexual energy.
The natural procreation made possible by the confluence of male and female
forces, however, explains the source of Presley's *artistic* impotence and also
informs a reading of the primary symbol of creation in the novel—the
wheat.[25] Presley's reliance on artificial, rather than organic, language—his
mistrust of "the plain story"—undermines his artistic capacity. In its emphasis on the almost mystical regenerative power of Nature, Norris's narrative suggests "the Wheat" not only as the inspiration for creative and philosophical insight but as a model for artistic production itself. Norris describes
the plowing of Annixter's ranch in language that explicitly corresponds to
sexual reproduction: "The rain had done its work; not a clod that was not
swollen with fertility, not a fissure that did not exhale the sense of fecundity"
(*The Octopus* 677). Norris further ascribes to the earth a human longing and
passion, claiming that "underfoot the land was alive; roused at last from its
sleep, palpitating with the desire of reproduction" (677). The fulfillment of
this desire occurs when the feminized earth prostrates herself before the masculine power of the plows—"man"-made machines designed to expedite the
natural cycle of reproduction: "Deep down there in the recesses of the soil,
the great heart throbbed once more, thrilling with passion, vibrating with
desire, offering itself to the caress of the plough, insistent, eager, imperious.
Dimly one felt the deep-seated trouble of the earth, the uneasy agitation of
its members, the hidden tumult of its womb, demanding to be made fruitful,
to reproduce, to disengage the eternal renascent germ of Life that stirred and
struggled in its loins" (677–78). The almost comical overdetermination of
the sexual language in this passage provides an inescapable link between the

masculine-feminine ethic, exemplified by Annixter and Hilma's complementary relationship, and the natural process of creation. In his role as spectator, Presley does not participate in the work of the ranch and the creation of the wheat. Similarly, the bachelor poet is unable to awaken within himself the primal, masculine desire necessary for either a sexual relationship or the creation of art.

The plowing of Annixter's ranch not only illustrates the masculine-feminine ideal for creation but also reveals the problematic consequences of this metaphor. Although the coupling of masculine machine and feminine earth produces the wheat and thereby perpetuates the eternal cycle, the procreative act itself is undeniably violent: "There, under the sun and under the speckless sheen of the sky, the wooing of the Titan began, the vast primal passion, the two world-forces, the elemental Male and Female, locked in a colossal embrace, at grapples in the throes of an infinite desire, at once terrible and divine, knowing no law, untamed, savage, natural, sublime" (*The Octopus* 680). The "terrible and divine" act of creation involves a disturbing degree of brutality and atavistic passion. Indeed, the language of this passage echoes earlier descriptions of that other beastlike machine—the railroad. Norris writes, "It was the long stroking caress, vigorous, male, powerful, for which the Earth seemed panting. The heroic embrace of a multitude of iron hands, gripping deep into the brown, warm flesh of the land that quivered responsive and passionate under this rude advance, so robust as to be almost an assault, so violent as to be veritably brutal" (*The Octopus* 680).

The violence of the plows, the "iron hands . . . gripping . . . the brown, warm flesh of the land," recalls Presley's impression of the locomotive that destroys Vanamee's flock, the "terror of steel and steam . . . with tentacles of steel clutching into the soil" (*The Octopus* 617). In this context, the ethical contrast between the creative act of the plows and the purely destructive act of the locomotive becomes clearer.[26] The "responsive and passionate" earth accepts the violence of the machines as part of the natural cycle of the wheat. The sexual violence that this cycle requires, however, indicates an essential component of the creative process, and Presley's inability, or unwillingness, to fulfill the masculine role reveals an anxiety within the text about this kind of aggression.[27] In submitting to "this rude advance, so robust as to be almost an assault, so violent as to be veritably brutal," the earth is effectively raped in the service of a greater purpose, the creation of the wheat.[28] This formula for hope and rebirth as a consequence of sexual violence reveals the troubling relationship between violence and creativity that *The Octopus* proposes.

Norris's consistent invocation of sexual impulses in the development of aesthetics, illustrative of the limitations and implications of gender and power, must also be read symbolically in the context of Norris's nationalist ideology. In his essays, Norris, like Presley, longs for the expression of "the story of the West, the epic of this wonder work of the nineteenth century" (*Criticism* 106). For Norris, the heroes of the "Epic of the West" (107) are "hard-grained, hard-riding, hard-working fellows, Anglo-Saxons, Americans" (106), much like Magnus Derrick and Buck Annixter. The dominating virility of these characters reflects their ability not only to create wealth and opportunity but also to participate in the conquest of the West. Their actions, like that of the "imperious" plow impregnating the earth, form the basis of the developing American empire. Magnus Derrick, "the one-time mining king, the most redoubtable poker player of Calaveras county" (*The Octopus* 813) represents the Rooseveltian idea of upper-class masculinity—imposing, uncompromising, and possessing a virile physicality that matches his intense ambition.

This investment in Anglo-Saxon dominance informs the problematic biases inherent in Norris's conception of western expansion and manifest destiny.[29] The racism, sexism, and nativism of Norris and his characters, however, obscure Norris's own conflicting anxieties about the nature of this conquest. Just as the depiction of the plows sowing the wheat fields recalls the brutal, dehumanized violence of the railroad, so does Norris's characterization of Derrick and the ranchers at times connect them to the destructive and amoral power of S. Behrman and the railroad operatives. "At the very bottom, when all was said and done," Norris writes, "Magnus remained the Forty-Niner" (*The Octopus* 813). Despite his essential honesty and charity, Derrick embodies the same short-sighted greed behind the railroad trust:

> It was the true California spirit that found expression through him . . . ; the miner's instinct of wealth acquired in a single night prevailed, in spite of all. It was in this frame of mind that Magnus and the multitude of other ranchers of whom he was a type, farmed their ranches. They had no love for their land. . . . They worked their ranches as a

quarter of a century before they had worked their mines. To husband the resources of their marvellous San Joaquin, they considered niggardly, petty, Hebraic. To get all there was out of the land, to squeeze it dry, to exhaust it, seemed their policy. (813–14)

The "instinct" of the "true" Californian stems from his Anglo-Saxon essence: harsh, brutal, loveless, opposed to the "Hebraic" instincts belonging to other races. For the ranchers, *their* San Joaquin has been drained of its nonwhite character and infused with the spirit of arrogant conquest. Norris's recurring description of the land as a body echoes in the reflections of Lyman Derrick, who will ultimately help the railroad destroy his father. When Lyman sees a map of California depicting the railroad as red lines on a white background, Norris writes, "it was as though the State had been sucked white and colourless, and against this pallid background the red arteries of the monster stood out, swollen with life-blood . . . gorged to bursting" (*The Octopus* 806). The virile, masculine impulse that compels Derrick to violate the land has been duplicated in the even stronger force of the railroad and its conquest of the West. This imperial model of conquest involves simultaneous production and consumption—the sexualized drive to create is matched by the need to engulf, subsume, and destroy.

Like the powerful locomotive that destroys Vanamee's flock, a "jack-rabbit drive" held by the ranchers prefigures the larger themes that emerge later in the novel. When the inhabitants of the valley all converge "in their Sunday finery" (*The Octopus* 967) to witness the capture and slaughter of the rabbits that infest their wheat fields, the scene foreshadows the lethal actions taken by the railroad against the ranchers and highlights the fundamental rules of "force" that govern Nature. The scene also reveals the racial and class distinctions implicit in the empire building that serves as the novel's backdrop. The ranchers, on horseback, drive the rabbits into a large holding pen, and "men and boys reaching over the sides of the corral, picked up a jack in each hand, holding them by the ears, while two reporters from San Francisco took photographs of the scene" (977). The landowners, the natural aristocracy of the frontier, then step away from the spectacle and allow the largely nonwhite farmhands to perform the actual killing: "The Anglo-Saxon spectators round about drew back in disgust, but the hot, degenerate blood of Portuguese, Mexican, and mixed Spaniard boiled up in excitement at the wholesale slaughter" (978).[30] Like Shelgrim and the other industrialists, Derrick and his fellow ranchers rely on others to perform the necessary dirty work, and Presley, along with the other white spectators, looks away briefly before joining in the festive barbecue some distance away. The scene also echoes the dynamics of a typical boxing match, in which primitive contestants provide a violent form of amusement for the leisure class. Like any anonymous member of the audience, Presley plays no role here, as the photographers from San Francisco serve to document the proceedings.

At last, faced with the imperial authority of the railroad, yet possessing himself none of the masculine or creative impulse with which to continue the struggle, Presley leaves California. As a chronicler of injustice, Presley has failed. As a passenger on the freighter *Swanhilda*,[31] whose name invokes "the blood of the race that has fought its way out of a swamp in Friesland," Presley becomes part of the growing American empire envisioned by capitalists such as Magnus Derrick and Cedarquist and carried out by industrial powers such as Shelgrim's Trust. As Presley leaves, Cedarquist tells him, "The Swanhilda is the mother of the fleet, Pres. I had to buy her, but the keel of her sister ship will be laid by the time she discharges at Calcutta. We'll carry our wheat into Asia yet. The Anglo-Saxon started from there at the beginning of everything and it's manifest destiny that he must circle the globe and fetch up where he began his march" (*The Octopus* 1094). Cedarquist's plans for shipping wheat to China and the Far East, in fact, recall Magnus Derrick's vision of the promise of a new frontier to be conquered: "The whole East is opening, disintegrating before the Anglo-Saxon" (830). It is the wheat, the product of the masculine-feminine relationship between "man" and Nature, that provides the means for imperial conquest. Derrick imagines its effect: "He saw his wheat, like the crest of an advancing billow, crossing the Pacific, bursting upon Asia, flooding the Orient in a golden torrent" (831).[32] For Norris, the proper vehicle through which to document this inevitable progression is the naturalistic novel—an aesthetic form that itself embodies the masculine force it depicts. Like Derrick's wheat, the novel represents both the product of a masculine-feminine aesthetic and the vanguard of subsequent cultural production.

If the imperial impulse finds proper expression in Norris's novel, however, Presley's fate reflects the anxieties present in the definition of artistry that Norris constructs. By refusing to embrace the same masculine impulses that drive the ranchers and the railroad, Presley is unable to chronicle the consequences of the inexorable course of empire. Despite his eventual understanding of "force" and the progressive nature of history, Presley, as an artist, is powerless. By traveling to India on the same ship with the San Joaquin wheat, Presley has become a silent and passive commodity, shipped westward as imperial cargo.[33] Norris, in contrast, finds expression for the experience of the ranchers and succeeds where Presley has failed. Although Presley's bomb cannot kill S. Behrman, whose name suggests a "Hebraic" Other, the "poetic justice" of Norris's novel can, burying him in the hold of the *Swanhilda* beneath a sea of symbolic wheat. The metaphorical sexuality of a naturalist aesthetic serves as the proper, potent outlet for the literature of the nascent American empire. As Walter Benn Michaels observes, Norris's novel, ostensibly about the *production* of wheat, ends up a chronicle of *consumption*.[34] The "hungry maw" of the railroad consumes the ranchers and their land, the reading public consumes Presley's verse, and the wheat itself consumes the hapless S. Behrman. In the increasingly complicated economy of the late nineteenth century, the line between production and consumption is blurry indeed, and Presley's capitulation to the system mirrors his chronic inability to fulfill the manly role of artist that seems open to him.

Though less overtly concerned with the Anglo-Saxon historicism that runs throughout *The Octopus,* Wharton's novels *The House of Mirth* and *The Age of Innocence* also reveal the anxieties that surrounded the social upheaval of the Progressive Era. Through the fates of two women, these works collectively trace the emergence of New York as the center of an emergent commercial empire and as the turbulent melting pot of American identity at the end of the nineteenth century. *The Age of Innocence* focuses on the patrician society of the 1870s—a closed world of tradition, secure in its preeminence and outwardly impervious to change. The introduction of alien ideas, in the person of Ellen Olenska, is met with suspicion, aversion, and her eventual ostracism. The end of the novel, however, revisits its male protagonist, Newland Archer, some thirty years later, in a much-changed social climate—the era, in fact, of *The House of Mirth.* The challenges to the cultural hegemony of "Old New York" have taken an irreversible hold by the turn of the century, and these challenges stem from a common cause: money. The infusion of new capital has broken down many of the barriers that dominated the culture of Archer's young manhood and contributed to Ellen's exile in Europe.

The Age of Innocence opens with a night at the opera, followed by a ball at the garish and elaborate home of Mr. and Mrs. Julius Beaufort, whom

Wharton describes as "not exactly common; some people said they were even worse" (1030). The opening chapters establish not only the performative nature of New York society but the rituals that enforce its outermost boundaries. The artifice surrounding Archer's life, although apparently arbitrary and decorative, is anything but meaningless. Beaufort, whose first name suggests a Jewish lineage but who "passed for an Englishman" (1030), has never been fully accepted as a member of the social elite, a consequence of his vaguely-defined "foreign" background and his "regrettable" past. According to rumor, Wharton declares, "he had been 'helped' to leave England by the international banking house in which he had been employed" (1031). Not merely a "common" transgressor of class lines, Beaufort's *passing* suggests membership in an entirely distinct race. Although the racial implications of Beaufort's undesirable connection to international banking are only indirectly described, a younger Wharton is less circumspect in her characterization of Simon Rosedale in *The House of Mirth*. She presents Rosedale as "a small, glossy-looking man with a gardenia in his coat . . . a plump, rosy man of the blond Jewish type, with smart London clothes fitting him like upholstery, and small sidelong eyes which gave him the air of appraising people as if they were bric-a-brac" (14). As with Norris's description of Hartrath's velvet coat, the clothes make the man, and Rosedale clearly represents the questionable progress made by such interlopers within the ranks of New York's upper classes. Although her typically ironic narrative voice takes aim at multiple targets, Wharton does not hide her distaste for such "types" despite an implicit critique of the narrow and repressive societies Beaufort and Rosedale both disrupt. Such is the ambivalence of Wharton's attitude toward the social mobility of the Progressive Era—an era in which the expanding literary marketplace allows her own emergence as a "professional" writer.

The same economic changes that have facilitated Wharton's entrance into the arena of authorship also bring with them crass and vulgar commercialization, associated among members of Wharton's class with suspicious outsiders in general, and Jews in particular.[35] *The Age of Innocence* concludes in the age of Lily Bart, as Newland Archer awaits the marriage of his own son Dallas to the daughter of the same Julius Beaufort whose boorishness he once condescendingly tolerated. Archer recalls the words of the hypocritical avatar of "Christian manhood," Lawrence Lefferts, who had wondered about the consequence for a society that opens "its doors to vulgar women" like Beaufort's mistress: "If things go on at this pace . . . we shall see our children fighting for invitations to swindler's houses, and marrying Beaufort's bastards" (1284). With the wisdom of his later years, Archer notes wryly that the latter is precisely what his son is doing, but his acquiescence to the relaxed customs of this "new land" is not without misgivings. Discussing the fact that "nobody was surprised when Dallas's engagement was announced," Wharton writes, "Nothing could more clearly give the measure of the distance that the world had traveled. People nowadays were too busy—busy with reforms and 'movements,' with fads and fetishes and frivolities—to bother much about their neighbors" (1296). Although the novel clearly exposes the cruelty and raw power behind the elaborate rituals of her childhood world, Wharton demonstrates, through Archer's reactions, her own reservations about the crass materialism and selfishness of the new order.

Paramount among Wharton's concerns and central to masculine anxieties of the Progressive Era, the rise of the "new woman" offers a useful prism through which to distinguish the nature of Norris's and Wharton's ambivalence about social change. Although the cult of masculinity arose, in large part, as a reaction to the women's rights movement and its repercussions, Norris's incorporation of women into his fiction hardly recapitulates the one-sided dismissal of women so evident in the work of his literary idol, Kipling. Maisie, in *The Light That Failed,* provides a paradigmatic example of Kipling's attitude toward the folly of female empowerment. Possessed of minimal artistic talent, Maisie offers inadequate competition for Dick's authentic craftsmanship and instead merely encourages him into a life of artistically barren domesticity. For Kipling, the domestic and artistic realms must remain entirely separate, and any attempt to reconcile the two amount to creative suicide. The adventure genre allowed authors such as Kipling and Robert Louis Stevenson to write female characters out of the text completely, because they had no place at sea or on the battlefield. Norris, in contrast, finds rather far-fetched ways to include women in his adventure novels *Moran of the Lady Letty* and *A Man's Woman,* and as the books' titles indicate, he places the women at the center of the narrative. In his synthesis of male and female forces, Norris attempts to resolve the conflict between domesticity and adventure, between the feminized world of leisure and the masculinized world of action. Hilma Tree, instead of trapping the hypermasculine Buck Annixter in a "fee-male" prison of lace and china, offers him the stability and virtue needed to civilize his brutish impulses. Presley's failure to achieve a similar union is evidence of his own ethical and artistic short-comings. Wharton, through her characterizations of Selden and Archer and the roles that they play in destroying the lives of the central female charac-ters, levels an even stronger charge of inadequacy at her problematic male protagonists.

Laurence Selden, Lily Bart's would-be suitor in *The House of Mirth,* and Newland Archer, whose essential conventionality overwhelms his love for Ellen Olenska in *The Age of Innocence,* have provided consistent challenges to critical analyses of Wharton's novels. Critics have traditionally viewed Selden and Archer in one of two roles: as either perpetuators of the societal constraints on women or unsuccessful liberators who fall prey to the same social forces as Lily and Ellen.[36] All together, these contradictory appraisals of Selden and Archer suggest the complexity of Wharton's characterizations and the pivotal roles of these figures in the novels.

Certainly, Wharton locates these characters sympathetically in the frame-work of the narrative itself, as well as within the often distasteful and brutal circle of fashionable New York society. Although Selden and Archer fail as Lily's and Ellen's saviors, Wharton spells out their oppositional position vis-à-vis their contemporaries. Moreover, she describes this opposition as funda-mentally interpretive and aesthetic in nature. For example, Selden's status as a connoisseur of beauty is clearly quite unlike the obsessive collecting of his peers. In *Displaying Women: Spectacles of Leisure in Edith Wharton's New York,* Maureen E. Montgomery describes the cultural rituals of female display and notes the "overt parallel between the collection of inanimate objects and the collection of women" in Wharton's short story "The Daunt Diana" (71). In *The House of Mirth,* Selden himself suggests this parallel in his aesthetic pro-nouncements to Lily: "I'm not really a collector. . . . Your real collector val-ues a thing for its rarity. I don't suppose the buyers of Americana sit up reading them all night—old Jefferson Gryce certainly did n't" (11). Selden's refinement of his nature in this manner resonates with Lily, who, at the time, considers Jefferson Gryce's son, Percy, as her likely husband. Like Percy Gryce, Selden admires objects of beauty and value, but, unlike his coarser peers, Selden's desire for such objects is motivated, and to some extent justified, by his ability to use and understand them.

Newland Archer also imagines himself as distinct from his peers. Whar-ton writes, "Archer tried to console himself with the thought that he was not quite such an ass as Larry Lefferts . . . but the difference was after all one of intelligence and not of standards. In reality they all lived in a kind of hieroglyphic world, where the real thing was never said or done or even thought, but only represented by a set of arbitrary signs" (1050). Archer is distinguished from louts such as Larry Lefferts by his sensitivity to meaning and his capacity to see through the artifice of his culture. He fails, however, in his attempts to transcend this artifice. Although he recognizes the arbitrariness of the "hieroglyphics," he continues to live by them.

Wharton aligns the readers' sympathy with Selden and Archer by making clear their status as social critics, but she also recognizes that such awareness does not necessarily lead to successful intervention on behalf of the female protagonists. When, at the farewell dinner for Ellen, Archer achieves a growing awareness of his powerless position and feels "like a prisoner in the centre of an armed camp" (*Age of Innocence* 335), he is also aware that it is Ellen who must leave. Similarly, when Selden realizes that "all the conditions of life had conspired to keep [him and Lily] apart" (*House of Mirth* 329), he remains free to live his life as before, whereas Lily lies dead in her squalid room. In truth, Selden and Archer are both villains and victims to a certain extent, but a purely social or moral critique of these characters fails to explain their actions, and their significance, in the novels. To dismiss these characters is to ignore the prominence Wharton gives them in the novels. It is primarily Newland Archer, after all, whose perspective governs *The Age of Innocence,* and *The House of Mirth* begins and ends with Wharton's narrative voice enveloping and interpreting Selden's consciousness. As is the case with Presley in *The Octopus,* these central characters function as the spectators whose view mediates the reader's perspective on the action of the novels. According to Candace Waid, "Both Archer and Selden represent men with literary interests who at crucial moments in their lives have pulled back from the threshold of the women they associate with art and poetry" (14). Indeed, Archer and Selden fail as "interpreters," to invoke Crane's definition of that term, and Wharton allows them to serve as negative examples of her own critical and literary objectives. By "pulling back" from direct involvement, Selden and Archer reveal their ultimate inadequacies. As David Holbrook observes, in Wharton's novels, "often the growth of a love is frustrated by the failing of the man to commit himself or to develop" (13). In order to understand Selden's and Archer's failure to commit themselves to Lily and Ellen, one must adopt an *aesthetic,* rather than a social, model. Throughout the novels, Wharton consistently defines Selden and Archer as aesthetes whose flaccid detachment from the actualities of life prevents them from transcending the prevailing perception of women as mere objects of beauty.

Selden's and Archer's disengagement from the manly world of the business arena is reflected in their mutual choice of the law as a profession and in their strong connections with the world of women. A lawyer, although engaged in a respectable, gentlemanly occupation, nonetheless remained distinctly removed from the rough arena of finance and speculation in which fortunes were won and lost. Selden and Archer also manifest symptoms of that dreaded condition in late nineteenth-century America: the "mollycoddle" confined by a mother's apron strings. Having been left fatherless at a young age, both Selden and Archer retain what many observers of the time might describe as an unhealthy attachment to their mothers. Wharton writes of the avowed bachelor Selden that "his views of womankind in especial were tinged by the remembrance of the one woman who had given him his sense of 'values.' It was from her that he inherited his detachment from the sumptuary side of life: the stoic's carelessness of material things, combined with the Epicurian's pleasure in them" (*House of Mirth* 161). Of the Archers, Wharton writes, "Mother and daughter adored each other and revered their son and brother; and Archer loved them with a tenderness made compunctious and uncritical by the sense of their exaggerated admiration, and by his secret satisfaction in it" (*Age of Innocence* 1043).[37] These descriptions reinforce the impression of Selden and Archer as something less than the "redblooded" men of action who served as exemplars of American manhood. The "Epicurian" sensibilities that Selden and Archer bring to their relationships with women, in fact, signal their allegiance with an aesthetic tradition antithetical to the "strenuous life" of the Progressive Era.

Wharton's own relationship with the tenets of late-Victorian aestheticism is a complicated one.[38] As the editor of a volume entitled *Eternal Passion in English Poetry,* Wharton chose to include the works of Rossetti, Swinburne, and Browning among the "most beautiful passages of love-poetry in the language" (vi). In the preface to this volume, Wharton explains the "problem of the relative importance of love-poetry": "The only emotion to which 'all thoughts, all passions, all delights' minister in the average man is but one among the many in the breasts of those who, Admirals on the high seas of poetry, thrill to all the tremors sent below by breezes striking the higher sails" (vii). Wharton's rather labored metaphor distinguishes between the modest "delights" of love poetry and the higher aims of great art. More meaningful literature, Wharton argues, addresses those "tremors sent below," the work of invisible and mysterious forces on the human condition.

Wharton's first published book, *The Decoration of Houses,* an 1897 work on interior design cowritten with Ogden Codman Jr., reveals an aesthetic philosophy that translates to her poetics. In *The Decoration of Houses,* Wharton criticizes the ornamental qualities of Art Nouveau and bemoans the "gilded age of decoration" (196) that then dominated American tastes. Furthermore, she blames this condition on the fact that "house decoration has ceased to be a branch of architecture" (xx). In *The Social Construction of American Realism,* Amy Kaplan points out the feminist implications of Wharton's argument: "Her metaphor of 'interior architecture' suggests the goal of appropriating a traditional male discourse of architecture to transform a traditional female discourse of interior space" (80). This appropriation, although used to critique the patriarchal society, ultimately reiterates the gendered aesthetic principles that govern naturalist principles of artistry and authorship. Although she would agree with the Victorian aesthetes on the absence of beauty in much contemporary art, she connects this problem to a loss of purpose and a misplaced emphasis on ornamentation over functionality—symptomatic of an overall shortage of vitality and vigor in American culture.

Wharton finds in architecture the unity of form and function so lacking in other artistic endeavors. Architecture plays an overtly important role in Wharton's work, from the "House of Mirth" that stifles Lily's (and Selden's) future to the cluttered library into which Newland Archer invariably retreats. The former book's title is taken from Ecclesiastes 7:4: "The heart of the wise is in the house of mourning; but the heart of fools is in the house of mirth"; the phrase further suggests a financial "house," such as those run by Gus Trenor, Simon Rosedale, and the novel's other capitalists. Furthermore, however much he may believe otherwise, Selden, as a part of the machinery of capitalism and as a literal resident in one of his landlord's apartment buildings, lives in the "house of Rosedale." The multiple resonances of the book's title reinforce the unity of morality, economics, and aesthetics implicit in Wharton's critique of Selden. By refusing to take his place in the male arena, Selden allows himself to be controlled by the society he disdains. Moreover, Wharton locates much of the miscommunication and subsequent tragedy of both novels in the dissociation of thought and action in Selden's and Archer's approach to the world.

The aesthetic habit of mind exhibited by Newland Archer and Lawrence

Selden contrasts starkly with the principles Wharton advocates in *The Decoration of Houses.* Judith Fryer, in *Felicitous Space,* has noted the similarities between Wharton's book and the ideas of architect Louis Sullivan, designer of the world's first skyscrapers. Both Wharton and Sullivan support the unity of form and function, and in her writings on decorating Wharton continually stresses the importance of a room's use in considering its appointments. This "organicism" of form bears little resemblance to the championing of artifice undertaken by Archer and Selden. Furthermore, as Fryer observes, Sullivan's aesthetic notions fell into step with the "new kingdom of force" of his era: "Abandoning the East of the Beaux Arts architects for the more open and aggressive city of Chicago, he had begun in the late 1880s to build the skyscrapers which, rooted in the ground and ornamented along their shafts with an elegance that emphasized their verticality and grew more elaborate at their skyward tips, were raw celebrations of phallic energy" (14). Like the majority of artists, writers, and critics of their time, both Sullivan and Wharton identified aesthetic characteristics as either masculine or feminine, and those qualities marked as feminine, they felt, offered nothing of value to a burgeoning and vital American culture. According to Sullivan, successful architecture relied upon the successful architect: "A man that lives and breathes, that has red blood; a real man, a manly man; a virile force—broad, vigorous and with a whelm of energy—an entire male" (qtd. in Fryer 14). In her fiction, Wharton peels away the artifice of New York society to reveal its cruel machinations, and she further indicts the bloodless men who, faced with a vision of reality, retreat into a safe world of fancy and aesthetic amusement.

Wharton connects these characters to the British aesthetic tradition in a variety of ways. *The Age of Innocence,* although published in 1920, depicts New York of the 1870s, and, in this sense, chronologically precedes *The House of Mirth.* Newland Archer, a product of the education and training expected for men of his status in society, emerges from a family that considers "architecture and painting as subjects for men, and chiefly for learned persons who read Ruskin" (1042). In a significant passage depicting Archer's reaction to Ellen's self-described "bits of wreckage" filling her small apartment, Wharton presents Archer's aesthetic credentials:

Newland Archer prided himself on his knowledge of Italian art. His boyhood had been saturated with Ruskin, and he had read all the latest books: John Addington Symonds, Vernon Lee's "Euphorion," the essays of P. G. Hamerton, and a wonderful new volume called "The Renaissance" by Walter Pater. He talked easily of Botticelli, and spoke of Fra Angelico with a faint condescension. But these pictures bewildered him, for they were like nothing that he was accustomed to look at (and therefore able to see), when he traveled in Italy; and perhaps, also, his powers of observation were impaired by the oddness of finding himself in this strange empty house, where apparently no one expected him. (1071)

Wharton's identification of Archer with these major and minor Victorian critics depicts him as an attentive follower of art criticism. Pater's volume in particular, published in 1873, helped to shape subsequent views, not only on Italian art but on the principles of aesthetics, for many years. Archer's background, however, does not prepare him for Ellen Olenska and the challenge her presence provides to his aesthetic sense. The pictures contain no transparent or transcendent qualities, but require certain "powers of observation" to be understood—powers that Archer clearly lacks.

The strangeness of this empty house parallels the challenge to Newland Archer's sensibility that Ellen presents. Emily Orlando notes that "Wharton shows us Ellen's bookshelves as a way of constructing a counter-reading to Archer's fictions" (66). Among her possessions are books by "such new names" to Archer as the Goncourts and Huysmans, whose uncompromising naturalism is utterly alien to his aesthetic sensibilities. Although Archer's preferred habitat is within the confines of his orderly and cloistered library, he sees Ellen's books "scattered about her drawing room," open and accessible to her guests (*Age of Innocence* 1098). Orlando further claims, "Another important feature of Olenska's books is that they are all authored by men. Wharton seems to be saying Olenska understands the 'male' perspective from which these books are written" (67). In other words, Ellen is more of a "man"—aesthetically speaking—than Newland can ever hope to be. In her insistence on personal freedom, her willingness to receive male visitors (including Archer) at "inappropriate" times, and her desire to live in the "Bohemian" quarter with the artists and writers, Ellen represents a prototype of the "new woman" that emerges at the end of the nineteenth century.[39] To Archer, however, her attitudes are merely a source of confusion. As he studies her books, Archer ponders the difference in their understanding of the world: "Ruminating on these things as he approached her door, he was once more conscious of the curious way in which she reversed his values, and of the need of thinking himself into conditions incredibly different from any that he knew if he were to be of use in her present difficulty" (1098). Ultimately, he proves unable to "be of use," and what he perceives as Ellen's "masculine" sensibilities render her compelling, yet finally incomprehensible, to the effete Archer.

Archer's reaction to Ellen's belongings reflects an interpretive failure to "understand" duplicated by his inability to comprehend Ellen herself. Archer follows Ellen to the van der Luyden's country house, Skuytercliff, in a scene in which he both realizes their growing love and misinterprets her relationship with Beaufort. The setting for Archer's encounter with Ellen at Skuytercliff is not the transcendent, pure "Nature" of the romantic tradition, but an artificial, constructed nature typical of Victorian society. The main house at Skuytercliff is a perverse "Italian villa": "Those who had never been to Italy believed it; so did some who had" (*The Age of Innocence* 1118). Ellen senses the artificiality of the house, the rarefied beauty so coveted by New York society. She pleads with Archer, "Is there nowhere in an American house where one may be by one's self? You're so shy, and yet you're so public. I always feel as if I were in the convent again—or on the stage, before a dreadfully polite audience that never applauds" (1121). Ellen chafes against the impossible contradictions in the role assigned to her, as well as the reactions of others.

They wander through the grounds of the estate, and in so doing, come upon the "Patroon's house," built by the family patriarch hundreds of years earlier. Even here, however, the rustic simplicity is an illusion. Through the "newly-washed windows," Archer sees the light of the fire lit by the van der Luydens so they might visit later in the day (1121). Upon entering, Archer ignores the truth and interprets the scene as the result of some enchantment: "The homely little house stood there, its panels and brasses shining in the firelight, as if magically created to receive them" (1121). The tension between the apparent simplicity, even homeliness, of the rustic location and the polished brass and immaculate windows is, for Archer, a sign of aesthetic perfection, rather than perverse falsehood. In this carefully constructed setting, Ellen claims, "I live in the moment when I'm happy" (1122), which Archer interprets as a promise of momentary ecstasy, like Pater's "gem-like flame."[40] He fantasizes about physical contact with Ellen: "Archer imagined her, almost heard her, stealing up behind him to throw her light arms about his neck" (1122). Ellen is correct when she says to Archer, "I don't speak your language" (1120). The mysterious "hieroglyphics" of Archer and his society, built upon artifice and illusion, clash with Ellen Olenska and the sober perspective she has gained through experience. The inability to communicate undermines the relationship between Archer and Ellen and reflects the distance between their aesthetic priorities. Ellen challenges Archer to abandon his accustomed role as observer and act.

Archer responds to this challenge by, quite literally, running away. Following their meeting at Skuytercliff, Archer leaves New York to visit his fiancée, May, in Florida. Before departing, however, Archer signals his retreat from reality in another way—through literature. In a brief passage, Wharton describes Archer's receipt of several books from London, among which he finds only one to capture his attention. Wharton identifies the work as *The House of Life,* a volume written by Dante Gabriel Rossetti, one of the founders of the Pre-Raphaelite Brotherhood.[41] Archer's reaction to this "small volume of verse" is profound: "He took it up, and found himself plunged in an atmosphere unlike any he had ever breathed in books; so warm, so rich, and yet so ineffably tender, that it gave a new and haunting beauty to the most elementary of human passions" (*Age of Innocence* 1125). Rossetti's poetry merges with Archer's dreams and, in so doing, transforms the reality of Archer's meeting with Ellen into an unattainable fantasy. The vision he pursues is not a real person, but "a woman who had the face of Ellen Olenska," and the next morning "his hour in the park of Skuytercliff became as far outside the pale of probability as the visions of night" (1125–26). Archer's aestheticism intensifies his desires but precludes any chance for their consummation. The "haunting beauty" of the poetry, in essence, "unmans" Archer, rendering him incapable of action.

Like Newland Archer, Lawrence Selden responds aesthetically, not actively, to his surroundings in general, and to Lily Bart's predicament in particular. Wharton describes his view of Lily as that of a detached observer: "As a spectator, he had always enjoyed Lily Bart" (*House of Mirth* 4). It is not Lily's company, but Lily herself that Selden enjoys, as one would a work of art. Selden, "conscious of taking a luxurious pleasure in her nearness," admires details such as "the crisp upward wave of her hair—was it ever so slightly brightened by art?" (4). For Selden, there is no contradiction in Lily's natural appearance and the artifice behind it. He reflects upon the "wildwood grace to her outline—as though she were a captured dryad subdued to the conventions of the drawing room," yet recognizes that "the same streak of sylvan freedom in her nature . . . lent such savour to her artificiality" (13). Lily's reconstruction of Nature attracts Selden to her through his recognition of the skillful craft behind it.

Selden insists that his interest in Lily differs from that of her suitors, who see her as a commodity to be purchased. Although Selden's interest in Lily is not strictly commercial in nature,[42] even he recognizes the materialism inherent in his aesthetic judgments:

> He had a confused sense that she must have cost a great deal to make, that a great many dull and ugly people must, in some mysterious way, have been sacrificed to produce her. He was aware that the qualities distinguishing her from the herd of her sex were chiefly external: as though a fine glaze of beauty and fastidiousness had been applied to vulgar clay. Yet the analogy left him unsatisfied, for a coarse texture will not take a high finish; and was it not possible that the material was fine, but that circumstance had fashioned it into a futile shape? (5)

In this passage, Wharton exposes the objectification inherent in Selden's gaze: like a curious museum-goer, Selden puzzles over the nature of the material beneath Lily's "fine glaze." He also interprets her appearance through an economic model in which beauty exists as a limited resource, acquired only at great expense. Though Selden revels in the artificiality of Lily's appearance, he longs to retain a faith in the "fine material" underneath. This belief in the spiritual essence of beauty distinguishes his Victorian aesthetics from the conspicuous consumption of objets d'art that he criticizes. Selden senses the "futile shape" that Lily must assume to become, like the rare volumes of Americana accumulated by old Jefferson Gryce, a desirable piece in someone's collection. Selden's insistence on the primacy of beauty, for its own sake, foolishly ignores the rules of the marketplace that envelop him and Lily. Indeed it is the very "futility" of her artistic creation that drives up Lily's market value, and Selden lacks the successful speculator's stomach for risk.

The discrepancy between aestheticism and realism demonstrated by Archer and Ellen's fruitless discourse at Skuytercliff unfolds in Selden and Lily's liaison at Bellomont. Like Skuytercliff, the Trenors' country estate, Bellomont, is an artificial reconstruction of nature. The omnibus that departs, empty, each Sunday morning with the pretence of carrying the residents to church symbolizes the shallow artifice and spiritual emptiness of this world. This setting provides the backdrop for Lily's rejection of Percy Gryce and her dangerous attraction to Selden's detached aestheticism. At Bellomont, Selden offers his definition of success for Lily as "personal freedom . . . from everything—from money, from poverty, from ease and anxiety, from all the material accidents. To keep a kind of republic of the spirit—that's what I call success" (70–71). To defend his position, Selden constructs an exclusive "republic," formed by an explicit disdain for the materialism of society. This rejection is, of course, purely theoretical—Selden has in no way sacrificed his career or social position. When Lily confesses her inability to find this "country" on her own, Selden replies, "Ah, there are sign-posts—but one has to know how to read them" (*House of Mirth* 68). Citizens of Selden's "republic" must follow his own narrow aesthetic guidelines, and political currency is granted to those elite interpreters with impeccable taste.[43] Like Archer, Selden recognizes the artificiality of society and, in so doing, feels superior to it. He asks Lily, "Why do we call all our generous ideas illusions and the mean ones truths?" (70). With his retreat into the "republic of the spirit," Selden consciously rejects the distinction between reality and illusion. Furthermore, by challenging Lily to join him, he ignores the very real restraints on "personal freedom" that Lily must endure as a penniless, unmarried woman.

By simultaneously rejecting the coarse materialism of his society, yet admiring the "high finish" on Lily's beauty, Selden reveals the source of his "confused sense" of perception. Despite his avowed spirituality, Selden remains a prisoner of his limited understanding of only the outermost surfaces. Wharton emphasizes the visual in her description of Selden's growing romantic interest in Lily:

> Selden was still looking at her, but with a changed eye. Hitherto he had found, in her presence and her talk, the aesthetic amusement which a reflective man is apt to seek in desultory intercourse with pretty women. His attitude had been one of admiring spectatorship, and he would have been almost sorry to detect in her any emotional weakness which should interfere with the fulfillment of her aims. But now the hint of this weakness had become the most interesting thing

about her. He had come on her that morning in a moment of disarray; her face had been pale and altered, and the diminution of her beauty had lent her a poignant charm. *That is how she looks when she is alone!* had been his first thought. . . . From whatever angle he viewed their dawning intimacy, he could not see it as a part of her scheme of life; and to be the unforeseen element in a career so accurately planned was stimulating even to a man who had renounced sentimental experiments. (*House of Mirth* 71–72)

Even in his reappraisal of Lily as something more than attractively shaped "clay," Selden is "still looking at her," and his insight never transcends the most superficial level. "A reflective man," Selden is defined by his intellect, his capacity for reflection; Lily, however, exists purely as a "pretty woman," the object of men's objectifying gaze. Selden feels most attracted to Lily when he spies her in "a moment of disarray," without her customary "fine glaze." His thrill at seeing "how she looks when she is alone" hints at the oppressive surveillance under which Lily must operate in the looking glass of upper-class society, and Selden revels in his privileged vantage point. In defying society's expectations for marriage, Lily breaks the mold set for "clay" of her kind, and Selden, accustomed to a perspective of "admiring spectatorship," feels that she is asking him to break with his own pattern as well. Like Archer, however, Selden responds to this challenge by turning inward. His "republic of the spirit" has no tangible reality, no *use* in the "real" circumstances of his life or Lily's.

Wharton's disclosure of the amorphous idealism that governs Selden's critical inaction invites comparison with a conversation before Ellen's "farewell dinner" in *The Age of Innocence*. Ellen urges Archer to "look, not at visions, but at realities" and asks, "Is it your idea, then, that I should live with you as your mistress—since I can't be your wife?" (1245). Archer claims, "I want—I want somehow to get away with you into a world where words like that—categories like that—won't exist," to which Ellen simply responds, "Oh, my dear—where is that country? Have you ever been there?" (1245). In the country where "words like that" do matter, Archer and Selden insulate themselves from direct involvement and remain unable to act because of their misunderstanding of what is "real." They fail to "read" Ellen and Lily correctly, and this failure has tragic consequences. At the end of *The

Age of Innocence, Archer has the opportunity to see Ellen, many years after her departure. May is dead, and social custom no longer precludes their romance, but Archer chooses to remain outside Ellen's door. He again retreats inward: " 'It's more real to me here than if I went up,' he suddenly heard himself say; and the fear lest that shadow of reality should lose its edge kept him rooted to his seat as the minutes succeeded each other" (1302). For Archer, his shadowy memories of their unconsummated romance are more "real" than Ellen herself. The intensity of his imagination exceeds any satisfaction to be gained from actual contact. As ever, Archer remains paralyzed by his disengagement from the hard facts of life.

Although he remains content within the confines of his imagination, Archer is left with a mere "shadow of reality" that is ultimately unsatisfying. In the final chapter, Wharton describes the accomplishments of Archer's career but writes, "Something he knew he had missed: the flower of life" (*Age of Innocence* 1291). In his idealized and detached relationship with his own life, Archer fails to achieve anything approaching true understanding. Even his memories of his once-passionate feelings for Ellen are oddly distant: "When he thought of Ellen Olenska it was abstractly, serenely, as one might think of some imaginary beloved in a book or a picture: she had become the composite vision of all that he had missed" (1291). In his memories, Archer has completed the transformation of Ellen into an aesthetic object that represents his own lost "flower of life." Likewise, his wife now exists only as the "first photograph of May, which still kept its place beside his inkstand" in the sanctum sanctorum of his library—the only place Archer has ever felt at home. Despite the mimetic authority of photography, the image defies Archer's attempts at insight:

> There she was, tall, round-bosomed and willowy, in her starched muslin and flapping Leghorn, as he had seen her under the orange-trees in the Mission garden. And as he had seen her that day, so she had remained; never quite at the same height, yet never far below it: generous, faithful, unwearied; but so lacking in imagination, so incapable of growth, that the world of her youth had fallen into pieces and rebuilt itself without her ever being conscious of the change. This hard bright blindness had kept her immediate horizon apparently unaltered. (1292)

What Archer failed to see at the time, and continues to misapprehend, is May's ability to manipulate the outcome of Archer and Ellen's relationship. As the reader discovers, May's sudden capitulation to an early wedding date, her premature notification of Ellen about her pregnancy, and the carefully orchestrated "farewell dinner" all result from May's understanding of the potential threat posed by Archer and Ellen's presumed affair. Wharton's ironic narration reveals Archer's own *willful* blindness: he simply refuses to recognize either May or Ellen as anything more than superficial visions, competing representations of two worlds between which he has chosen.[44] Archer never confronts the possibility that his own flawed perceptions and overall weakness left him with no real choice to make. If his name recalls Isabel Archer, the heroine of James's *The Portrait of a Lady,* Newland Archer's story suggests that Wharton's focus is not on his inanimate, idealized portraits of Ellen and May, but on her critical portrait of a *man* who remains unwilling or unable to confront his own limitations. Wharton's *The Age of Innocence* shares its title with a Joshua Reynolds painting depicting an angelic young girl. The parallel between Reynolds's neoclassical image and Archer's vision of May as the embodiment of the blissful ignorance of an earlier age further suggests the reification and distortion that result from Archer's misguided aestheticism. Ironically, it is Archer who remains frozen in a disconnected, childlike state, even as he projects this image on May and the society she represents.

The consequences of Selden's failure to acknowledge material reality and respond vigorously are even more tragic. From the outset of the novel, Selden sees "the real Lily" in his detached observation of her ideal beauty, and despite his growing attachment to Lily, Selden never transcends this crucial limitation. At an extravagant party given by the nouveau-riche Wellington Brys, Lily appears in one of a series of *tableaux vivants* in which actors portray characters from well-known paintings. Lily's tableau depicting *another* Joshua Reynolds portrait, "Mrs. Lloyd," elicits a variety of responses from the audience, including the prurient snickers of hypocritical gentlemen, but in this performance Selden distinguishes a beauty in Lily that he "lost the sense of when he was not with her" (*House of Mirth* 142). Selden believes that "for the first time he seemed to see before him the real Lily Bart" (142). This reaction is both insightful and ironic: he correctly sees Lily's successful performance as an artistic triumph, but he fails to understand the context of her achievement as a means of increasing her value on the marriage market.[45]

Indeed, in imitating a woman carving her husband's surname on a tree, Lily is, at least in part, attempting to inscribe her own future as a wife. For a woman in Lily's position, the line between reality and artifice is necessarily thin, because the appearance of desirability is the objective. In this setting, Selden is only window-shopping, unwilling to risk his own capital on Lily, yet disdainful of those who recognize the true purpose behind her performance. In economic terms, he has mistaken exchange value for something more ephemeral. For Selden, Lily's aesthetic value is immediate and powerful, and his feeling for her dissipates when she is not before him. When Lily dies, Selden cannot reconcile the reality of her condition with his vision of her: "That it was her real self, every pulse in him ardently denied" (343). But it *is* her real self, and Selden must withdraw to his aesthetic detachment to absolve himself of guilt. Despite his contempt for the vulgar tastes of his contemporaries, it is as an ornament that Selden most appreciates Lily. Although he believes he can choose to escape the crude machinations of the marketplace, he fails to realize that, acknowledged or not, the market will come to him.

In both Archer's and Selden's objectification and idealization of women, their perspective represents something in between the typically male gaze of desire and possession and the disinterested scrutiny of a detached observer. The discourse of spectator sports, so central to definitions of manhood in the Progressive Era, helps explain the curious position occupied by Archer and Selden. In both novels, women partake in both literal and figurative gamesmanship for the benefit of male spectators, and their actions are frequently linked, directly and indirectly, with the spectacle of athletic contests. In *The Age of Innocence,* May's eventual victory over Ellen is prefigured by descriptions of her athletic prowess: "As she walked beside Archer with her long swinging gait her face wore the vacant serenity of a young marble athlete" (1127). During her honeymoon, May shows little interest in the museums of Europe, seeing her travels "as merely an enlarged opportunity for walking, riding, swimming, and trying her hand at the fascinating new game of lawn tennis" (1170). From the beginning, the typically masculine and feminine characteristics of Archer and May are inverted: "He delighted in the radiant good looks of his betrothed, in her health, her horsemanship, her grace and quickness at games, and the shy interest in books and ideas that she was beginning to develop under his guidance" (1051). She exemplifies the vigorous athlete; he the introverted bookworm. May, not her husband, is the true "archer" in the family, and her skill with a bow and arrow makes her the center of attention. "Archer," Wharton writes, "looked down in wonder at the familiar spectacle" of his wife competing at the Newport Archery Club (1177). By the 1870s, archery had become popular with upper-class women as a physical activity that allowed for outdoor exercise without threatening established feminine standards of decorum and attire. Wharton notes that archery provides women with a perfect "opportunity to show off pretty dresses and graceful attitudes" (1177), even as May competes with "tense muscles and happy frown" (1182). When she emerges from a tent in a delicate white dress, prepared to do battle with her opponents, May projects "the same Diana-like aloofness as when she entered the Beaufort ball-room on the night of her engagement" (1182). At this point, Archer has not yet fully realized that May has mastered more games than those played with a bow and arrow. "Diana-like" in her warrior skills beyond the archery range, May consistently defies Archer's expectations, yet only at the end of the novel does he begin to perceive the role May has taken in vanquishing Ellen and ensuring the stability of her own marriage and position in society.

When Wharton first invokes the Greek goddess to describe May, she also suggests Archer's lamentable interpretive skills.[46] While speaking with Ellen at the van der Luyden's dinner party, Archer spots his fiancée:

> The drawing-rooms were beginning to fill up with after-dinner guests, and following Madame Olenska's glance Archer saw May Welland entering with her mother. In her dress of white and silver, with a wreath of silver blossoms in her hair, the tall girl looked like a Diana just alight from the chase.
> "Oh," said Archer, "I have so many rivals; you see she's already surrounded." (*Age of Innocence* 1067)

In fact, as Wharton's allusion implies, it is May who must do combat with her rival, but Archer reveals the combination of egocentrism and sexism that will lead him to underestimate May throughout the novel. He assumes his own agency in determining the course of his life and overlooks his true identity as a mere spectator.

Throughout the novel, the spectacle of female competition provides entertainment for male spectators. Upon Ellen's first arrival at the opera, Archer notices that the box containing May and Ellen is "attracting the undivided attention of masculine New York" (*Age of Innocence* 1024). The consumers of this ongoing spectacle are those men whose collective gaze determines the value of the women on display. The commercial implications of such spectacles place emphasis on both the female bodies and the nature of the transaction, as Montgomery notes in *Displaying Women: Spectacles of Leisure in Edith Wharton's New York:* "The gender dynamics of display and spectatorship in such venues as the opera house is in some ways suggestive of brothel behavior, with men ogling women framed and contained in boxes in darkened auditoriums. Theaters had not entirely rid themselves of associations with prostitution" (128). As costly goods on the market, unmarried women invested much in the public display of their value, and this display focused on their physical attractiveness as much as their behavior or attire.

Whereas male authors such as Norris or Jack London emphasize the place of the white male body of the athlete at the center of the battle for national identity, Wharton highlights the role of the white woman as the embodiment of Anglo-Americanism. When the Welland family matriarch, Mrs. Manson Mingott, holds forth on the topic of May's wedding ring, she notes, "Her hand is large—it's these modern sports that spread the joints—but the skin is white" (1038). The older woman recoils at the potential vulgarity of athletic display but is reassured by the purity and strength of character that May epitomizes.

Likewise, Lily's appearance in the tableau of Reynolds's "Mrs. Lloyd" calls attention to the interconnected narratives of commerce, race, and gender in female display. The "dryad-like curves" of her body, covered only by "pale draperies" (*House of Mirth* 142), elicit gasps from the audience, but as Selden sees the tableau as further evidence of the "sylvan grace" he has earlier detected in Lily, the other men interpret the performance as part of the sexual economy of the marriage market. Ned Van Alstyne leers at Lily and later remarks, "Gad, what a show of good-looking women; but not one of 'em could touch that little cousin of mine. Talk of jewels—what's a woman want with jewels when she's got herself to show?" (145–46). Another of Lily's cousins, Jack Stepney, denounces the idea of Lily "standing there as if she was up at auction" (166). Jennie Kassanoff explores the tableau scene as part of a larger narrative of "eugenic superiority" (62) running through Wharton's novel, in which Lily embodies the virtues and desires of Anglo-Saxon destiny. According to Kassanoff, Lily "projects what Alan Trachtenberg calls 'an official American version of reality'—the natural reconceived by the upper classes and recast as an emphatic rejection of ethnic and racial pluralism" (63). More her "real self" than ever when she inhabits the neoclassical portrait of a vanishing notion of Anglo-Saxon wifehood, Lily's appearance at the *tableaux vivants* represents one successful sortie in the staged battle put on by women for the amusement of the male audience.

The cut-throat competition among women for wealth and prestige through successful marriage is a central theme throughout *The House of Mirth,* and in the end Lily Bart proves much less "Diana-like" than May Welland. "The Dying Gladiator in bronze who occupied the drawing-room window" of Lily's Aunt, Mrs. Peniston, serves as a stark reminder of the stakes of this contest (103). When Lily flirts with Selden in the book's opening scenes, he wonders why "she would waste her powder on such small game," revealing both Lily's role as hunter and his own as an unlikely target (8). Her dead mother, Lily recalls, had taught her to regard her beauty as the "weapon" with which she would reclaim the family's rightful fortune, and at the proper moment, Mrs. Peniston "had simply stood aside and let her take the field" (40).[47] When Lily, an inveterate and unlucky card player, amasses a substantial gambling debt, she brokers a deal with Gus Trenor, but in life as in cards, Lily is a poor bluffer, and her fortunes unravel when Trenor attempts to collect an amorous return on his investment. After she refuses his advances, Trenor rages, "But, by gad, that ain't playing fair: that's dodging the rules of the game. Of course I know now what you wanted—it wasn't my beautiful eyes you were after—but I tell you what, Miss Lily, you've got to pay up for making me think so" (154). Before releasing her, Trenor nearly rapes Lily, thereby making her return his investment with the currency she possesses—her body.[48]

Unfortunately, Lily's success never matches her love for the many games she undertakes. Wharton describes Lily's poor luck at cards: "Once or twice of late she had won a large sum, and instead of keeping it against future losses, had spent it in dress or jewelry; and the desire to atone for this imprudence, combined with the increasing exhilaration of the game, drove her to risk higher stakes at each fresh venture" (*House of Mirth* 28). The "exhilaration" of her various gambits only leads her further toward her own downfall, and any stakes she has wagered on Selden never come to fruition. After Lily's reputation has been irrevocably tarnished by a jealous Bertha Dorset, she returns to Simon Rosedale, whom she had earlier rebuffed, hoping to find his proposal still on the table. Now unwilling to settle for such damaged goods as Lily, Rosedale calls her "a dead game sport," admiring her intrepid attitude, if not her proficiency (269). She plays by an honorable set of rules when she refuses to blackmail Bertha Dorset with some incriminating letters that document Bertha's onetime liaison with Selden. The notion of "fair play" and sportsmanship looms large in Progressive-Era rhetoric, and Gus Trenor—whose very name suggests the emperor Augustus and a powerful earthquake—adopts a Rooseveltian posture when he accuses Lily of "dodging the rules of the game." In the end, Lily's sportsmanship outweighs her gamesmanship, and she loses out to less principled competitors. Trenor, like the industrialists of *The Octopus,* represents the apotheosis of the manly appetites that propel the economic and social hierarchy of the emergent American empire. His is the unsavory face of success, contrasted with the unscathed but untested detachment practiced by "small game" such as Selden.

The ongoing perspective of privileged spectatorship taken by Selden and Archer and the associated level of emasculation that this position entails point to their classification as prototypical neurasthenic men, according to the diagnostic criteria of the Progressive Era. In their embrace of the "feminine" world of novels, art, and the home, as well as their aestheticized detachment from the rough world of men, they fail as heroic counterparts to the female protagonists of these novels. E. Anthony Rotundo's explanation of male neurasthenia from what he defines as the era of "passionate manhood" aptly describes Selden and Archer's shortcomings:

Looked at in terms of gender, male neurasthenia amounted to a flight from manhood. It not only meant a withdrawal from the central male activity of work, but it also involved a rejection of fundamental manly virtues—achievement, ambition, dominance, independence. . . .

Moreover, the neurasthenic man was retreating into the feminine realm. By going home to rest, he was seeking out the domestic space of women. He was also finding refuge in roles and behaviors marked "female": vulnerability, dependence, passivity, invalidism. Even a man who traveled to recuperate was pursuing the life of cultivated leisure which was associated with women. Unwittingly, a neurasthenic man was inverting the usual role of the sexes, rejecting "male" and embracing "female." (190)

Despite their position of privilege in the patriarchal society of New York, Selden and Archer abdicate those responsibilities deemed masculine by their culture. Their desultory attitude toward work, their attachment to their mothers, and their comfort in the home all signal distinctly neurasthenic proclivities. For example, when George Dorset confides in Selden about his dangerous infatuation with Lily, Wharton describes Selden's response in terms that mark his role as passive bystander: "Selden saw that for the moment all he could do was to soothe and temporize, to offer sympathy and to counsel prudence. He let Dorset depart charged to the brim with the sense that, till their next meeting, he must maintain a strictly noncommittal attitude; that, in short, his share in the game consisted for the present in looking on" (*House of Mirth* 218–19).[49] One can hardly imagine Gus Trenor, or any other prospective rival for Lily's affection, "soothing," "offering sympathy," or "counseling prudence" in this manner. Selden not only is a weak contestant but is never really "in the game" at all.

Whereas Selden consistently remains on the outside looking in at the brutal machinations of Gus Trenor, Bertha Dorset, and the other architects of Lily's demise, Wharton suggests that Archer briefly enters the ring of decisive action. Near the end of the novel, Archer looks back on particular occasions in his beloved library and remembers that

it was in that library that the Governor of New York, coming down from Albany one evening to dine and spend the night, had turned to his host, and said, banging his clenched fist on the table and gnashing his eyeglasses: "Hang the professional politician! You're the kind of man the country wants, Archer. If the stable's ever to be cleaned out, men like you have got to lend a hand in the cleaning.

"Men like you—" how Archer had glowed at the phrase! How eagerly he had risen up at the call! It was an echo of Ned Winsett's old appeal to roll his sleeves up and get down into the muck; but spoken by a man who set the example of the gesture, and whose summons to follow him was irresistible. (*Age of Innocence* 1290)

Most readers would surely recognize the governor "gnashing his eyeglasses" as Theodore Roosevelt, a member of Wharton's extended social circle and the object of Wharton's admiration for both his policies and his decisive public posture.[50] This intrusion of the "real" into Wharton's fiction serves to accentuate the strong impulse Archer has always felt to "get down into the muck," but it also highlights his inability to follow this impulse fully. Wharton continues,

> Archer, as he looked back, was not sure that men like himself *were* what his country needed, at least in the active service to which Theodore Roosevelt had pointed; in fact, there was reason to think it did not, for after a year in the State Assembly he had not been re-elected, and dropped back thankfully into obscure if useful municipal work, and from that again to the writing of occasional articles in one of the reforming weeklies that were trying to shake the country out of its apathy. (1290)

Tellingly, Wharton portrays Archer's writing as something far removed from the "active service" that Roosevelt's Progressivism demanded.[51] As his relationship with Ellen Olenska indicates, Archer inevitably "drops back" from the strenuous involvement that he acknowledges to be necessary. Unlike Roosevelt, who "cured" the nervous tendencies of his youth through athletics, hunting, and other manly rituals, Archer never overcomes the predisposition toward neurasthenia that his characterization indicates.

Naturally, Wharton's depiction of nervous tendencies in Selden and Archer must be considered in light of her own bout with neurasthenia, which coincided with the inception of her career as a professional writer. Beginning in 1894, Wharton displayed symptoms that included a loss of appetite, severe headaches, and recurring depression, and she eventually underwent a version of S. Weir Mitchell's "rest cure" in 1898. Mitchell's treatment, memorably depicted in Charlotte Perkins Gilman's harrowing short story "The Yellow Wallpaper," proposed that women suffering from neurasthenia should refrain from any physical or intellectual activity for a month or more. As Lutz notes in *American Nervousness, 1903,* "Neurasthenia was a highly gendered discourse" (31). Although male neurasthenics were often perceived as suffering from too little physical exercise and active involvement in real-world matters, popular perception held that females contracted neurasthenia through too much "masculine" activity. In his own writing, Mitchell blamed the onset of female neurasthenia on "the woman's desire to be on a level of competition with man and assume his duties" (*Doctor and Patient* 13). R. W. B. Lewis points out the incidents and experiences that might have contributed to Wharton's condition, most notably those surrounding her disintegrating marriage and the struggle to publish her short fiction. Lewis writes, "These various factors came together in the challenging question that could no longer be postponed. What, at the age of thirty-two, was her fundamental role in life: wife, social hostess, observer of foreign parts—or, drawing on all of these, a writer of fiction?" (76). For Wharton, questions of gender and authorship presented themselves not merely as abstract notions, but as practical hurdles to be overcome.

During this period, Wharton endured setbacks in her writing career, as Edward Burlingame, her editor at Scribner's, rejected several stories for a proposed collection. In an 1895 letter to Burlingame, Wharton tentatively writes, "Since I last wrote you over a year ago, I have been very ill, & am not yet allowed to do any real work. But I have been scribbling a little & I have sent you a few pages which I hope you may like" (*Letters of Edith Wharton* 35). Lacking the confidence of her later correspondence, this letter reveals its author's dilemma as the very kind of "scribbling woman" long derided by the literary establishment. Burlingame, in fact, rejected the work that Wharton enclosed with this letter—a collection of brief parables entitled "The Valley of Childish Things and Other Emblems." The title story describes a little girl who lives in a valley populated entirely by children who spend their days "playing all manner of delightful games, and studying the same lesson-books" (467). The little girl ventures out of the valley and discovers a harsh adult world in which "she saw cities and men, and learned many useful arts, and in so doing grew to be a woman" (467). She returns to the valley, and on the journey back, she encounters a man who has made a similar excursion out into the "cold, bleak table-land beyond the mountains." Together, they plan to teach their former playmates what they have learned and improve their valley. When they arrive, however, all of the residents are still children, playing the same games and exhibiting no interest in the knowledge they possess. When the woman exhorts her male comrade "to set to work with her building bridges, draining swamps, and cutting roads through the jungle," she discovers that he is on his knees making a little decorative garden for a "dear little girl with blue eyes and a coral necklace" (467). Although the woman remains committed to "the work" that needs to be done, the man has reverted to the "childish things" of his past. Wharton's parable exposes the regression then considered characteristic of neurasthenic men, even as she proposes that her own salvation may be found in the work she feels compelled to perform. Unlike the protagonist of Gilman's "The Yellow Wallpaper," however, Wharton is not forbidden from writing altogether, and her emergence as a professional author coincides with her "recovery" from neurasthenic illness under Mitchell's care in 1898.[52] Key to establishing her independence from the stifling expectations placed upon her by her class and gender is Wharton's understanding of the power of the literary marketplace, and her ability and willingness to play by its rules precipitates her artistic and commercial success.

Wharton's ambivalence about the business of authorship, revealed in "The Descent of Man" and elsewhere, surfaces in her depiction of journalism.[53] The panoptic gaze of male spectators, suggested by the opera house in *The Age of Innocence* and in Lily's tableau, also resonates in Wharton's satirical depiction of the popular press in Lily's appearance in *Town Talk* after her performance at the Brys' party. Reminded that "*Town Talk* was full of her this morning," Ned Van Alstyne furtively snickers, "Yes: lively reading it was" (*House of Mirth* 166). The society scandal sheet, based on the real-life periodical *Town Topics,* maintains constant surveillance on the members of the upper class, in particular marriageable debutantes such as Lily Bart or outré married women such as Ellen Olenska. As Amy Kaplan notes, Wharton's portrait of the mass media invites obvious comparison with her own chronicling of these same subjects and events.[54] The unforgivable event that precipitates Lily's banishment from the Fifth Avenue bridge tables is not her improper relationship with George Dorset during her travels in Europe, but the publication of a story about this relationship by "that horrid little Dabham who does 'Society Notes from the Riviera'" (208). To distinguish the valid work of authorship from the tawdry gossip column, Kaplan suggests that Wharton "poses Selden as a model for the realist who has one foot in the gilded cage but still seems to keep the other outside by the power of detached, objective observation" (*Social Construction of American Realism* 97). Selden, however, fails to act upon the observations that he makes. He knows the truth about Lily but is powerless against the narratives established by Dabham's scandal sheet and Bertha Dorset's whispers. In adopting her own narrative strategy, Wharton understands the contradictory power of storytelling as both empowering labor and reifying practice.

Wharton's characterizations of Selden and Archer, with their neurasthenic withdrawal from robust activity, reveal important similarities with Norris's characterization of Presley, particularly as these portraits show their authors' shared investment in the cult of masculinity and its tenets. One significant difference, however, helps illuminate Wharton's revision of Norris's anti-aesthetic principles. Whereas Presley occupies the dual role of creative artist and reflective critic, Selden and Archer serve as critics only—Lily and Ellen are the potential artists in these novels.[55] Lily's performance as Reynolds's Mrs. Lloyd and Ellen's ties with the writers and painters of New York's bohemian community suggest their artistic allegiance. Like athletes on the playing field, Lily and Ellen provide the spectacle upon which society members gaze with awe, envy, and disdain. Selden and Archer merely observe and, as critics, possess neither the potential nor the desire to produce art themselves. Although Presley fails because he consumes rather than produces, Selden and Archer—consumers by nature—only have the power to undermine the real artists, that is, the women whose production has no market value in a culture built on ornamentation and frivolous display. Paradoxically, the feminization of Selden and Archer serves to further debilitate the "new women" Lily and Ellen. In the consumer culture of the Progressive Era, male critics reserve the right to devalue the work of female artists. Conversely, Wharton, as a woman and an artist, must either embrace a masculine aesthetic model to compete on the battlefield of the literary marketplace or capitulate to the diminished role assigned to her female forebears, such as Jewett and Freeman.

The tragic disengagement of Selden and Archer recalls the Easterner's confession at the conclusion of Crane's "The Blue Hotel." In the final analysis, Selden and Archer fail as interpreters. Just as the Easterner's silence helps seal the fate of the Swede, so does Selden and Archer's complicity with a society they claim to criticize contribute to Lily's death and Ellen's exile. The Easterner, however, finally admits his own responsibility and changes his interpretation of the events he has witnessed. Selden and Archer never fully come to terms with their interpretive shortcomings, and, to the end, persist in a misguided reading. Standing over Lily's dead body, Selden recollects their final conversation and last kiss: "Yes, he would now read into that farewell all that his heart craved to find there: he could even draw from it courage not to accuse himself for having failed to read the height of his opportunity" (*House of Mirth* 347). Like Presley's musings about "force" at the end of *The Octopus,* Selden's reflections offer a staunchly deterministic view of the universe, but in Selden's case, these reflections are self-serving and unconvincing. Wharton writes, "He saw now that all the conditions of life had conspired to keep them apart; since his very detachment from the external influences which swayed her had increased his spiritual fastidiousness, and made it more difficult for him to live and love uncritically. But at least he *had* loved her—had been willing to stake his future on his faith in her—and if the moment had been fated to pass from them before they could seize it, he saw now that it had been saved whole out of the ruin of their lives" (347).

To the last, Selden continues to aestheticize his experiences, clinging to a "fleeting victory" (*House of Mirth* 347) instead of his own part in the tragedy. As someone who understands the "conditions of life" arrayed against Lily, he had the responsibility to act, but now prefers to dwell upon the gemlike flame that has been extinguished. Like Crane's Easterner, he refuses to "stand up and be a man" at the crucial time, yet his deepest flaw is his inability to recognize this fact. For Wharton, as for Crane, the duty of the writer depends on a willingness to depict the irresolvable struggle between autonomy and determinism, and the gendered discourse of the Progressive Era inevitably defined this willingness. Norris and Wharton, with their characterizations of failed spectators, argue for "masculine" aesthetic standards that shun decadence and ornamentation in favor of function and vitality. This message helps establish a highly charged and problematic definition of the writer as an engaged, active presence, even as it consistently evokes its repressed mirror image: the aesthete, pen in hand, converting the hard facts of life into entertainment for the "hungry maw" of the marketplace, for "a public long nurtured on ice-cream sodas and marshmallows."

4 / "A Man Only in Form"

The Roots of Naturalism in African American Literature

It is not the positive propaganda of people who believe white blood divine, infallible, and holy to which I object. It is the denial of a similar right of propaganda to those who believe black blood human, lovable, and inspired with new ideals for the world.

—W. E. B. Du Bois, "Criteria of Negro Art"

"How does it feel to be a problem?" This is the question posed by W. E. B. Du Bois near the beginning of *The Souls of Black Folk* (1). Writing at the turn of the twentieth century, Du Bois addresses the conditions of African Americans at the point known among historians as the "nadir" of American race relations,[1] the period following the collapse of Reconstruction noted for the strict codification of Jim Crow segregation, increased incidence of lynching and other forms of racial violence, and widespread evaporation of the hopes that had accompanied the end of slavery. The moral conviction behind the abolitionist movement had mutated into the uncertainties of "the Negro problem": what to do with the millions of people freed from bondage but as yet denied full participation in the promise of American idealism? For Du Bois, as for other African American intellectuals, the dilemma of racial identity intersected unavoidably with the definition of manhood during the Progressive Era. If the so-called crisis of masculinity that haunted middle-class white men during this period created tensions for writers and artists in general, the gender-based pressures on black authorship were compounded exponentially by the volatile racial climate infusing turn-of-the-century American culture. The persistent and calculated "feminization" of the black race and the fear-driven negation of black manhood made the establishment of masculinity both exceedingly difficult and—paradoxically—*necessary* for leaders in the struggle for racial justice. In this context, the naturalistic novel proved attractive, as well as highly problematic, as an avenue for African American creative expression.

The development of American literary naturalism, as practiced by Stephen Crane, Frank Norris, Jack London, among others, reflected the racialized nationalist discourse of the day, and the pseudoscientific understanding of race plays a central role in the explicit celebration of Anglo-Saxon destiny found in such works as Norris's *The Octopus* and London's *The Sea-Wolf.* In such an environment, any embrace of literary naturalism by African American writers would seem an unlikely development. For a variety of reasons, however, naturalism did prove attractive. In part, black authors were drawn to this approach for the same array of reasons as any other author: naturalism was, to a degree, fashionable within the broader American literary community. Furthermore, its emphasis on social problems and economic forces would have had immense appeal for African Americans, who knew, perhaps better than anyone, the debilitating effects of such forces on the aspirations of the individual and the exercise of free will. In spite of the link between naturalism and overtly racist social theory, several pivotal texts appropriate naturalist discourse in an effort to argue ideological positions opposed to the doctrine of Anglo-Saxon cultural and political supremacy. I choose to examine the reconfiguration of literary naturalism in four novels: Charles Chesnutt's *The Marrow of Tradition* and Paul Laurence Dunbar's *The Sport of the Gods,* both published in 1901, as well as Du Bois's *The Quest of the Silver Fleece* and James Weldon Johnson's *The Autobiography of an Ex-Colored Man,* published in 1911 and 1912, respectively. To some extent, each of these authors seeks to redefine racial destiny as a cultural rather than biological concept and to critically examine the rigidly circumscribed lives of African Americans at the beginning of the twentieth century. The terms of this redefinition, however, are set by the radically masculinist discourse of this era and reflect the anxieties over manhood that inhabit the genre of American literary naturalism as a whole. The crucial link between these texts and those of the canonical Anglo-American naturalists lies in the shared preoccupation with the pervasive rhetoric of masculinity endemic to this period, and the legacy established by these texts demonstrates their place among the naturalists as well as the unresolved tensions over gender present throughout the canon of African American literature.

In adopting the discourse of "manliness," African American writers sought to combat the crippling effects of nativism, racism, and imperialism through the construction of a nation within a nation—the revitalization of a culture alternately demonized and emasculated by the accumulated injustices of legal segregation and the extralegal ritualized violence of lynching. When Du Bois, in *The Souls of Black Folk,* calls for "the assertion of the manhood rights of the Negro" (35), the term "manhood" carries with it implications of gender as well as citizenship. As Hazel Carby explains, "Du Bois constructed particular personal, political, and social characteristics of a racialized masculinity to articulate his definition of black leadership" (11).[2] *The Quest of the Silver Fleece,* in fact, draws parallels between the political progress of African Americans and the fulfillment of an unwritten code of virtuous, heterosexual manhood by the novel's protagonist. In constructing this relationship, Du Bois revisits and, to some degree, reinscribes the problematic connection between virility and racial destiny that dominates the ideology of Anglo-Saxon superiority. Although Du Bois rejects the biological dogma of the Progressive Era as it pertains to the black race, his novel reinforces the biological imperatives of gender. Although the dynamics of gender and ideology are not identical across the racial divide of Jim Crow America, the parallels invite further investigation and suggest a more complex relationship between canonical naturalist authors and their African American counterparts than traditional criticism of the genre has explored. This apparently simultaneous repudiation and embrace of biological determinism highlights the complexities and contradictions at the heart of naturalism as a literary form in general, and its use by African American authors at the beginning of the twentieth century in particular.

In this period, the establishment of professional spectator sports on a large scale put forth an attempt to simultaneously appropriate "the primitive" from racial Others and exclude these Others from direct participation in the spectacles themselves. Such phenomena as the "gentlemen's agreement" among club owners to ban African Americans from major league baseball; John L. Sullivan's declaration of a "color line" in championship boxing; and the rise of college athletics and amateurism as "pure" sport, untainted by either commercial interests or the lower classes, all reflected the same complex cultural tensions that found other outlets in the rise of fraternal orders, the legislative doctrine of segregation, and the Progressive reforms of heavy industry and the marketplace. According to official statistics compiled by Robert Zangrando, 3,446 African Americans were lynched between

1882 and 1968; the number of these recorded lynchings peaked in 1892 at 161 and declined gradually over the next few decades.[3] In this environment, the corresponding emergence of both lynching and prizefighting as forms of public ritual and violent entertainment offers some insight into the troubling impulses lurking behind America's growing attachment to sport. The color line in boxing ensured that the heavyweight champion, the most recognizable symbol of the virile masculine impulse, would remain white. Boxing matches provided audiences with the opportunity to view dangerous, often lethal, displays of violence, and the sexual potency embodied by the prizefighter came to represent the masculinized nationalism of the so-called strenuous age.

Indeed, the ascent of Jack Johnson as heavyweight contender, then champion, in the first decade of the twentieth century, culminating with his stunning defeat of Jim Jeffries in 1910, served as a pivotal cultural event in the formation of both white and black notions of masculinity, class, and racial identity. If Johnson served as a thorn in the side of the ideologues of Anglo-Saxon destiny such as London, his presence on the cultural landscape was equally problematic for the African American cultural elite. Johnson's victory over Jeffries made possible the widespread acceptance of a concept of black manhood that reflected both the hypermasculine physicality and competence of "the strenuous life" and the transgressive "badman" of African American folklore. Johnson's explosive rise presented the literal embodiment of a version of black cultural identity that met white fears face to face. Lawrence Levine writes: "It was not Johnson's physical prowess alone that infuriated whites; it was his entire life style: his fast cars, fancy clothes, ready tongue, white wife (the first of three white women he married), and white mistresses. Johnson ruptured role after role set aside for Negroes in American society, and, despite the criminal charges which forced him into exile from his own country for seven years, he made the whites accept it" (432).

His aggressive masculinity invoked black folk heroes, both real and fictitious, from Railroad Bill to John Henry, but found its expression within the world of the bachelor sporting culture that arose in urban America during the 1890s. Defined as powerful and defiant, such "badmen" carry with them an aura of virility and sexual potency that matches their authority in other areas and further targets them for retribution by white society.[4] The emergence of a heroic figure of Johnson's stature and type during this volatile period offers some insight into the shifting cultural backdrop for the early development of African American literary naturalism. Moreover, Johnson occupied a problematic hypermasculine position in African American culture that had already found voice in the narrative struggles of Dunbar and Chesnutt. If Johnson's ascent exploited the notion of "play" in the trope of the black male as sexual predator, brute, and outlaw, the seeming embrace of biological determinism in African American naturalism must be read as something more than the mere acceptance of received wisdom on racial difference, as defined in the Progressive Era.

In *Modernism and the Harlem Renaissance,* Houston Baker notes that "efforts of turn-of-the-century black spokespersons provide tactics, strategies, and sounds that mark a field of possibilities for an emergent Afro-American *national* enterprise" (71). This enterprise, Baker further argues, requires "a shrewd combination of formal mastery and deformative creativity" (71–72). Baker describes the appropriation of the minstrel mask as a trope within the work of Booker T. Washington, Chesnutt, Dunbar, and others as a tool with which to reshape the notion of artistry within the African American cultural tradition. In his own attempt to reconcile vernacular and literary cultures, *The Signifying Monkey,* Henry Louis Gates suggests that "several of the canonical texts in the Afro-American tradition seem to be related to other black texts primarily in terms of substance or content, whereas they seem to be related to Western texts in terms of form" (122). Gates explains this "curious two-toned Harlequin mask of influence" (122) within the context of the African American rhetorical practice of "signifying"—the strategy of repeating "with a difference" the language and tropes of both traditions to create a new text. In this way, "signifyin[g] is the black trope of tropes, the figure for black rhetorical figures" (51). Baker's and Gates's contributions to an understanding of the particularities of African American literary production inform my argument about the "blackness" of African American literary naturalism. By incorporating those assumptions of biological determinism associated with naturalist discourse, African American writers engage those determinist tropes central to naturalism and, employing a "deformative creativity," reshape the form in ways that serve the establishment of a "national" identity within the larger nation of the United States.

The adoption of the naturalistic novel by black writers begins at the turn of the twentieth century with Dunbar's *The Sport of the Gods* and Chesnutt's *The Marrow of Tradition.* Each of these books marked the culmination and effective end of its author's career as a novelist. Dunbar died in 1906 without publishing another novel, and Chesnutt, despite publishing *The Colonel's Dream* in 1905, never regained the level of popular and critical support he enjoyed with his earliest works. Both Dunbar and Chesnutt earned their literary reputations with dialect stories and poems reflecting the motifs and plots of folktales and the plantation slave tradition, a literary novelty popularized in the 1890s by Joel Chandler Harris's "Uncle Remus" tales. In this context, social criticism and philosophical reflections on race and identity lay concealed by the veil of humor and the racial expectations of a white middle-class audience. With their late novels, however, Dunbar and Chesnutt entered into the fashionable genre of social protest fiction, made famous by muckraking journalists such as Lincoln Steffens and David Graham Phillips and simultaneously explored by Norris, Upton Sinclair, and others. Critics and readers alike greeted this move with suspicion, if not outright hostility.[5] Although dialect stories and poems might be alternately praised or dismissed as examples of "local color," naturalistic novels could not. With this turn toward naturalism, Dunbar and Chesnutt confront the double bind of the black artist in the Progressive Era—to be a serious writer, one must engage with social reality, but in doing so, one also makes visible the threat of black manhood—the very subject whose ominous visage gave rise to the oppressive laws and ritual violence of the time. If naturalism had been defined by its adherents as a "masculine" genre, then its adoption by a group for whom masculinity constitutes a perceived threat is itself a political act, and a dangerous one.

The problem of depicting the struggle for African American civil rights through the lens of naturalism leaves unresolved some of the basic questions these novels seek to address, at least in part because Dunbar and Chesnutt combine elements of sentimental melodrama with the naturalistic study of their characters' fates. An overview of the novels' plots reveals parallels, as well as critical distinctions, among these works and the works of white naturalists that they most closely resemble. In its plot, *The Sport of the Gods* aggressively debunks the genteel plantation mythology so pervasive at the turn of the century through the story of the intersection and degeneration of two families, one white and one black, in the turbulent South of the Jim Crow era. A proud inheritor of the aristocratic tradition celebrated in fiction by Thomas Nelson Page, Thomas Dixon, and others, Maurice Oakley belongs to the generation that has survived the Civil War and its aftermath beaten but unbowed, and he retains a paternalistic racism, along with the diminished trappings of wealth that constitute his birthright. When his dishonest and wayward half brother, Frank, falsely accuses Maurice's loyal servant Berry Hamilton of the theft of some money, Maurice allows him to be convicted of the crime. The crux of the novel, however, traces the journey of Berry's wife and children from the false Eden of the South to the urban crucible of New York City, site of radical demographic and cultural shifts during this period as a result of foreign immigrants and oppressed African Americans alike seeking work in the industrialized North.

In its depiction of New York as a dangerous and corrupting place, the novel invites comparisons with such canonical naturalistic works as Crane's *Maggie* and Theodore Dreiser's *Sister Carrie.* As with Maggie and Hurstwood in those novels, Berry Hamilton's children, Joe and Kitty, succumb to the temptations of the city and are ultimately destroyed by them. Dunbar describes the allure and danger of the northern metropolis in memorable terms:

> To the provincial coming to New York for the first time, ignorant and unknown, the city presents a notable mingling of the qualities of cheeriness and gloom. If he have any eye at all for the beautiful, he cannot help experiencing a thrill as he crosses the ferry over the river filled with plying craft and catches the first sight of the spires and buildings of New York. If he have the right stuff in him, a something will take possession of him that will grip him every time he returns to the scene and will make him long and hunger for the place when he is away from it. Later, the lights in the busy streets will bewilder and entice him. . . . The subtle, insidious wine of New York will begin to intoxicate him. Then, if he be wise, he will go away, anyplace—yes, he will even go over to Jersey. But if he be a fool, he will stay and stay on until the town becomes all in all to him; until the very streets are his chums and certain buildings and corners his best friends. (*Sport of the Gods* 76–77)

In his use of language—the world-weary voice of experience speaking in detached terms of the city's effect—Dunbar recalls Crane's typically ironic, bemused narrator.[6] Likewise, the description of a new arrival in a dazzling urban landscape echoes Dreiser's account of Carrie's first glimpse of Chicago in similarly generalized terms: "To the child, the genius with imagination, or the wholly untravelled, the approach to a great city for the first time is a wonderful thing. . . . What does it not hold for the weary! What old illusion of hope is not here forever repeated!" (*Sister Carrie* 6–7). Like Crane and Dreiser, Dunbar concerns himself with the effects of this powerful environment on weak characters, predisposed by a combination of background and circumstance to fall under the spell of corrupting forces.[7] Unlike Maggie or Hurstwood, however, the Hamilton children in *The Sport of the Gods* are not completely destroyed—at the story's end, all the family members are alive, but condemned to a kind of purgatory: Berry, finally vindicated of his crime, is reunited with his unfaithful wife Fannie and returns to the ruined Southern plantation to live in shame, whereas Joe sits in prison for murder and Kitty tours the country as an actress in a somewhat scandalous revue.[8] Berry's "manhood," his status as the head of his household, has been entirely shattered. When Hurstwood's masculine desire has been undermined, he fades from Carrie's life and story entirely. Berry Hamilton, however, remains as the ostensible leader of a family in disarray. The concluding lines of the book, in which Dunbar describes the sad fate of the Hamilton family, explicitly invoke the stark determinism that traditionally defines literary naturalism: "It was not a happy life, but it was all that was left to them, and they took it up without complaint, for they knew they were powerless against some will infinitely stronger than their own" (195). Dunbar fails to elaborate on the nature of the "will" that defines their lives. Thus the novel ends with an uneasy stasis, the lives of the characters having come full circle, though now much diminished, and the condition of Berry Hamilton as deposed master of his own household reflects the emasculating effects of Jim Crow "justice" on the black race.

The plot of *The Marrow of Tradition* adheres to a naturalistic penchant for authenticity and the fictional recreation of real-life events. Just as Dreiser's *Sister Carrie* incorporates details from the Brooklyn streetcar strike of 1895, and Norris's *The Octopus* fictionalizes the 1880 Mussel Slough Massacre involving ranchers in the San Joaquin Valley, Chesnutt bases the setting and central crisis of his novel on the Wilmington "race riot" of 1898, during which white mobs attacked and killed blacks in response to a virulent campaign in the city's white newspaper against "Negro domination" of North Carolina politics.[9] The main storyline follows the novel's protagonist, William Miller, introduced as a "mulatto" whose "erect form, broad shoulders, clear eyes, fine teeth, and pleasingly moulded features showed nowhere any sign of that degeneration which the pessimist so sadly maintains is the inevitable heritage of mixed races" (*Marrow of Tradition* 49). A doctor educated in the North and Europe, Miller has returned to Wellington, North Carolina, to open a "colored" hospital. With his characterization of Miller, Chesnutt directly challenges the simplistic theories of race and genetics popularized by figures such as Joseph LeConte and Cesare Lombroso and immediately distinguishes his naturalistic vision from the biological determinism of contemporaries such as Norris and London.

The growing racial antagonism of the city erupts alongside the evolving story of the parallel families of Miller and Philip Carteret, editor of the newspaper and architect of the racist violence that envelops the characters' lives.[10] At the story's end, as Dr. Miller agrees to save the life of Carteret's young son, even as his own son lies dead at the hands of the angry mob, he inquires as to the child's condition. The answer to this question and the book's final line, "There's time enough, but none to spare" (329), looms over the novel as Chesnutt's warning and rallying cry for the "race problem" in the United States. Like *The Sport of the Gods,* however, one of the novel's crucial subplots reiterates the conventions of Victorian melodrama and involves theft and mistaken identity that implicates an innocent black man. This juxtaposition of apparently contradictory generic norms reveals some of the unresolved formal tension in Chesnutt's work, which, as Samira Kawash remarks, "does not conclude so much as it disappears" (119). Also like *The Sport of the Gods,* Chesnutt's novel ends in a kind of limbo, with equal amounts of hope and fear looming on the horizon.

The aesthetic tension between sentimental and naturalistic forms in *The Sport of the Gods* and *The Marrow of Tradition* is revealed in most compelling fashion by the unresolved problem of masculinity that haunts these novels.[11] Like the "problematic men" in the novels of Norris and Wharton discussed in chapter 3, the pivotal figures in these books do not fit the traditional profile of degeneration, but rather exist as diminished men, left to sort through the pieces of their shattered lives. In these novels, however, Dunbar and Chesnutt both tackle cultural fears of white degeneration directly, through the trope of the effete, dissipated artist. If much of the male anxiety in the work of Crane, Norris, and London reflects widely held misgivings about the changing status of white men in the United States, this problem held particular sway in the context of post-Reconstruction Southern manhood. The then-growing body of popular novels offering revisionist views of the Confederacy and alarmist visions of racial insurgency revealed the nexus of race and gender that defined the Jim Crow society to which Dunbar and Chesnutt reply with their works.[12] Although the downfall of the Southern aristocracy occurred within a particular set of historical and cultural circumstances, the popularity of works such as Dixon's *The Clansman* in both North and South and the ongoing currency given to plantation mythology in the twentieth century demonstrate a willingness to accept these fallen aristocrats as emblematic of race and class anxieties across geographic lines. One way that Dunbar and Chesnutt capture and portray Anglo-Saxon fear is through dissipated characters whose absence of manliness prefigures their roles as both villains and corruptors. Not coincidentally, Frank Oakley and Tom Delamere are first depicted in these novels as aesthetes with artistic pretenses, if very little talent. Dunbar portrays the weaker of the Oakley brothers in terms that echo Frank Norris's account of Hartrath in *The Octopus:*

> At the first intimation that Francis had artistic ability, his brother had placed him under the best masters in America, and later, when the promise of his youth had begun to blossom, he sent him to Paris, although the expenditure just at that time demanded a sacrifice which might have been the ruin of Maurice's own career. Francis's promise had never come to entire fulfillment. He was always trembling on the verge of a great success without quite plunging into it. Despite the joy which his presence gave his brother and sister-in-law, most of his time was spent abroad, where he could find just the atmosphere that suited his delicate, artistic nature. (29)

Here Dunbar characterizes Frank as a perfect example of the aesthetically inclined, insufficiently masculine specimen so derided by Progressive Era observers, from Theodore Roosevelt to G. Stanley Hall. Further described as "a great favorite both with men and women," Frank has "the face and brow of a poet, a pallid face framed in a mass of dark hair. There was a touch of weakness in his mouth, but this was shaded and half hidden by a full mustache that made much forgivable to beauty-loving eyes" (30).[13] The language used to describe Frank's decidedly unmanly demeanor—"trembling," "delicate," "pallid"—not only calls into question his normative sexuality but offers a physiological indication of the moral weakness that the novel later reveals, with the framing of Berry for the theft of money actually lost to gambling debts.

Although a quite different novel in its scope and complexity, *The Marrow of Tradition* contains an important subplot that also involves a black servant framed for a crime by the ne'er-do-well scion of the book's archetypically aristocratic family. Furthermore, this character, Tom Delamere, is defined by his artistic temperament and effete appearance as well: "Slender and of medium height, with a small head of almost perfect contour, a symmetrical face, dark almost to swarthiness, black eyes, which moved somewhat restlessly, curly hair of raven tint, a slight mustache, small hands and feet, and fashionable attire, Tom Delamere . . . was easily the handsomest young man in Wellington. But no discriminating observer would have characterized his beauty as manly" (16). Here Chesnutt includes many of the same code words suggesting, if not sexual deviance, certainly a lack of masculinity, operating in accord with a propensity for dissipation and degeneracy. Furthermore, like Frank Oakley, Tom Delamere's insufficiently manly exterior presages his moral shortcomings. His theft and ensuing murder of an elderly spinster are blamed on his uncle's loyal valet, Sandy, after Tom deliberately impersonates Sandy's appearance when fleeing the scene of the crime. This episode, in fact, offers Tom's second impersonation of Sandy; the first occurs during a "cakewalk" contest incongruously won by Tom in a blackface caricature of Sandy, a serious, stern, and submissive servant respectful of the traditions and conventions held over from the antebellum South.[14] This series of events, rife with irony and suggestive of the paradox of white minstrelsy, reenacts on a smaller scale the hypocrisy of the white supremacists who decry the bestiality of blacks even as they incite white mobs to violence. Unlike old Mr. Delamere, who in his struggle to stop Sandy's lynching reveals the sense of honor, however inadequate, that accompanies his outdated paternalism, Tom is an outright fraud—an unqualified criminal hiding behind his racial and familial mask of respectability.

The appropriation of primitive masculinity suggested by white minstrelsy parallels the evolution of spectator sports, and the confluence of minstrel performance, ritual violence, and greed in Tom's behavior suggests the constellation of forces behind the rise of sporting culture during this era. Driven by the need to "play primitive" through the display of brute force, physical prowess, and atavistic violence, upper- and middle-class white men took to the football gridiron and immersed themselves in the gritty saloons, pool halls, and sporting clubs that offered drinking, gambling, boxing, and the other fraternal rituals of the day. Out of this impulse emerged not only an attraction to the "action" of the ring, the racetrack, and the stadium, but also a big business—an escalating supply of consumable manliness to meet the demands of a restless and sedentary leisure class.

As a representation of the upper-class male's embrace of the primitive, the tragic absurdity of Tom Delamere's performance as Sandy functions not only as a critique of the hypocrisy behind the Jim Crow South, but also as a bitter caricature of the Anglo-Saxon cult of masculinity that fueled the sporting culture of the Progressive Era. Like the "pure" sport on display in the ring or on the field, what appears as the unmotivated act of appropriation actually occurs within the context of a commercial enterprise. Tom's cakewalk occurs at an event staged for Northern investors in the town's cotton industry whom Wellington's leaders wish to give "a pleasing impression of Southern customs, and particularly of the joyous, happy-go-lucky disposition of the Southern darky and his entire contentment with existing conditions" (117). When Ellis, a newspaper reporter, watches Tom in his award-winning performance, "the grotesque contortions" seem to him "somewhat overdone, even for the comical type of negro" (119).[15] "The vague suggestion of unreality about this performance" leads Ellis to reflect upon the "two widely varying phases of [negro] character": "No one could tell at what moment the thin veneer of civilization might peel off and reveal the underlying savage" (119). Of course, as Chesnutt's ironic narrative makes clear, it is actually Tom Delamere's "savagery" that has been revealed here, as well as in the subsequent murder of Polly Ochiltree. The paradoxical drive to outdo the "darky" at his own game recapitulates the brutality of the boxing ring, in which representatives of Anglo-Saxon civilization expose their primitive essence and thereby preserve the manliness of the race. All of this occurs, unsurprisingly, in a commercial venue, the spectacle sold to an audience in an act of capitalist exchange that reminds the participants of the power relationship at work. The Wellington cakewalk, intended to displace the demeaning dependence of the South on Northern capital by making visible the compliant "darkies," instead reveals (to the reader, at least) the venial desperation of the degenerate aristocrat and his willingness to prostitute his alleged dignity for quick money. The mob violence that spills onto the streets in the wake of black assertions of manhood simply reenacts Tom's performance on a larger stage.

Although both *The Sport of the Gods* and *The Marrow of Tradition* offer pointed exposés of white male degeneration among the genteel Southern aristocracy, Dunbar and Chesnutt are less than willing to fully embrace the hypermasculine model for identity fed by the sporting culture of the era and epitomized by the "badman" figure of Jack Johnson. In *The Marrow of Tradition,* the intellectual grace of William Miller proves ineffectual in the face of white dishonor and brutality. In a chapter revealingly entitled "How Not to Prevent a Lynching," Miller argues with "big Josh Green," a working-class leader who, Miller notes, "has been in court several times for fighting" (188–89). After Sandy Campbell's arrest for murder, Josh comes forward with an alibi proving Sandy's innocence. Miller and Watson, the town's "colored lawyer," convince Josh to remain silent, lest his information further provoke the lynch mob that is forming. Chesnutt's use of dialect in Josh's speech emphasizes the class distinction between him and the professional men: "Dr. Miller, is we-all jes' got ter set down here, widout openin' ou' mouths, an' let dese w'ite folks hang er bu'n a man w'at we know ain' guilty? . . . Ef you'all won't he'p, I'll do somethin' myse'f! Dere's two niggers ter one white man in dis town, an' I'm sho' I kin fin' fifty of 'em w'at 'llfight, ef dey kin fin' anybody ter lead 'em" (189).

In his depiction of Josh Green, Chesnutt creates an uneasy distance from his character through a reliance on black dialect conventions, with all of its protocols and inconsistencies (sometimes "w'ite"; other times "white," for instance). The doctor and lawyer successfully silence Josh at this point, but during the eventual unleashing of white rage that consumes the town, Josh rises as perhaps the only leader able to rally the black citizens in defense of their lives and property.[16] While Miller looks for his wife and child in the midst of the riot, he encounters Josh leading a group of armed laborers. Miller incorrectly argues that the whites would never destroy the black schoolhouse or hospital, and counsels the men to turn around: "Josh—men—you are throwing your lives away. . . . Resistance only makes the matter worse. The odds against you are too long" (295). Josh, however, insists, "We'd ruther die fightin' dan be stuck like pigs in a pen" (*Marrow of Tradition* 295). In his description of Miller's thoughts after leaving Josh and the men, Chesnutt reveals his own ambivalence about the quandary faced by his characters: "The colored men might win a momentary victory, though it was extremely doubtful; and they would as surely reap the harvest later on. The qualities which in a white man would win the applause of the world would in a negro be taken as the marks of savagery. . . . Or, if forced to admire, they would none the less repress. They would applaud his courage while they stretched his neck, or carried off the fragments of his mangled body as souvenirs, in much the same way that savages preserve the scalps or eat the hearts of their enemies" (295–96).

Although Miller's ideas are depicted through indirect discourse, Chesnutt fully articulates the problem of masculine identification felt by black men in general, and by writers such as himself in particular. Black manhood is, like any other performance, something to "applaud"—a show presented to an unwilling and hypocritical audience. Josh's compulsions to tell the truth and to stand up and fight are explicitly intertwined, and the consequences of his actions within the story, like the lynch law then pervasive in the United States, prove the thesis expressed earlier. African Americans who manifest the masculine characteristics so highly valued during the Progressive Era construct the inverse of minstrelsy: whereas the blackface minstrel adopts and defuses the mysterious, comical, or threatening characteristics of the other race for the purpose of entertainment, the "badman" revokes the white man's appropriation of blackness, thereby exposing the savagery behind the minstrel's act.

Josh Green's ultimate failure to stop the white rioters confirms the futility behind violence that Miller expresses, but Chesnutt also makes clear the appeal of the violent transgressive hero in his final description of Josh, who leads the men in a desperate charge against Captain McBane—the sadistic leader of the white mob: "Josh Green, the tallest and biggest of them all, had not apparently been touched. Some of the crowd paused in involuntary admiration of this black giant, famed on the wharves for his strength, sweeping down upon them, a smile on his face, his eyes lit up with a rapt expression which seemed to take him out of mortal ken. This impression was heightened by his apparent immunity from the shower of lead which less susceptible persons had continued to pour at him" (309). This passage documents the transformation of Josh Green from working-class roughneck to folk hero in the aftermath of the violence. Josh stabs McBane in the heart as he is shot and killed, and the two men die in a perverse embrace, each fulfilling his last wish to kill the other. "When the crowd dashed forward to wreak vengeance on [Josh's] dead body," Chesnutt writes, "they found him with a smile still on his face" (309).

This language suggests nothing so much as London's grudging, puzzled admiration of Jack Johnson in the wake of his victory over Jeffries some nine years after Chesnutt's novel appeared: "Johnson is a wonder. No one understands him, this man who smiles. Well, the story of the fight is the story of a smile. If ever a man won by nothing more fatiguing than a smile, Johnson won to-day" (*Jack London Reports* 301). Above all, the "badman's" power to distress and dismantle white supremacy rests with his ability to meet force with force and do so with apparent cheer and confidence. The danger, Chesnutt's novel warns, is that such victories come at a tremendous price.

Furthermore, the titanic struggles of legendary heroes such as Josh Green leave little room for mere intellectuals such as William Miller, who, after the white insurrection, have no place, either commonplace or mythic, in Wellington. In the aftermath of the Wilmington riot upon which Chesnutt based his work, Glenda Gilmore describes the response of the local examples of the African American leadership famously defined by Du Bois as the "talented tenth": "Black Best Men would have to leave North Carolina or outwardly conform to a place in society that was less than 'manly'" (*Gender and Jim Crow* 117).[17] If the only assertion of manhood can come through suicidal violence, Chesnutt suggests, what place is there for the rational portrayal of events, characterized in the novel by Miller's ineffectual analysis and further represented by the work of the novelist himself?

The Sport of the Gods likewise reveals its author's ambivalence toward the Progressive Era notion of masculinity as demonstrated by physical prowess, manly ritual, and primitive displays. Dunbar's depiction of the saloons and sporting clubs of New York suggests both the seductive allure and destructive power of this demimonde on Joe and Kitty alike. Kitty, like Crane's Maggie, falls prey to the dazzling, if tawdry, spectacle of consumption and glamour that the nightclubs provide. Joe is similarly seduced, like Crane's George Kelcey, by the fraternal kinship and manly rituals of the murky underworld. Dunbar explains the unusual mingling of classes that defined the male urban subculture of that era in his description of one such nightclub:

> The Banner Club was an institution for the lower education of Negro youth. It drew its pupils from every class of people and from every

part of the country. It was composed of all sorts and conditions of men, educated and uneducated, dishonest and less so, of the good, the bad, and the—unexposed. Parasites came there to find victims, politicians for votes, reporters for news, and artists of all kinds for color and inspiration. It was the place of assembly for a number of really bright men, who after days of hard and often unrewarded work came there and drunk themselves drunk in each other's company, and when they were drunk talked of the eternal verities. (100–01)

For men of all races and ethnicities, the saloon offered a sense of community and a source of identity free from the emasculating influence of both the home and the workplace, and for African American men, whose jobs often reinforced the subservient position of their race, places such as the "Banner Club" provided a way to participate in the masculine rituals established by the larger culture. In a study of the rise of saloon culture, Jon Kingsdale argues, "The saloon supported and reinforced a stereotypically masculine character and a self-sufficient all male culture separate from the prissy world of women and the constraints of family" (*Sport of the Gods* 273). Furthermore, such clubs supplied working-class black men such as Joe with an occasion to rub elbows with "politicians," "reporters," and "artists"— black and white—and such contact proved as intoxicating as the alcohol for impressionable men with little experience beyond the farm or factory.

Despite the obvious attractions of such an environment, in which the boundaries of race and class are challenged though ultimately reinforced, Dunbar expresses his distaste for the club in phrases that betray his place in the nineteenth-century genteel tradition: "Of course, the place was a social cesspool, generating a poisonous miasma and reeking with the stench of decayed and rotten moralities. There is no defense to be made for it. But what do you expect when false idealism and fevered ambition come face to face with catering cupidity?" (101). In his description of the Banner Club, Dunbar reveals not only his adherence to attitudes toward the "decayed and rotten moralities" of the saloon that belong to an earlier era but a discomfort with the lower-class characters who populate his novel. This detached indignation obeys the conventions of naturalistic descent narratives, such as *Maggie* or Emile Zola's *L'Assommoir*, but ultimately leaves unresolved the book's narrative perspective on its subject: African American life and culture at the turn of the century. Although Chesnutt offers William Miller as an alternative, however problematic, to the "other" class of "Negro," Dunbar provides no options for his characters or his readers.

The transgressive folk figure in *The Sport of the Gods* is appropriately named "Sadness," and his world-weary account of the lynching of his father reveals Dunbar's interpretation of the "badman's" place in black culture. When Joe gives a "gasp of horror" at an offhand remark about the lynching, Sadness responds, "Oh, yes, but it was done with a very good rope and by the best citizens of Texas, so it seems that I really ought to be very grateful to them for the distinction that they conferred upon my family, but I am not. I am ungratefully sad. A man must be very high or very low to take the sensible view of life that keeps him from being sad. I must confess that I have aspired to the depths without ever being fully able to reach them" (121). Lacking the violent rage that defines Josh Green, Sadness instead demonstrates a bitter resignation, seeing his only escape in the sordid underworld of New York's Tenderloin. For Dunbar, as for Chesnutt, the challenge for black artists and cultural observers is to adopt a "sensible view of life" that precedes meaningful action. *The Sport of the Gods* and *The Marrow of Tradition* raise this problem, but they finish in disarray and uncertainty. Dunbar's novel ends with a bleak portrayal of the Hamiltons' reconstituted family, living out their days in diminished circumstances, and their hard-won insight would be all too familiar to Dunbar's black readers at the nadir: "They knew they were powerless against some will infinitely stronger than their own" (195).

If their ambivalence about the perceived biological underpinning of primitive masculinity separated Dunbar and Chesnutt from their white literary counterparts, so did their attitude toward the emergence of popular or "yellow" journalism, which owed more to William Dean Howells and Henry James than to those naturalists, including Crane, Norris, and London, who practiced it themselves. Although the older generation of realists looked upon professional journalism as a lesser art than fiction, naturalist authors generally saw the role of reporter—particularly war correspondent or sports reporter—as a more appropriate manly vocation than that of author. Furthermore, Dunbar's and Chesnutt's antipathy toward the popular press stemmed from the openly racist editorial slant of many newspapers, as well as from their own exclusion as African Americans from the journalistic enterprise. Among the myriad consequences of the widespread institutional segregation of American society was the emergence of a vital and influential African American press with a national audience. Between 1900 and 1910, several periodicals emerged that catered to black readers, including *The Colored American Magazine, Voice of the Negro, Horizon,* and the NAACP's *Crisis.* In fashioning a journalistic response to the white supremacist doctrines of the day, these journals provided an outlet for writing that presented a de-romanticized view of race and social inequity. For both Du Bois and Johnson, these periodicals provided a platform for the dissemination of their views on art, politics, and culture, and their involvement with journalism gave them a somewhat different view of writing as a professional endeavor.

In both *The Sport of the Gods* and *The Marrow of Tradition,* the novels' climaxes hinge on a newspaper article. For Berry Hamilton, justice is delivered only after Skaggs, a reporter for the New York *Universe,* uncovers the truth about Frank Oakley's theft. Skaggs's introduction into the story and into the Hamiltons' lives occurs—not coincidentally—at the Banner Club, where he meets Joe and hears the story of his father's imprisonment. Although described as "a monumental liar" whose feigned familiarity and fondness for "darkies" proves superficial at best (103–04), Skaggs convinces his editor to send him South to investigate Joe's story. Joe's destructive attraction to the "yellow-skinned divinity" Hattie Sterling (105) proves no less complex than his friendship with the yellow journalist Skaggs, whose motives for revealing the truth about the Oakleys have more to do with material rewards than altruism. Dunbar's description of Skaggs's newspaper could easily apply to Pulitzer's *World* or Hearst's *Journal:* "The *Universe* was yellow. It was very so. But it had power and keenness and energy. It never lost an opportunity to crow, and if one was not forthcoming, it made one. In this way it managed to do a considerable amount of good, and its yellowness became forgivable, even commendable" (182).[18] Dunbar recognizes the power of the press to do good or ill but remains ambivalent about its role in promoting real progress.

Chesnutt's novel presents an even more troubling portrait of the press in its depiction of the *Morning Chronicle.* Although the Wilmington riot had been encouraged by a series of editorials by Josephus Daniels in the Raleigh *News and Observer* as well as articles in the Democratic organ, the Wilmington *Messenger,* Chesnutt places Major Phillip Carteret's paper at the very center of the plot to strip black citizens of their rights in Wellington.[19] By reprinting an editorial from the "negro newspaper" condemning lynch law and referring to "voluntary acts" of miscegenation (84–85), the *Chronicle* sets in motion the events that lead to mob violence: "The reproduction, in the Chronicle, of the article from the Afro-American Banner, with Carteret's inflammatory comment, took immediate effect. It touched the Southern white man in his most sensitive spot. . . . To meet words with words upon such a subject would be [to] acknowledge the equality of the negro and his right to discuss or criticise the conduct of the white people" (248).

As in *The Sport of the Gods,* the printed word leads to direct action, but in this case, the action is neither commendable nor forgivable. As Eric Sundquist observes, "Forty years before Richard Wright would make the journalistic caricature of Bigger Thomas a central feature of *Native Son,* Chesnutt put the power of the white press under scrutiny" (*To Wake the Nations* 423–24). When Carteret sees the horrific scope of the violence, he attempts to restrain the mob, but his words are useless: "In vain the baffled orator gesticulated and shrieked in the effort to correct the misapprehension" (306). In the end, Carteret disavows any responsibility for the riot and leaves the lower classes, white and black, to destroy themselves.

The hypocrisy and cruelty of Carteret and other inheritors of the paternalistic system offer the broadest target for Chesnutt's critique, but in the character of the reporter Ellis, Chesnutt presents a sympathetic portrait of the shortcomings of Progressivism. Ellis enters the story as Tom Delamere's rival for the affections of Carteret's half sister Clara in one of the novel's many subplots. Ultimately, however, his role as a member of Carteret's staff at the *Chronicle* proves significant. It is Ellis who wrongly identifies Sandy when he mistakes Tom Delamere for the servant on the dark streets. When he learns of the plan to lynch Sandy for the crime, Ellis feels "a sudden sense of responsibility . . . for his had been the final word to fix the prisoner's guilt" (216). Despite his personal opposition to lynch law and his authorship of several editorials against it Ellis finds himself implicated in its imminent application. Upon realizing the truth, Ellis resolves to speak to old Mr. Delamere about his nephew's guilt. When Mr. Delamere asks him plainly, "Who was it?" however, Ellis responds weakly. "'I do not wish to say at present,' replied Ellis, with a remorseful pang, 'unless it becomes absolutely necessary, to save the negro's life" (221). His reluctance to speak out on this occasion prefigures Ellis's ineffectual response to the riot at the novel's close. When Clara asks him what he can do to "stop this terrible affair," Ellis finds few words: "'I wish I could do something,' he murmured fervently"

(311). The inaction of the reporter recalls the Easterner in Crane's "The Blue Hotel," who withholds comment and stands aside while others attack the Swede. Despite good intentions, Ellis fails to "report" anything in the story. Although the power of the press can be harnessed for sinister purposes by Carteret and his Democratic allies, it can also fail to achieve any effect whatsoever.

In *The Marrow of Tradition,* Chesnutt bases his description of the black editor of the *Afro-American Banner,* Barber, on Alexander Manly of the *Wilmington Daily Record,* whose editorial response to the publication of a speech supporting lynching as a legitimate response to the rape of white women by black men began the war of words in the press and the call for white retribution. In both the historical and fictional versions of events, the African American editor and newspaper paid dearly for daring to speak the truth about lynch law. The offices of the *Daily Record,* the only black daily newspaper in North Carolina, were destroyed, and public officials called for the lynching of Manly himself.[20] The fictional Barber and his *Afro-American Banner* suffer a similar fate, and Miller expresses reservations about Barber's writing comparable to those he feels toward Josh Green's more physical assertion of his "manhood rights." After seeing the reaction to Barber's "obnoxious editorial" in the white newspaper, Miller reflects on its impact: "The right of free speech entitled Barber to publish it; a larger measure of common-sense would have made him withhold it" (277–78). As in Miller's guidance of the headstrong and doomed Josh Green, the extent to which Chesnutt reveals his own attitudes remains unclear, but the passage certainly illustrates the author's awareness of the power of free speech to capture the attention of an audience. As the fate of Chesnutt's novel itself would show, however, this attention may come at a steep price.

Throughout his early career, W. E. B. Du Bois demonstrated his own willingness to speak directly about issues of race in America, and his first novel, *The Quest of the Silver Fleece,* served as an inevitable extension of his earlier works of scholarship, biography, and cultural criticism. According to Arnold Rampersad, "From the start, Du Bois saw his fiction as flowing naturally out of his scholarly and political concern with black life and culture in the United States" (Foreword 5). A hint at Du Bois's interest in naturalistic fiction appears in the penultimate chapter of *The Souls of Black Folk,* entitled "Of the Coming of John," a fictional account of the tragic fate awaiting an educated black man in the Deep South. In this story, an idealistic young man who has returned from his intellectual awakening in the North to work at the "Negro school" chafes at the limitations of Jim Crow society and ends up murdering his white doppelganger—a judge's son, also named John, and who has also returned from a Northern education—when he sees "his dark haired sister struggling in the arms of a tall fair-haired man" (534). As the lynch mob closes in on him, he stoically rises to meet them, "softly humming" a line from Wagner's *Lohengrin* (535). This fictional version of the "truth" behind lynching exposes the same subject as the editorial behind the Wilmington riots and resonates strongly with the African-American literary canon—from Frederick Douglass's exploration of the bitterness that comes with knowledge to the grim inevitability of Bigger Thomas's fate in Richard Wright's *Native Son*. Encouraged by his publisher to pursue the writing of fiction, Du Bois would turn to the model afforded by the naturalists of the day to explore the issues of economics and race that *The Souls of Black Folk* introduces.[21]

As David Levering Lewis notes, the novels upon which Du Bois drew for inspiration included Sinclair's exposé of the meat-packing industry, James Allen's *The Reign of Law, A Tale of the Kentucky Hemp Fields,* and Norris's unfinished "epic of the wheat," *The Octopus* and *The Pit.*[22] Of these, the intersections with Norris's *The Octopus* are particularly instructive. Like *The Octopus,* Du Bois's work combines elements of realism and romance[23] and involves a number of plots and subplots centered around the production of a single crop—in this case, cotton.

Du Bois parallels a study of the socioeconomic forces driving rural "Tooms" County, Alabama,[24] with a love story between the novel's two protagonists, Blessed Alwyn and Zora Cresswell. "Bles," a hard-working, upwardly mobile member of the "talented tenth," falls in love with Zora, who bears the same last name as the white plantation owner and is the daughter of a notorious prostitute, raised in a cabin in the swamp at the outskirts of a cotton plantation. As children, Bles and Zora attend a school run by a sympathetic New Englander, Miss Smith, and their love matures as they work together on a secret cotton crop planted in the fertile soil of the swamp. The characters' paths diverge after Bles learns that Zora has been raped by white men and is thus not "pure." Simultaneously, the "silver fleece" that Zora brings to the cotton market is stolen by Colonel Cresswell, who claims ownership of all cotton grown by his "niggers." As Northern industrialists exploit racial antagonisms to transform Toomsville into a thriving factory town, both Bles and Zora receive a further "education" up North in Washington, Bles as a civil servant and Zora as the maid of a rich white woman, Mrs. Vanderpool. After gaining valuable experience, both characters discover the corruption and hypocrisy behind the system that governs the lives of their people, and they resolve to return to Miss Smith's school outside Toomsville to struggle against the repressive forces that preserve the inequities of the rural South.

As in "On the Coming of John," Du Bois's narrative combines a didactic indictment of capitalism with the travails of enlightened heroic characters, although in *Quest,* the outcome is far from tragic. Instead, Bles and Zora are reunited as the Creswell property and fortune pass into the hands of Emma, the Colonel's mulatto granddaughter, and eventually to Miss Smith's school. Although his earlier work of fiction ends, like Dunbar's and Chesnutt's novels, in an uneasy limbo, in his epic of cotton, Du Bois attempts not only to deflate the spurious Southern mythology of Page and Dixon, but to construct an idealized countermyth to the dominant plantation romances of the day. In his essay "W. E. B. Du Bois as a Man of Literature," Rampersad claims, "The immoral stasis of the world in 'Of the Coming of John' gives way to the exposition of culture as process, and history and the world as both scrutable and stimulant to optimism" (69). In this active composition of culture, Du Bois draws upon the themes and devices of literary naturalism as articulated most aggressively by Norris.

In shaping the idealistic design of *The Quest of the Silver Fleece,* Du Bois effectively revises the "masculine-feminine ethic," a trope identified by Donald Pizer in Norris's popular fiction and represented in *Octopus* by the Annixter-Hilma Tree relationship. In Norris's fiction, the brutishness of men is properly focused and harnessed by the support of a strong-willed, untraditional woman, who in turn surrenders some of her mannish characteristics and assumes a more feminine role. Such is the arrangement when the headstrong but heroic rancher "Buck" Annixter is "tamed" by Hilma, a robust and independent milkmaid. Likewise, Bles Alwyn, despite his intelligence and ambition, needs the guidance and inspiration provided by Zora to achieve his potential as a "race man." The emergence of their love occurs as they prepare to harvest their glorious crop of cotton, grown to extraordinary size and quality in the fertile swamp. Also raised in the lush and mysterious swamp, Zora takes on the characteristics of the "silver fleece" as she reaches sexual maturity:

She would, unhindered, develop to a brilliant, sumptuous woman-hood; proud, conquering, full-blooded, and deep bosomed—a passionate mother of men. Herein lay all her early wildness and strangeness. Herein lay, as yet half hidden, dimly sensed and all unspoken, the power of a mighty all-compelling love for one human soul, and, through it, for all the souls of men. All this lay growing and developing; but as yet she was still a girl, with a new shyness and comeliness and a bold, searching heart.

In the field of the Silver Fleece all her possibilities were beginning to find expression. These new-born green things hidden far down in the swamp, begotten in want and mystery, were to her a living wonderful fairy tale come true. All the latent mother in her brooded over them; all her brilliant fancy wove itself about them. They were her dream-children, and she tended them jealously. (125)

Whereas the growth of the cotton elicits from Zora a newfound maternal sense, the "new-born green things" awaken a complementary sense of purpose in Bles: "The sun burned fiercely upon the young cotton plants as the spring hastened, and they lifted their heads in darker, wider luxuriance; for the time of hoeing was at hand. . . . Strength and ambition and inarticulate love were fighting within [Bles]. He felt, in the dark thousands of his kind about him, a mighty calling to deeds" (*Quest* 126). Du Bois purposely links the growth of the cotton with the nascent sexual feelings between Bles and Zora and further connects these impulses with the "strength and ambition" necessary to perform important work on behalf of the race. Whereas Norris, in *The Octopus,* presents three potential "heroes," Presley, Vanamee, and Annixter—each of whom possesses heroic aspects to his character, specifically artistry, spirituality, and masculinity—Du Bois weaves the defining characteristic of all three into Bles. Virtuous, intellectual, and virile, Bles represents the kind of gifted man "blessed" with the heroic qualities needed for the survival of the dreams Zora envisions. As he contemplates their cotton and his feelings for Zora, Bles realizes "they were drifting to a silenter, mightier mingling of souls" (126). The mystical "stirring of a mighty force" described by Du Bois recalls Norris's language when chronicling the majestic power of "the Wheat." Like Norris, Du Bois was heavily invested in various forms of mysticism, and indeed a sense of racial destiny, which—unlike Norris—belied his background as a rationalist and a social scientist.

Just as Norris's invocation of a male-female ethic in defining the development of heroic character suggests the fashioning of a male-female aesthetic to define the proper role of the artist, so does the union of Bles and Zora suggest Du Bois's understanding of the proper adoption of a voice to speak the truth about racial oppression and injustice. The passages quoted earlier repeatedly refer to the silent and inarticulate nature of both Bles's and Zora's feelings of love and responsibility, and only through their common influence on each other can these impulses find expression. A gifted orator, Bles discovers a path to power and prestige in the Republican Party during his extended sojourn in the nation's capital. At a debating club meeting on "The Democratic Party and the Negro," Bles rises and speaks of "the government and conditions in the Black Belt, of the lying, oppression, and helplessness of the sodden black masses" (*Quest* 262). His moving narrative of his childhood education under Miss Smith wins over his erudite and sophisticated audience, unused to hearing such words from a "Southern country Negro" (254): "He spoke for nearly an hour, and when he stopped, for a moment his hearers sighed and then sprang into a whirlwind of applause" (262).[25] Bles's speech also impresses Caroline Wynn, a fair-skinned socialite who takes on Bles as a political protégé and, later, fiancé. Cynical and worldly, with "little faith in the world or its people" (253), Caroline provides a stark contrast to Zora's earthy, dark, and idealistic influence.

Bles's growing involvement in Republican politics, under the tutelage of Caroline Wynn, leads to the consideration of his name for the position of Treasurer of the United States, to this day a largely symbolic political appointment. Voicing the distrust of petty materialism typical of Progressive Era manhood, Bles worries, "I don't somehow like the idea of seeming to have worked hard in the campaign simply for money or fortune" (277). Miss Wynn, understanding how to manipulate Bles, says to him, "Here's your chance to lead your people, and here you stand blinking and hesitating. Be a man!" (277). Forced to moderate his criticism of the party on its support for an education bill reforming black schools, Bles must decide between following his conscience and achieving professional success. At the same time, Zora has urged her patron, Mrs. Vanderpool, to pressure her husband's Republican associates to appoint Bles: "Make him Treasurer of the United States without sacrificing his manhood or betraying his people" (298). In spite of Zora's machinations, Bles must renounce his criticisms of the party in order to secure the appointment, and his refusal to do so leads to his professional downfall and the subsequent loss of Caroline Wynn's affections: "And Carrie Wynn—poor Carrie,[26] with her pride and position dragged down in his ruin: how would she take it? He writhed in soul. And yet, to be a man, to say calmly, 'No'; to stand in that great audience and say, 'My people first and last'" (318).

As Bles contemplates his course of action, he opens an anonymous note (sent by Zora) that contains a few unattributed lines of poetry: "It matters not how strait the gate, / How charged with punishments the scroll; / I am the master of my fate, / I am the captain of my soul" (318). The source for these words is, of course, "Invictus," by William Ernest Henley, whose reputation as a Tory defender of British imperialism and the "white man's burden," as much as any other evidence, suggests the paradoxical nature of Du Bois's countermythology of race building in *The Quest of the Silver Fleece*. Bles chooses to tell the truth and thereby relinquishes his chance at personal and romantic "success." When Carrie Wynn redirects her affections to Bles's rival, the opportunistic Samuel Stillings, she admits admiration for "Bles Alwyn, the Fool—and the Man. But, by grace of the Negro Problem, I cannot afford to marry a man" (323–24). For Du Bois, as for naturalist writers in general, truth telling and manhood are inextricably linked, and Bles triumphs where others, such as Chesnutt's William Miller, have failed. Furthermore, the seduction and near destruction of Bles by a fair-skinned temptress, and his return to the darker heroine, Zora, conforms to Du Bois's political agenda, as expressed in numerous essays on the integrity and direction of the black race.

The Quest of the Silver Fleece, as several critics have observed, is remarkable for its focus on heroic protagonists who are distinctively working class and dark skinned. Whereas earlier "serious" fiction by African American writers tended to examine the problem of the color line from the point of view of those on its boundaries, Du Bois (though himself light-skinned, Northern, and with a family history free from the memory of North American slavery) chooses to celebrate the very "blackness" of Bles and Zora and in so doing redefines the color lines within black society. His depiction of their speech seldom reflects the condescending taint of dialect, and their actions are consistently more honorable than the middle-class blacks epitomized by Caroline Wynn and her allies.[27] Bles and Zora are members of the "Talented Tenth" by virtue of their natural abilities and intelligence, rather than their proximate whiteness. Du Bois's investment in the rhetoric, if not the popular intent, of social Darwinism is made clear in the following passage from his essay "The Talented Tenth" itself, published in 1903:

> From the very first it has been the educated and intelligent of the Negro people that have led and elevated the mass, and the sole obstacles that nullified and retarded their efforts were slavery and race prejudice; for what is slavery but the legalized survival of the unfit and the nullification of the work of natural internal leadership? Negro leadership, therefore, sought from the first to rid the race of this awful incubus that it might make way for natural selection and the survival of the fittest. (*Writings* 842–43)

In denouncing the intraracial racism of skin tone, Du Bois presents a notion of racial "purity" that, in some ways, merely inverts the usual formula. Bles is "yellow" in terms of neither courage nor appearance, and this correlation, within the literary landscape of Du Bois's novel, is far from coincidental. Even more important is the blackness of Zora, who provides Bles with the direction necessary to become a true leader. According to Dickson Bruce, "It is the character of Zora that holds the book together, serving as the emotional focus of the novel and as the chief medium for conveying Du Bois's concerns" (218). Zora's dark, maternal spirit is, as Felipe Smith notes, "in keeping with Du Bois's emphasis on black womanhood's latent, unconscious spiritual gift" (297). In his well-known 1897 essay "The Conservation of Races," Du Bois argues that the black race "must be inspired with the Divine faith of our black *mothers,* that out of the blood and dust of battle will march a victorious host, a mighty nation, a peculiar people, to *speak* to the nations of the earth a Divine truth that shall make them free" (*Writings* 823, italics added). In emphasizing the role of women as repositories of racial integrity, Du Bois transforms slave law governing race based on the "condition of the mother" into a source of pride and unity. Moreover, Du Bois's linkage of racial destiny with artistic duty vividly plays upon the pleas for Anglo-Saxon responsibility in Norris's literary essays, as well as his vague, spiritual rhetoric. Du Bois calls for leaders, for a gathering of "the talented, unselfish men, the pure and noble-minded women, to fight an army of devils that disgraces our manhood and our womanhood. There does not stand today upon God's earth a race more capable in muscle, in intellect, in morals, than the American Negro" (825). For Du Bois, it is the duty of black leaders to meet the muscular force of white racism with equal firmness and resolve, and *The Quest of the Silver Fleece* attempts to do just that.[28]

The problem of defining racial identity and black authenticity serves as a contentious issue for African Americans to this day, and the positions represented by Dunbar, Chesnutt, Du Bois, and Johnson offer a complex and divergent set of approaches. Of the four, only Dunbar could be described as having a dark complexion—a disparity reflected throughout the black intelligentsia of the time, as well as throughout the literary concerns of much African American fiction.[29] For his part, Chesnutt, most famously in an essay entitled "The Future American," suggested that the eventual intermixing of all races to form a single, multiracial identity would bring about the only viable resolution to the problem of the color line in the United States. Du Bois, in contrast, sought to remind black Americans of their inevitable blood ties to Africa and to encourage and maintain the distinctions between the races.[30] In this regard, Du Bois inevitably reflects the deeply ingrained racial essentialism of his era, at least at this early stage in his career. Du Bois's championing of heroic figures such as Bles and Zora in his novel further reflects the awareness of his own outsider status so plainly chronicled in *The Souls of Black Folk*. Fear of becoming merely a "car-window sociologist," as he calls it in the chapter of *Souls* entitled "Of the Quest of the Golden Fleece" (469), compelled Du Bois to enter the arena of naturalist fiction, to participate in the discourse about the fate of his race.

This same participatory impulse informs the characterization of the failed artist who narrates James Weldon Johnson's *The Autobiography of an Ex-Colored Man*.[31] Furthermore, it is through the discourse of masculinity that Johnson advocates his aesthetic sensibility, or more precisely, shows the failures of the wrong approach. Published anonymously in 1912, and later reprinted in 1927 under Johnson's name, the influential novel traces the picaresque journey of a man through a series of roles: as the child of a black mother and an absent white father in New England, a cigar-roller in Florida, a gambler and ragtime pianist in New York's Tenderloin, a successful musician and composer in Europe, and finally as a prosperous businessman passing for white in an international wholesale firm. In the end, the protagonist abandons an ambitious project to elevate popular ragtime music into a respected art form when he decides to marry a white woman and enter the New York business establishment. Johnson's novel serves not only to elucidate the issues of identity confronting African Americans in the twentieth century and expose the social construction of race, but also to articulate the author's views on the ethical and aesthetic responsibilities of the artist.

Johnson's novel, in fact, turns the Anglo-Saxon "cult of masculinity" against itself. Whereas Du Bois appears to validate the racial essentialism behind the glorification of the muscular "Teutonic" hero through the creation of his own racial propaganda, Johnson, by showing one man's inability to rise to the occasion, as Bles had done, underscores the anxieties behind the masculine authenticity for which Du Bois strives. In fashioning his own rejoinder to the predominant theories of Anglo-Saxon dominance embedded in the fiction of London, Norris, and others, Johnson effectively employs the masculinist discourse of these texts toward a quite different purpose.[32] The ex-colored man's failure is not lack of *understanding,* but rather of strength, an absence of manly fortitude—a "yellow streak" in the language of the boxing ring—which manifests itself in his inadequate artistry. In the context of Johnson's novel and its racial concerns, the narrator, of course, might also be described as "yellow," in that term's vernacular usage, as his light skin allows him to pass easily for white.[33] In fact, these two definitions of "yellow" have some inherent connection, at least for the narrator. In his failure to "stand up and be a man," as the Easterner in Crane's "The Blue Hotel" says, by publicly acknowledging the truth of his black blood, the novel suggests that the protagonist is not only no longer "colored" but also no longer a "man."

Among the novel's innovations are two formal characteristics that set it apart from earlier works by African Americans, even as they place the text squarely within the tradition. First, as a fictional "autobiography," the book invites comparison with the slave narratives that constitute the foundation of African American literature, with Douglass's 1845 *Narrative of the Life of Frederick Douglass, An American Slave* as the primary point of reference.[34] Second, the book's central theme, the biracial dilemma of its protagonist, evokes the dominant trope of the earliest black novelists, the "tragic mulatto" represented in many works, from the first published novel by an African American, William Wells Brown's *Clotel,* to Chesnutt's *The House Behind the Cedars.* Both of these literary associations indicate the importance of gender in the formulation of Johnson's novel. The turning point of Douglass's *Narrative* comes after his fight with the brutal slave-breaker Mr. Covey, about which Douglass writes, "You have now seen how a man was made a slave; you shall see how a slave was made a man" (65–66). Although formulation of black manhood serves as one of the crucial legacies of Douglass's text, the novels of the color line normally exposed the injustices of black woman-hood. Indeed, in literature, the "tragic mulatto," the masculine noun ending notwithstanding, is almost exclusively a *female* whose uncertain identity and desirability to men of both races left her vulnerable and isolated. By playing freely with the conventions of both genres, Johnson's novel occupies an im-portant position, linking the experimental fiction of the later Harlem Ren-aissance with the earlier contributions of African American writers, as well as placing its aesthetic properties and the question of gender at the forefront of any careful reading of the text.

The failure experienced by the protagonist of *The Autobiography* repre-sents something greater than an individual's artistic career, in this case as a pianist and composer who fuses black folkloric and European classical mu-sical forms, reflecting the hybrid culture that defines African American iden-tity. Although Johnson's book challenges the dominant genetic theories of race of his day, it also suggests the need to construct and maintain a distinct racial identity through cultural production. Whereas the novels of London and Norris call for a "masculine" art to uphold the obligations of Anglo-Saxon empire building, Johnson's novel employs a similar aesthetic strategy in direct response to this ideological impulse. Although the pursuit of racial assimilation served as an important goal for Johnson and other members of the "talented tenth," elements of the novel reflect the often contradictory impulse to preserve the integrity of racial or cultural identity in spite of integrationist aspirations.[35]

As an artist, the ex-colored man uses his unusual position in society to drift between worlds. He moves seamlessly from playing ragtime for gam-blers in the Tenderloin to interpreting Chopin in European salons, just as he uses his fair complexion to "pass" between black and white. In his depiction of the dark and seductive world of the Tenderloin, Johnson paints a more inviting portrait than does Dunbar in *The Sport of the Gods,* but the narra-tor, unlike Joe, never truly becomes a part of the underworld he inhabits. Instead, as an entertainer, he remains an outsider. From his youth, the ex-colored man plays the role of detached artist, and his detachment from his peers, his musical talent, and his questionable masculinity are all inter-twined. From the start, the narrator describes himself as the epitome of a "mama's boy," a self-concept well established before he becomes aware of his racial identity: "My mother and I lived together in a little cottage which seemed to be fitted up almost luxuriously. . . . My mother dressed me very neatly, and developed that pride which well-dressed boys generally have. . . . As I look back now I can see that I was a perfect little aristocrat" (*Autobiography* 275). The narrator remembers that his mother's sewing customers would "tell [his] mother what a pretty boy [he] was" and encourage him to undertake lessons in piano (275). Leading "a rather unwholesome life," he lives "in a world of imagination, of dreams and air castles—the kind of atmosphere that sometimes nourishes a genius, more often men unfitted for the practical struggles of life. I never played a game of ball, never went fishing or learned to swim; in fact the only outdoor exercise in which I took any interest was skating" (292). A veritable prototype of the kind of flat-chested weakling fretted over by social reformers such as Ernest Thompson Seton, George M. Beard, and Joseph Lee, the narrator fails to engage in the typical boyish pastimes, instead clinging to his mother's apron strings and artistic visions.[36] Later, despite his immersion in the hypermasculine world of the gambling hall and barroom, he never fully participates in the manly rituals of the saloon referred to simply as "the Club," the walls of which prominently display portraits of Frederick Douglass and the black Australian boxer Peter Jackson, and whose patrons include various "notables of the ring, the turf, and the stage" (316–17). Here, as elsewhere, the worlds of sport, spectacle, fraternity, and racial leadership are interwoven.

The narrator's boyhood friend Shiny serves as his double—a dark-skinned boy, gifted and resourceful, who stands up for the narrator and wins his "undying gratitude" when the other children call him "nigger" (*Autobiography* 280). Shiny's stirring oration of Wendell Phillips's "Toussaint L'Ouverture" at their grammar school graduation awakens the narrator's sense of racial pride and obligation, and his performance also elicits a powerful reaction from the gathered audience. The narrator likens Shiny's effect on the crowd to that "of others who would have played on the varsity football and baseball teams" and suggests that "the explanation . . . lies in what is a basic, though often dormant principle of the Anglo-Saxon heart, love of fair play" (291). Shiny's fate as a "race man" seems secure, but the protagonist's experience with audiences is far more ambiguous.

Although he succeeds as a ragtime pianist, catering to the primal urges of a mixed audience, the narrator finds a pathway to artistic expression only after he falls under the patronage of an unnamed white benefactor. After hiring the narrator for a dinner party, this "millionaire friend," whom the narrator first observes "languidly puffing cigarettes" at "the Club" (*Autobiography* 321), gives him twenty dollars and offers him steady work, "his only stipulation being that I should not play any engagements such as I had just filled for him, except by his instructions" (323). When the narrator witnesses the murder of one of his white female "admirers" at the Club by a black "bad man," the mysterious millionaire takes the narrator for a carriage ride in the park and invites him to take the place of his "valet" on a trip to Europe. As Philip Brian Harper observes, the relationship between the two men extends beyond that of employer and employee and "most nearly approximates a homosexual coupling" (110). When the narrator grows weary of their endless travel, despite the cultural and artistic avenues it has opened up for him, he dreads "the ordeal of breaking with my millionaire. Between this peculiar man and me there had grown a very strong bond of affection" (332).[37] In the dynamics of this relationship, Johnson suggests not only the narrator's willingness to capitulate to a form of volunteer slavery and to an overtly "female" role vis-à-vis a white man, but also the emasculating effect upon a black artist of the demands of a predominantly white audience.

Johnson himself was well acquainted with the role of white patrons in the world of music, having worked with his brother Rosamond and their partner Bob Cole composing "coon songs" on Broadway.[38] Full of dialect, "low" humor, and racial stereotypes, such songs offered Johnson the opportunity to showcase the possibilities of black musical forms but also presented dire limitations for expressing the range of experiences that Johnson writes about elsewhere. Johnson knew firsthand the expectations that black-face minstrelsy had placed on the African American artist, and the fate of the ex-colored man reflects his awareness of the difficulties in confronting these expectations.[39]

The novel's violent climax precipitates the final artistic and ethical downfall of the protagonist. Passing for white in the rural South, the narrator witnesses a brutal lynching, the "transformation of human beings into savage beasts" (351). This pivotal scene captures what Kenneth Warren identifies as the central theme of the novel: "The making of a man into less than a man" (*Autobiography* 273). The ex-colored man watches as a mob brings in its black victim, "a man only in form and stature, every sign of degeneracy stamped upon his face" (351). As the man is reduced to "blackened bones" and "charred fragments," the protagonist says, "I was fixed to the spot where I stood, powerless to take my eyes from what I did not want to see" (352).

The grotesque spectacle leaves its spectator paralyzed with "a great wave of humiliation and shame" and renders him impotent in the face of the white mob's savagery (352). The lynching not only reduces its victim to mere fragments but leaves the ex-colored man as "a man only in form" as well.

The ritualized violence of lynching described so vividly by Johnson is recapitulated in the remarkable spectacle of the Jack Johnson-Jim Jeffries boxing match that had occupied the national spotlight only two years before the publication of *The Autobiography*.[40] The sense of disgrace felt by the novel's narrator captures the effect upon black audiences intended by the promoters of the Johnson-Jeffries fight. Indeed, by violating the primary principle of Jim Crow society—marrying a white woman (in fact, several)—Jack Johnson exposed himself to the very real threat of lynching. Although promoters confiscated dozens of handguns from the audience in Reno, Johnson's predicted defeat at the hand of Jeffries would have been a symbolic lynching itself, reinforcing African American humiliation and shame in the face of Anglo-Saxon superiority. Jack Johnson's refusal to submit to this fate—even in his honorable defeat by Jess Willard in 1915—not only undermined the ideology of white supremacy but also suggests the importance of Johnson's manliness in shaping the construction of African American identity. Johnson became something of a folk hero, a prototypical "badman" who defied and outwitted the authorities at every turn. For James Weldon Johnson, the challenge remained to do with his pen what Jack Johnson had done with his fists, to "get in the ring" with adherents of Anglo-Saxon superiority and show the hollowness of their ideas. The fate of the ex-colored man stands as a cautionary tale of the failure to do so. Rather than stand up and confront the "brutality and savagery" of white society, he reveals his true "yellow"-ness and retreats and, in so doing, denies his own identity.

For Progressive Era writers, the proper response to society's violence is an art that avoids the feminized "culture" of drawing rooms and salons and harnesses the masculine authority of nation building, whether that of Norris's venture capitalists, London's socialists, or what Johnson's narrator calls the "small but gallant band of colored men who are publicly fighting the cause of their race" (*Autobiography* 362). Instead, the ex-colored man descends to insignificance, subsumed by the manly game of commerce, but having little power to control it. He recalls his lost aspirations with regret: "When I sometimes open a little box in which I still keep my fast yellowing manuscripts, the only tangible remnants of a vanished dream, a dead ambition, a sacrificed talent, I cannot repress the thought that, after all, I have chosen the lesser part, that I have sold my birthright for a mess of pottage" (362). The narrator's confession evokes Bles Alwyn's response to the offer of a political appointment in *The Quest of the Silver Fleece:* "I wonder if I'm selling my birthright for six thousand dollars" (Du Bois 316).

Both of these passages, moreover, resonate with Du Bois's offhand criticism of Chesnutt, who returned to the lucrative profession of court stenographer after the commercial failure of *The Marrow of Tradition.* As Joseph McElrath points out in his introduction to the recent *Critical Essays on Charles W. Chesnutt,*

> Aware from their correspondence that the disappointing sales of *Marrow* had driven Chesnutt back into his much more lucrative stenographic work, Du Bois was not at all sympathetic but chided him for being interested in "money making," asking the readership of *Booklovers Magazine*—subtitled *Advance Guard of the Race*—the loaded question: "Why leave some thousands of dollars a year for scribbling about black folk?" The obvious answer, that Chesnutt had abandoned his role, or duty, as one of the "advance guard of the race" for the sake of looking out for number one, was a severe indictment. (9)

The ex-colored man's retreat from his racial obligation for a "mess of pottage" has clear implications for the African American artist as "race man" and a combatant for his people.[41] The resolution of Johnson's novel further reinforces the gendered associations of racial identity. Ironically, by following the path of his white *father* into material wealth and cultural insignificance, the ex-colored man surrenders any shot at the spectacular manhood so powerfully embodied by Jack Johnson.

James Weldon Johnson's own relationship to the racial struggles from which the ex-colored man retreats in shame remains implicit in the text of the novel itself. Although the *real* author of *The Autobiography* did not deny his identity as a black American in his life, and in fact worked vigorously for racial justice, as a writer of fiction he necessarily maintains a certain distance from his subject, not unlike that of the social scientist. Johnson's narrative technique, however, sets *The Autobiography* apart from the other naturalistic novels discussed in this chapter. Whereas Dunbar, Chesnutt, and Du Bois employ a detached third-person narrator for their novels, Johnson's first-person narration renders the author's attitude toward his characters somewhat difficult to ascertain. Despite the ambiguities of this approach, the ironic distance between the novel's author and its narrator remains essential to understanding the didactic power of Johnson's work.[42] Eric Sundquist claims that the novel must "demonstrate simultaneously the distance that Johnson has on his cowardly protagonist *and* the degree to which he stands in judgment on those characteristics that he has in common with him" (*The Hammers of Creation* 13). What Johnson has in common with his narrator is the perspective on the text that creates a spectatorial distance between the artist and his subject. Johnson provides what Robert Stepto calls the narrator's "rhetoric of detachment" as "a thing to be explored, as well as used, in the course of a narrative" (108). At novel's end, the narrator confesses, "Sometimes it seems to me that I have never really been a Negro, that I have been only a privileged spectator of their inner life; at other times I feel that I have been a coward, a deserter, and I am possessed by a strange longing for my mother's people" (*Autobiography* 361).

Here Johnson reminds us that it is his *mother's* people for whom the ex-colored man longs, reiterating the notion of women as reservoirs of cultural identity so central in Du Bois's "The Conservation of Races." The embrace of matrilineal identity effectively confronts the trope of feminized blackness embedded in slave-era "condition of the mother" statutes and perpetuated by Jim Crow segregation. Johnson suggests the connection between the roles of spectator and deserter, both willfully standing outside the ring in which the battles for identity are fought. Rather than pursue his vision of synthesizing ragtime and classical music, the ex-colored man ultimately trades his artistic duty to his race for the opportunity to become "an ordinarily successful white man who has made a little money" (*Autobiography* 362). Like Norris's Presley, the narrator is emasculated by his apparent "success"—merely subsumed by the world of commerce instead of rising to command it.

Robert Stepto suggestively compares the narrator's reaction to the lynching with his earlier response to the sight of a mule being dragged from the mud, among the first memories he cites when describing his arrival in the South for college, observing that "in both instances the Ex-Coloured Man is not a guide but a bystander—an observer in the most unambiguous sense, who is transfixed and inarticulate before the horror conjured by his momentary yet acute empathy with either victim" (116). The subtexts behind the sight of a helpless mule invite the reader to perceive the racist characterization of black men as dumb brutes, suitable for physical labor only, as well as the narrator's identity as a "*mul*atto"—a word that carries with it not only the implication of unnatural mixed ancestry but inert sexuality. I would argue that the ex-colored man's refusal to identify himself with the dehumanized brute who was lynched before him constitutes a particularized form of "spectatoritis," leaving the narrator paralyzed with inaction despite his clear sense of duty to his race.[43]

In the end, the naturalist writer must contend with the question "Is writing a form of action or not?" In one of many editorials for the New York *Age,* Johnson argues that the future of the race depends on a willingness "to struggle in physical conflict if it becomes necessary" (qtd. in Levy 154). In the opening paragraph of *The Autobiography,* Johnson makes clear his intentions for the narrative:

> I know that in writing the following pages I am divulging the great secret of my life, the secret which for years I have guarded far more carefully than any of my earthly possessions; and it is a curious study to me to analyze the motives which prompt me to do it. I feel that I am led by the same impulse which forces the un-found-out criminal to take somebody into his confidence, although he knows that the act is likely, even almost certain, to lead to his undoing. I know that I am playing with fire, and I feel the thrill which accompanies that most fascinating pastime; and, back of it all, I think I find a sort of savage and diabolical desire to gather up all the little tragedies of my life, and turn them into a practical joke on society. (274)

This passage, which explores the psychological impulses behind the narrator, simultaneously reveals much about its author. The ex-colored man suggests that, by writing *The Autobiography,* he might invert the choice he has already made—to value his "earthly possessions" above his "secret." The narrator fashions himself into a "criminal," violating the sacred laws of racial identity, not through his actions (which are more common than the white audience might expect) but by telling his story, which is an "act" itself. The "savage and diabolical desire" that provokes him conjures up the image of the "bad-man" who, like Jack Johnson, flaunts his transgressive behavior and turns the law itself into a joke.

For his part, James Weldon Johnson offers up the text itself as a "practical joke" by publishing it anonymously and suggesting, through the artificial Publisher's Preface, that the novel is in fact a "true" autobiography, its author an actual "ex-colored man" hidden like a ticking bomb deep in the heart of white America. Johnson's authorship thus raises the questions at the core of naturalism's aesthetic quandary.[44] Does the transformation of "life" into "literature" merely recapitulate the passivity of the spectator, or does it, in the hands of the naturalist, break free from the emasculating intimations of "art"? These same questions haunt the naturalistic narratives of writers with contradictory interests in the social change at the turn of the century, and Johnson's effort to define and sustain a culture in opposition to the Anglo-Saxon nationalism of Norris and London paradoxically repeats and reconfigures their discourse, even as it challenges their cultural authority and exposes the anxieties behind their ethical principles. Understood within the narrative strategies of African American culture, the reconfiguration of naturalism that occurs under Johnson and Du Bois not only invigorates the genre but perpetuates its efficacy beyond the particular biological discourse of race in the Progressive Era.

The theme that most clearly unifies these four novels by Dunbar, Chesnutt, Du Bois, and Johnson is the desire to document and describe the injustices suffered by African Americans at the turn of the century. Moreover, each novel confronts the specter of white violence against blacks through direct depiction of or indirect reference to the horrors of lynching.[45] For African Americans at the "nadir," the fact of lynching served as an omnipresent threat as well as a symbolic reminder of the debilitating effects of segregation and inequality. In *The Autobiography*, the narrator's pivotal gesture comes when he turns away from the lynching he witnesses on his journey South—for the ex-colored man, this event prompts his ultimate decision to pass as a white man permanently. After witnessing the gruesome scene, the narrator says, "I was as weak as a man who had lost blood" (353). What he loses, Johnson implies, is acknowledgment of his "black blood," and the false identity he has toyed with becomes a "general plan well fixed in [his] mind" (353). "I understood," he continues, "that it was not discouragement of fear or search for a larger field of action and opportunity that was driving me out of the Negro race. I knew that it was shame, unbearable shame" (353). Significantly, with this refusal to recognize his racial identity, the narrator also sacrifices his artistic vision and loses his place among the "small but gallant band of colored men" at the vanguard of change.

Epilogue

"I'll Get It All In": The Naturalist Imperative

An enlightening contrast to the lynching scene in *The Autobiography of an Ex-Colored Man* and an evocative complement to the aesthetic argument behind James Weldon Johnson's narrative can be found in a short story by Theodore Dreiser entitled "Nigger Jeff." As the grating title makes clear, this story concerns the "making of a man into less than a man," but it also demonstrates its author's views on the necessary role of the writer in documenting this process. In his essay "Theodore Dreiser's 'Nigger Jeff': The Development of an Aesthetic," Donald Pizer argues that the story establishes an artistic credo in its closing words, in which the protagonist, a Midwestern newspaper reporter sent to a nearby town to cover the manhunt and subsequent lynching of a black rapist, vows, "I'll get it all in" ("Nigger Jeff" 165).

The reporter, Elmer Davies, enters the story as "a vain and rather self-sufficient youth who was inclined to be of that turn of mind which sees in life only a fixed and ordered process of rewards and punishments" ("Nigger Jeff" 142). When he first hears of the pursuit of Jeff for assaulting a nineteen-year-old girl, Davies thinks, "No doubt such a creature ought to be lynched," and he enthusiastically accepts his editor's assignment: "What a nice ride he would have!" (142). Like Skaggs in *The Sport of the Gods*, however, Davies is redeemed by the story itself and by his compulsion to tell the truth about injustice. He investigates the crime and speaks to Jeff's family, learning of their compassion for the accused criminal.[1] When Jeff, "a groveling, foaming brute," is dragged from the sheriff's house by the angry mob, Davies "clapped his hands over his mouth, almost unconscious of what he was doing." Unable to stop the crowd's actions, the reporter stands feebly by: "'Oh, my God!' he whispered, his voice losing power" (158). After witnessing the murder and speaking once again to Jeff's grieving mother, Davies resolves to expose the entire episode as a cruel subversion of the "fixed and ordered process of rewards and punishments" he once believed in:

> Davies swelled with feeling. The night, the tragedy, the grief, he saw it all. But also with the cruel instinct of the budding artist that he already was, he was beginning to meditate on the character of story it would make—the color, the pathos. The knowledge now that it was not always exact justice that was meted out to all and that it was not so much the business of the writer to indicate as to interpret was borne in on him with distinctness by the cruel sorrow of the mother, whose blame, if any, was infinitesimal. (164–65)

In his exploration of the meaning of the "it" in "I'll get it all in," Pizer connects Davies's newfound understanding of the complexities of the episode to Dreiser's approach to the emotional and expositional content of naturalist writing, and he points out that Dreiser claimed to have based the story on his own experiences as a novice reporter.[2] What the previous passage also reveals is the anxiety with which Dreiser approaches the job of "interpretation" that is naturalist storytelling. Just as the role of "interpreter," as suggested by Crane's "The Open Boat," simultaneously suggests an objective intermediary and a critical observer, so does Davies's recognition of the "business of the writer" admit to an inevitable detachment, even cruelty, in the job of professional author. African American writers such as Johnson might well question whether they could afford such detachment from such immanent struggles. Is the cost of artistic success, as defined by Dreiser, too high a price for the black writer in this period?

Indeed, for African Americans, a different relationship altogether exists vis-à-vis the profession of authorship. By adopting the stance of a professional brotherhood—as that of a fraternal social organization—white writers sought to soothe anxieties about both the feminized notion of artistry and the growing concerns of sedentary "professional" working men in any field. For black writers, long excluded from the professional class in all areas, authorship remained an elusive goal, albeit one with the promise of fulfilling the masculine responsibilities that defined success for African American intellectuals. The union of manhood and artistry in the African American novel therefore reflects not only the personal or professional anxieties of a generation of men, but the necessary ambitions of a literary tradition that stretches from Frederick Douglass through the twentieth century. Only in recent years, with the increasing stature of women in the African American literary canon, has the assertion of alternative models of authorship somewhat displaced the hypermasculine discourse of literary authenticity. In this sense, the combined legacies of Paul Laurence Dunbar, Charles Chesnutt, W. E. B. Du Bois, and Johnson and the "problem" of masculinity in the black imagination have loomed large over subsequent generations of writers and artists. The adoption of literary naturalism by this group of African American writers thus raises inevitable questions about the consequences of this aesthetic strategy for the canon of African American literature.

Naturalism, as a narrative strategy, attempts to resolve the artistic and ethical dilemma summed up by Leo Tolstoy's question "What to do?" In constructing a model for writing that constitutes itself as a form of direct action, the naturalists employ the gendered rhetoric still ingrained in American culture, in which the desirable qualities of candor, integrity, and forcefulness are inscribed as "masculine." Within the African American canon, one perceives the consequences of this discursive quandary in the troubling misogyny of Richard Wright's *Native Son* and Chester Himes's *If He Hollers Let Him Go* or in the disruptive violence of important naturalistic works by African American women, including Ann Petry's *The Street* and Gloria Naylor's *The Women of Brewster Place*. Indeed, disruptive male violence has come to define contemporary reconfigurations of naturalism across generic categories—including novels by Joyce Carol Oates, Robert Stone, and Denis Johnson, plays by David Mamet and Sam Shepard, and films by Martin Scorsese. The search for form in naturalism takes place within the discourse of gender, and the anxieties of artistry and authorship create texts that are simultaneously alienating and riveting in their display of male violence and ritual.

In the end, Frank Norris's desire for "life, not literature" is an impossibly paradoxical goal for any writer of fiction. Naturalism has thus often been dismissed for a chronic failure to live up to its formidable objectives. In grappling with the problem of the writer as artist in a culture suspicious of the utility and efficacy of art, however, Norris and his contemporaries contribute to the modern redefinition of authorship and to our understanding of the place of literature in society. In response to his enduring question about what he, as an artist and a man, must do, Tolstoy suggests the following answer: "To renounce the consciousness of my righteousness, my prerogatives, my privileges in comparison with other men, and to recognize myself guilty" (*Complete Works* 9: 311). In its often arduous and contradictory effort to eradicate the spectatorial privilege of authorship, naturalism reveals the irreconcilable impulses at the heart of all storytelling, with more than enough guilt to go around.

Notes

Introduction

1. In "Darwin, Wharton, and 'The Descent of Man': Blueprints of American Society," MarySue Schriber investigates the implications of the second half of Darwin's full title *The Descent of Man and Selection in Relation to Sex* to reveal Wharton's critique of American gender relations, personified in the relationship between Professor Linyard and his wife.

2. Pater's refashioning of French philosopher Victor Cousin's phrase "l'art pour l'art" occurs most famously in the conclusion to his 1873 volume *The Renaissance:*

> Great passions may give us this quickened sense of life, ecstasy and sorrow of love, the various forms of enthusiastic activity, disinterested or otherwise, which come naturally to many of us. Only be sure it is passion—that it does yield you this fruit of a quickened, multiplied consciousness. Of this wisdom, the poetic passion, the desire of beauty, the love of art for art's sake, has most; for art comes to you professing frankly to give nothing but the highest quality to your moments as they pass, and simply for those moments' sake.

3. For an overview of Norris's flirtation with decadence, see Joseph McElrath, *Frank Norris Revisited* 11–24.

4. See R. W. Stallman, *Stephen Crane: A Biography* 57–63.

5. The nearly simultaneous publication, in the early 1980s, of Ronald Martin's *American Literature and the Universe of Force* and Harold Kaplan's *Power and Order: Henry Adams and the Naturalist Tradition* signaled a paradigm shift in the study of

this period. Both works attempt to connect naturalistic fiction both with the ideology of force that developed out of Herbert Spencer's popular reconfiguration of Darwinian science and with Henry Adams's concept of the dynamo as a unifying symbol for the emergent economic, political, and cultural power of the United States. Martin and Kaplan find, in key naturalist texts, confirmation of the ideological currents that dominated American culture during this era.

6. Howard revisits the study of naturalism's unresolved tension initiated in the 1950s by Charles Walcutt's *American Literary Naturalism: A Divided Stream*, which sought to place the movement firmly within the American tradition, exemplifying the ongoing tension between free will and determinism first explored by the Transcendentalists. Donald Pizer later articulated this theme in *Realism and Naturalism in Nineteenth-Century American Literature*, which suggests the persistence of two major tensions within naturalist fiction. These tensions involve, first, a contrast between the distinctly ordinary and mundane milieu of naturalism and the extreme, excessive emotions and behavior that arise, even within this setting, and, second, a clash between the individual characters' apparent lack of free will and the "seeking" imagination that propels them.

7. Mark Seltzer's *Bodies and Machines* and Philip Fisher's *Hard Facts* also offer gender-based readings of the naturalist model of production and consumption.

8. This is the view advocated, most notably, by Larzer Ziff's *The American 1890s* and Jay Martin's *Harvests of Change: American Literature, 1865–1914*.

9. On the connection between journalistic professionalism and masculinity, see also Cristophe Den Tandt, *The Urban Sublime in American Literary Naturalism* 190–94.

10. See Donald Pizer's editorial commentary in *The Literary Criticism of Frank Norris* 19–24.

Chapter One

1. See Ellmann, *Oscar Wilde* 438–79.

2. Bederman elaborates on the ideological origins of white male dominance as an explicitly racial construction:

> In itself, linking whiteness to male power was nothing new. White Americans had long associated powerful manhood with white supremacy. For example, during the first two-thirds of the nineteenth century, American citizenship rights had been construed as "manhood" rights which inhered to white males, only. Framers of state constitutions in sixteen northern and southern states explicitly placed African American men in the same category as women, as

"dependents." Negro males, whether free or slave, were forbidden to exercise "manhood" rights—forbidden to vote, hold electoral office, serve on juries, or join the military. (20)

3. During his year at Harvard in 1894, Norris—despite his efforts to write *McTeague* and *Vandover*—could not have failed to notice the curricular changes being undertaken at the university.

4. See Dubbert, *A Man's Place* 123.

5. For full accounts of the Sullivan-Kilrain bout, see Michael Isenberg, *John L. Sullivan and His America* 266–79; Elliot J. Gorn, *The Manly Art* 231–37; Jeffrey T. Sammons, *Beyond the Ring* 12–14; and William H. Adams, "New Orleans As the National Center of Boxing" 93–96.

6. Official condemnation of the fight notwithstanding, many of the city's leading citizens were eager members of the enthusiastic audience. Isenberg observes that "the Louisiana attorney general and the New Orleans chief of police rode one of the trains to the state line to ensure, as they said, that no fight would take place in Louisiana" (269). Furthermore, the referee for the fight was a future mayor of New Orleans.

7. See Gorn 239–47 and Isenberg 300–23.

8. Anti-Irish sentiment, along with other forms of ethnic and racial prejudice, continued to flourish in American society, but the idea that a working-class Irishman from Boston might become a popular celebrity in a predominantly Anglo-Saxon culture would have been unthinkable one generation earlier. According to Gorn, "What changed by the late nineteenth century . . . was the fact that boxers were no longer heroes exclusively to working-class and ethnic peoples. Now America's growing white collar population craved muscular demigods" (250).

9. Literary depictions of the Irish as a sort of caveman version of the Anglo-Saxon appear en masse soon after large-scale immigration from Ireland began in the mid-nineteenth century. Memorable examples include the "shiftless" farmer John Field in Thoreau's *Walden,* as well as Twain's characterizations of Huck Finn and his father.

10. Gorn explains the significance of athletic heroes such as Sullivan for Irish, and other, immigrants:

> To play sports seemed an archetypically American act, because they were freighted with the values of success, meritocracy, and competition; to buy a ticket to an athletic event was to learn the new role of consumer; to root for a team or a champion gave one a sense of having freedom of choice; to acquire knowledge about baseball or football or boxing was to be informed

about something distinctly American. . . . And when immigrants could applaud the deeds of one of their own countrymen, their sense of finding a place in America was doubly enhanced. (226)

The ethnic undertones of prizefighting evolved and reflected the nation's attitudes toward immigration and ethnicity. Thus, the 1849 championship bout between Irish immigrant James "Yankee" Sullivan and native-born Tom Hyer served as a focus for nativist sentiment, and Hyer's victory validated the anti-immigrant policies of the Know-Nothings. By 1860, however, John C. Heenan wore red, white, and blue trunks for his match with British champion Tom Sayers in London, and Heenan's Irish background proved less important than his role as the representative of American manliness. The two men fought for more than thirty-seven rounds, after which, in a controversial ruling, the British referee declared a draw. As the Union's relationship with England deteriorated during the Civil War, the Heenan-Sayers fight became a rallying point for Northern patriotism, particularly for the Irish Americans who would serve in large numbers in the Union army. See Gorn 148–61.

11. It is worth noting that Riis's book deliberately dissects the population and geography of New York's slums along strictly racial lines, noting that "the one thing you shall vainly ask for in the chief city of America is a distinctly American community" (21). The absence of the "native-born" American amid "Chinatown," "Jewtown," and the other ethnic enclaves of lower Manhattan makes explicit the racial difference of the dispossessed "other Half." Riis's own history, as a penniless Danish immigrant, is eclipsed by his identity as a journalist, an invisible interlocutor who serves as guide for the upper-class reader to the previously mysterious underworld of New York's tenements.

12. Donna Campbell points out the divided nature of the narrator in naturalist depictions of "fallen women": "As sympathetic interpreters, they function as social intermediaries, reaching an audience, in effect a market, otherwise inaccessible to the prostitute. But as questioner, they resemble the prostitute's customers, a role that the reader doubly reenacts by asking the question (why did this woman sell herself?) and by paying (buying the book) to have the question answered" (*Resisting Regionalism* 114).

13. In the Norton Critical Edition of *McTeague,* Donald Pizer provides two stories from the *San Francisco Examiner,* dated October 10 and 13, 1893, which describe the murder by Patrick Collins, "the savage of civilization," of his wife, a "janitress" at a kindergarten. The second article opens, "If a good many of Patrick Collins' ancestors did not die on the scaffold then either they escaped their desert or there is nothing in heredity. . . . Seeing him, you can understand that murder is as natural to such a man when his temper is up as hot speech is to the anger of the

civilized" (qtd. in Pizer, ed., *McTeague* 259). The language in these accounts emphasizes racial difference as an explanation for Collins's appearance and behavior and
draws a direct connection with Sullivan and the world of prizefighting:

> Collins is a young man in his early thirties, healthy and muscular. The hang
> of his arms, his blue shirt and the hitch that he gave his waistband with the
> backs of his hands all suggested the sailor. The face is not degraded, but brut-
> ish. That is to say, he is not a man who has sunk, but one who was made an
> animal by nature to start with. The face is broad, the brown eyes are set wide
> apart, the nose is flattened at the bridge and as broad as a negro's. The jaw is
> heavy and cruel. Fancy a first cousin of John L. Sullivan's in Collins dress and
> situation and you have the man. (qtd. in Pizer, ed., *McTeague*, 260)

Not only does this passage draw physiological connections between the Irish and the
"negro," but it also makes the crucial distinction between the "brutish" and the
"degraded" races. The Irish, though "healthy and muscular," are simply more primitive in nature than their Anglo-Saxon counterparts, however much the Anglo-Saxon
might debase himself. Although Irishmen such as Sullivan may, through their accomplishments, transcend the limitations of their race to some extent, when placed
in different "dress and situation," they are never far removed from brutishness.

14. See Gould 135–43.

15. Donald Pizer, in *The Novels of Frank Norris,* provides a thorough explanation
of LeConte's and Lombroso's influence on the novelist (12–22, 56–59).

16. Frank Norris, *McTeague,* in *Frank Norris: Novels and Essays,* ed. Donald Pizer
(New York: Library of America, 1986) 264. Subsequent references to the text refer
to this edition.

17. Dillingham, for instance, makes the connections between Norris's use of objective detail and his preoccupation with manliness:

> For [Norris's] details, gathered through experience, close observations, and
> hard work, objectified reality. . . . Norris's piling up of details actually repre-
> sented a rebellion against much of the literature of his time. . . . It was not
> merely a matter of effectiveness. It was also very much a matter of principle,
> for he associated specifics with the active, vital life and that, in turn, with force
> and masculinity. (128)

18. See John S. Haller, *Outcasts from Evolution* 160ff.

19. Critics have long disagreed on the value and significance of the Grannis-Miss
Baker story within the novel. Pizer, for instance, dismisses the subplot as inconsistent
with the themes of the work (*Novels* 74). William Dillingham sees the plot as evi-

dence for the triumph of deterministic "instinct" ("The Old Folks of McTeague" 172). Barbara Hochman claims that what "has consistently been seen as the most anomalous subplot of *McTeague* . . . fits clearly in the pattern of loss implicit in the novel" (*Art of Frank Norris* 66). Leonard Cassuto, contradicting Dillingham, asserts that their relationship offers a "fully realized portrait of free will" ("'Keeping Company' with the Old Folks" 46) in which the characters overcome the very forces propelling McTeague and Trina's unraveling relationship. Donna Campbell, however, reads the subplot as evidence for Norris's attitude toward the conventions of regionalism. Having demonstrated the enduring, if limited, value of local color fiction by allowing Grannis and Miss Baker to realize their romantic dreams, "Norris send them to their room for the remaining four chapters of the novel" (73). The tranquil union of the two old folks, although comforting, has no role in the fiery demise of the other characters, and their narrative fades away. For Norris, as Campbell notes, "neither the old couple, their story, nor local color fiction has anywhere else to go" (73).

20. Joe and Genevieve are described as "working-class aristocrats" (45), largely because of their racial identity. Genevieve, though orphaned, is "from a long line of American descent" (49), and her guardians, Jewish storekeepers named Silverstein, are "kindly aliens" (47) who fail to understand the purity and depth of the young lovers' relationship.

21. Although small professional leagues existed, mostly in the mining and steel-producing communities of the Northeast, the impact of professional football on the national cultural scene was insignificant until the formation of the precursor to the National Football League in the 1920s, and even thereafter college football would remain more popular until quite late in the century. See Benjamin G. Rader, *Sports* 260–62.

22. See Messenger, *Sport and the Spirit of Play in American Fiction* 92–100.

23. See Patrick Dooley, "Young Frank Norris as a Sports Journalist."

24. Messenger also provides readings of two short stories by Norris containing explicit sports themes, "Travis Hulett's Halfback" and "This Animal of a Buldy Jones." The former involves a football hero, defined as a brute on the field and a gentleman elsewhere, who saves the life of a beautiful girl by using his football rushing ability to carry her through a crowd in a burning theater. The latter story relates the equally improbable account of a collegiate baseball star who is challenged to a duel by an insulting Frenchman and, instead of taking up a pistol, uses a baseball to break the Frenchman's jaw. In both cases, Norris makes use of the popular dime novel tradition of the working-class sports hero and places the formula within the context of upper-class amateur athletics.

25. On the connection between "play" discourse and minstrelsy, see William Gleason, *The Leisure Ethic* 15–20.

26. As an illustration of the distinctions between healthy admiration of the male body and unhealthy "sensuality," consider the following passage from John Boyle O'Reilly's *Ethics of Boxing and Manly Sport*, published in 1888: "Your big-chested, bright-eyed large-shouldered athlete is never a vile sensualist. It is always your pot-bellied, purple-fleshed, dew-lapped, soft-handed creature, on the one hand, or your pallid, tremulous, watery-eyed specimen on the other" (151).

27. In his book *Monumental Anxieties,* Scott Derrick explores the homoeroticism in *The Red Badge* as evidence of Crane's notion that "relations between men are physical, bodily, desiring relationships" (175). Certainly the intense bonds formed between men in battle fascinated Crane, but Derrick's analysis does not delve into the role of sporting discourse in the formation of Crane's ideas about masculine relationships. The influence of sports, rather than contradicting Derrick's thesis, complicates it somewhat as the product not of Crane's individual sexuality, but of the cultural paradoxes involved in the definition of masculinity.

28. On Crane's claim about football and battle, see Stanley Wertheim and Paul Sorrentino, *The Crane Log* 178–79.

29. See Donald J. Mrozek, *Sport and American Mentality* 51–66.

30. A precursor to scouting in the United States was a boys' "tribe" modeled on James Fenimore Cooper's concept of the Indian ideal of manhood. The founder of this movement, Ernest Thompson Seton, along with Daniel Beard, the editor of *Recreation* magazine, which published adventure-laden tales of Daniel Boone and other frontier heroes, officially incorporated the Boy Scouts of America in 1910, bringing together a variety of like-minded clubs from around the nation into one centralized organization. The BSA, like its British precursor founded during the Boer War by Lord Baden-Powell, was deeply rooted in imperialist ideology but placed an even greater emphasis on the physical rigors required of scouts. See Hantover, "The Boy Scouts and the Validation of Masculinity" and Dubbert 149ff.

31. During this period, it was also widely known that a number of journeymen athletes essentially made careers of intercollegiate football, moving from one school to another and receiving salaries for their performance on the field. Only with the foundation of the National Collegiate Athletic Association (NCAA), in 1906, did this practice come under scrutiny. (On the establishment of the NCAA, see Ronald A. Smith, *Sports and Freedom* 191–94.)

32. Gail Bederman, who begins her study on masculinity with an account of the Johnson-Jeffries bout, asks, "Why should a mere prizefight result in riots and death?" In answer to this question, Bederman suggests that "during the decades around the turn of the century, Americans were obsessed with the connection between manhood and racial dominance" (*Manliness and Civilization* 4). Bederman insightfully probes the dependence of Progressive-Era notions of manhood on the definition of "whiteness" but does not consider the formal questions raised by the

sport of boxing as a forum in which such ideological concerns are displayed. It is, after all, not coincidental that a "mere prizefight" should figure so prominently in her discussion.

33. Detailed accounts of the Johnson-Jeffries fight and its aftermath, as well as Johnson's overall career, are described in Finis Farr's *Black Champion,* Al-Tony Gilmore's *Bad Nigger!,* and Randy Roberts's *Papa Jack.*

34. Burns, whose real name was Noah Brusso, had won the championship from Jim Jeffries's handpicked successor, an inauspicious contender named Marvin Hart, in Hart's first title defense. Contemporary critics saw the period following Jeffries's retirement as an embarrassment to the legacy of John L. Sullivan, and popular interest in the sport ebbed accordingly.

35. The color line in boxing was not absolute, even after Sullivan's decree. One notable exception to the exclusion of African Americans was the success of George "Little Chocolate" Dixon, who won the lightweight crown in 1892 at the same "Carnival of Champions" at which Sullivan lost his title. Because of its prestige and its establishment of a supreme champion, the possibility of a black heavyweight champion was a different matter. In the heavyweight classification, black contenders could face white opponents but could never receive a valid shot at the championship. For example, Jack Johnson fought and defeated former champion Robert Fitzsimmons, but he did so only in the late stages of Fitzsimmons's career as a boxer.

36. Stephen Jay Gould points out the illogic behind the doctrine of recapitulation, which dominated anthropologists' racial thinking in the nineteenth century. Equally illogical but contradictory is the turn-of-the-century notion of "neoteny," the idea that superior races "retain the traits of childhood" (Gould 120). Progressive-Era white masculinity, which celebrated men who played like boys (and like savages), even as it condemned the childishness of the "savages" themselves, exposes the logical incompatibility of these two doctrines. As Gould demonstrates, anthropologists manipulated physical characteristics and "scientific" data to fit whatever theory "proved" the superiority of the white race. See Gould 113–22.

37. For a discussion of Johnson's style in the context of African American intellectual history, see Early's *The Culture of Bruising* 27ff.

38. For a complete account of the match, see Sammons 39, Gilmore 42–44, and Farr 107–14.

39. See Roberts 108–10.

40. London himself contributed an article entitled "The Yellow Peril" to the San Francisco *Examiner* in 1904, based on his travels in Manchuria during the Japanese-Russian War. In this dispatch, London warns of the potential threat posed by a unified Japanese-Chinese-Korean alliance to the Western world. See *Jack London Reports* 340–50.

41. Interestingly, The *Oxford English Dictionary* identifies the first use of the

word *yellow* to describe cowardice or fear as occurring in the autobiography of P. T. Barnum, published in 1856. Barnum's role in the growing nexus of spectacle and commerce suggests the link between the colloquial evolution of the word and the performances required for its definition.

42. The Yellow Kid first appeared in Richard Outcault's "Hogan's Alley," a comic in Pulitzer's *World.* Initially given a yellow gown to test the new color presses of the *World,* for which yellow proved to be the most difficult to print consistently, the Kid became a popular sensation before Outcault and much of the *World*'s staff were lured away by Hearst's *Journal.* Eventually, both the *World* and the *Journal* featured competing versions of the comic strip, and Outcault later enjoyed greater fame as the creator of "Buster Brown." Featured prominently in advertising for both newspapers, the Yellow Kid became the unofficial symbol for the kind of journalism they presented, and the phrase "yellow journalism" fell into popular usage. See Edwin Emery, *The Press and America* 422–24, and Frank Luther Mott, *American Journalism* 424–26.

43. In the inconsistent, racist logic of the day, many thought that the mixing of blood through miscegenation resulted in a mongrel race weaker than either of its precursors (see Norris's "Among Cliff Dwellers" in *Complete Edition,* for instance). For African Americans, "yellow" skin often served to demarcate class distinctions, with the opposite implications.

44. Certainly, the "argument of force" finds its expression throughout Progressive-Era literature, from Henry Adams's "Virgin and the Dynamo" to Norris's metaphysical pronouncements about "FORCE" at the conclusion of *The Octopus.*

45. See Douglass, *Narrative* 65–66.

Chapter Two

1. Bill Brown, in "Interlude: The Agony of Play in 'The Open Boat,'" examines Crane's investment in the concept of play in the poststructuralist sense and observes that "play is never singular in Crane: the play *of* the world, play *in* the world are inextricable" (26).

2. *The Works of Stephen Crane,* ed. Fredson Bowers. Vol. 5 (Charlottesville: U of Virginia P, 1969–76) 68. Subsequent references to the stories from this collection are cited parenthetically in the text.

3. Halliburton discusses what he calls Crane's "aesthetics of war" and connects the admiration of beauty in Crane's work with Kant's notion of the sublime: "Crane brings to his portrayal an aestheticism that is the complement of his fascination with irony and the grotesque" (*Color of the Sky* 164). Halliburton compares Crane's and Pater's use of music as a measure of aesthetic qualities and suggests that this use reinforces the ways in which these authors aestheticize experience.

4. See Ellen Moers, *Two Dreisers* 42–56.

5. In "The Monster," Dr. Trescott's son has been saved from a fire by the family's African American servant, Henry Johnson. During the rescue, Henry suffers a horrible disfigurement, and, although first greeted by the people in the small town as a hero, he is eventually shunned by the community because of his appearance. The doctor's loyalty to Henry, and his refusal to institutionalize his son's rescuer, subsequently cost him his clients, respectability, and social standing.

6. See Michael Robertson, *Stephen Crane and the Making of Modern American Literature* 11–54.

7. Although the action of "A Man and Some Others" occurs somewhere in the borderlands of Southwest Texas and Mexico, the situation—that of white men literally surrounded by Mexicans—renders the political geography irrelevant.

8. For contrasting arguments on Crane's stereotypical use of Mexicans, see Raymund Paredes's "Stephen Crane and the Mexican" and Jamie Robertson's "Stephen Crane, Eastern Outsider in the West and Mexico."

9. The title of "One Dash—Horses" in fact not only refers to the race between Richardson's horse and those of his Mexican assailants, but it also suggests the colloquial use of the word *dash* to mean a throw of the dice. The stroke of luck by which Richardson escapes peril, therefore, is at least as relevant to the outcome as is the athleticism of the horse or Richardson's skillful riding.

10. For widely divergent critical views on whether or not Crane's statement reinforces, critiques, or ironically undermines the apparent bravery and will of "the Kid," see Frank Bergon, *Stephen Crane's Artistry* 97, Edwin H. Cady, *Stephen Crane* 175, Michael Collins, "Realism and Romance in the Western Stories of Stephen Crane" 142, and Walter Benn Michaels, *The Gold Standard and the Logic of Naturalism* 224–25.

11. Of course, the links between Crane and Hemingway are both obvious and complex and have been explored by several critics. The shared influence of Kipling forms one such link, and Kipling's work suggests the importance of the matrix of boys' games, adult diversions, and "real" life-or-death struggles. See, for instance, Martin Green's account of the influence of British "adventure" writers on Crane, Hemingway, and others in his book *The Adventurous Male* (26–30).

12. Illustrating this tension between feminine speech and masculine action and its relationship to journalism is William Randolph Hearst's oft-repeated assertion, mentioned earlier, that his reporters "act," whereas others "sit idly by" (qtd. in Christopher Wilson, *The Labor of Words* 28). To redefine writing as a manly enterprise, one must establish its basis in the world of action.

13. Carol Hurd Green comments on the gendered assumptions evidenced by this "brotherhood": "When men gather in Crane, they are seen to understand each other and to possess a comprehension of the large issues that precludes any unnec-

essary conversation. When women gather it is to cackle and rant, to exult in disaster" ("Stephen Crane and the Fallen Women" 107).

14. In "Fighting Words: The Talk of Men at War in *The Red Badge of Courage*," Alfred Habegger asks, "Why is manhood *quiet?*" and provides a provocative reading of the lines "Ah, there, Willie" in "The Open Boat." These words, attributed to no particular speaker, and spoken when the men on the boat are signaling in vain to a man on shore, might well be read as addressed to Billie, the oiler. Habegger, however, suggests that the phrase "Ah, there, Willie" is actually an insult, directed at the waving man on shore who misreads the survivors' gestures as friendly greetings, which calls into question his manliness, as implied by the vernacular term, "Willie-boy."

15. Cady also establishes the importance of recognizing the shifting points of view within the story: "The group viewpoint in the first, least usual, and most important of three points of view in the story. The other two are that of the neutrally observing narrator, who reports dramatically on the scenes which occur among the men, and that of the intellectual in the boat, the correspondent. It matters immensely to an understanding of the story that one see through which point of view events are conveyed" (*Stephen Crane* 152).

16. In painting, which serves as the primary subject of Dijkstra's study, the portrayal of demonic female figures is nowhere more prevalent than in the work of decadents such as Aubrey Beardsley, as in his illustrations for Wilde's *Salome*. The homosocial realm favored by Crane, Norris, et al. necessarily constructs itself as a hypermasculine alternative to the effete high aestheticism of Wilde, but shares with the aesthetes an adversarial relationship with the "feminine" forces of Nature.

17. Like the doggerel in "The Five White Mice," Norton's poem both contradicts and reinforces the events of the story.

18. The importance of "sympathy," the transmission of feeling, resonates with Rimvydas Silbajoris's explanation of Tolstoy's aesthetics: "Art does not really use feeling to convey some emotionally unmarked 'content' but makes that content itself a feeling—an emotion that comprehends the same dimensions as may be measured by the yardsticks of moral, social or philosophical ideas. Emotion, then, as contemporary structuralists might say, is the message" (108).

19. In *The Pluralistic Philosophy of Stephen Crane*, Patrick Dooley points out the interplay between observer and participant in Crane's narrative technique. Crane's cinematic descriptions and shifting point of view create constant shifts in perspective that place the reader alongside the characters as uncertain spectators of the narrative. See 26–34.

20. See Brown, "Interlude" 33.

21. An example of this pretension can be found in the behavior of reporters during the Spanish-American War, discussed at some length in the next chapter. Reporters, including Richard Harding Davis, Crane, and Frank Norris, made a great show

of carrying weapons alongside Roosevelt's Rough Riders, and William Randolph Hearst himself took up residence in Havana during the war to oversee the participation of his reporters in the conflict.

22. Indeed, Jack Potter and Scratchy Wilson reappear in "Moonlight on the Snow," this time in the somber roles of visiting marshal and deputy (!) from nearby Yellow Sky who are called in to arrest Tom Larpent.

23. In a different reading of the gendered language in the story, Daniel Weiss suggests that the Swede's paranoia in this male environment stems from his own repressed homosexuality and "the transformation of the repressed erotic attraction in favor of an overt sadistic aversion" ("The Blue Hotel" 52).

24. Thomas Kent notes that "the most sophisticated interpretation [of the Swede's death] is the Easterner's; he understands the murder to be a working out of naturalistic forces" ("The Problem of Knowledge in 'The Open Boat' and 'The Blue Hotel'" 266).

25. The story's epigram sets its date at 1875—well before Crane's journey west, and also before the "closing of the frontier" that signals the end of the "old West." Crane points out that the marketing of the Western frontier to Eastern capitalists is no new phenomenon, but something that has always been implicit in westward expansion.

26. An obvious "literary" source for this episode, ironically enough, is the Colonel Sherburn episode in *Adventures of Huckleberry Finn.*

27. Marston LaFrance, in his humanistic reading of "The Open Boat," rejects the traditional interpretation of Billie as Christ figure proposed by Edwin Cady, among others. LaFrance maintains that "the oiler is killed by mere chance, a death which could have come to any of the others with exactly the same significance in context" (*A Reading of Stephen Crane* 62). Although consistent with the humanistic philosophy behind the "brotherhood" in the story, this reading ignores the fact that the correspondent has emerged by the end of "The Open Boat" as the primary "interpreter," the person who will be expected to relate the remarkable story of the four men.

Chapter Three

1. Wharton mentions these earlier novels in the course of celebrating Sinclair Lewis's *Main Street* as a recent example of the greatness to which American novels should aspire.

2. In addition to Waid, Nettels, and Campbell, several other critics have examined Wharton's overtly hostile, yet covertly more complex, relationship to the popular conception of the "authoress." See, for instance, Amy Kaplan, *The Social Construction of American Realism,* and Katherine Joslin, *Edith Wharton.*

3. In his biography of Wharton, R. W. B. Lewis traces her relationship with Roosevelt. The two were products of New York's social elite and, as young adults, "had attended some of the same balls during the season" (112). Wharton knew Roosevelt throughout his life and, at a White House dinner, "sat not only at the President's table, as she was quick to mention, but at his right hand" (145). Politically, Wharton largely agreed with Roosevelt; she disagreed with her friend and Harvard president Charles Eliot Norton when he criticized the Spanish-American War as "criminal and idiotic" and declared herself a "rabid imperialist" in regard to the British campaign in the Boer War (139). Wharton's consistent investment in the Rooseveltian ideals of American expansion is the subject of Frederick Wegener's "'Rabid Imperialist': Edith Wharton and the Obligations of Empire in Modern American Fiction."

4. See Charles Brown, *The Correspondents' War* 329–32.

5. For an account of Crane and Norris as correspondents in Cuba, see Stanley Wertheim, "Two Yellow Kids."

6. Davis's popular first novel, *Soldiers of Fortune,* published in 1897 as the conflict with Spain drew nearer, presents the story of a brilliant, yet somewhat bookish American engineer, Robert Clay, sent by a mining company to oversee operations in a fictional South American country. Davis based the narrative on his experiences in Cuba a decade earlier, and in it, contributed to the image of Latin American insurgents as poorly organized, malleable, and shiftless and of the Spanish ruling class as debauched and incompetent.

7. To this day, the game of football, in its terminology and rhetoric, closely reflects the discourse of war. The game's object, to break through enemy lines into the opponent's territory, is achieved by the linemen's struggle in "the trenches," the quarterback's efforts as the "field general," who avoids "sack" and lets fly, from his "cannon" of an arm, long "bombs" and "bullet" passes.

8. During the Spanish-American War, newspaper reports consistently complained about the role played by guerilla warfare in Spanish military strategy. Seen as dishonorable and cowardly, ambushes by Spanish troops directly conflicted with the romantic notion of warfare as a rule-bound and orderly contest. See Crane, *Works* 9: 167.

9. Davis, an ardent supporter of Ivy League football, was first hired by Hearst himself to cover the 1895 Yale-Princeton game for the *Journal.*

10. Wegener quotes the following line from *The Gods Arrive:* "The fellows who 'grab' life . . . are the conquerors who turn it into form and colour" (qtd. in Wegener, "'Rabid Imperialist'" 805).

11. For a historical account of the massacre, see Pizer, *Novels* 118–21.

12. According to Ronald Martin, "The understanding that Presley finally achieves, viewing his whole experience in the light of both Shelgrim's and Vanamee's teach-

ings, is articulated in the long meditation with which the novel ends. With it his education is complete and man is reconciled to the universe of force" (171). Martin's resolute verdict, however, fails to confront the implications of Norris's use of indirect discourse in this passage. As McElrath indicates, "The point of view rendered there is that of the character Presley rather than Norris" (*Frank Norris Revisited* 98).

13. This tension between individual responsibility and collective "FORCE" leads to what Daniel Borus sees as "the difficulty in maintaining a stance of radical determinism" (*Writing Realism* 167). Borus contends that Norris fails to integrate these polarities and offers the reader conflicting conclusions as a result of this struggle. Like McElrath, Barbara Hochman points out the distinction between Presley and the narrative voice and suggests that this gap contributes to the confusion over the novel's ending. According to Hochman, "Evaluation of the text's concluding 'optimism' depends on the question of whether *The Octopus* as a whole supports or subverts Presley's final perspective" (*Art of Frank Norris* 4). For Hochman, the answer to this question is elusive due to the ambiguity of Presley's position in the text, as well as the difficulties in separating Norris's voice from that of Presley. Pizer, in *The Novels of Frank Norris,* establishes the consistency of Norris's evolutionary theism in *The Octopus.* Presley's final understanding only replicates the enlightenment of Annixter and Vanamee that has already occurred; the ambiguity upon which critics have seized stems from flaws in Presley himself. Pizer states, "It is therefore not Norris who varies between ideas of amoral force and triumphant good, as has often been charged, but rather Presley as Norris dramatized his gradual and troubled progress toward Truth" (139).

14. For an examination of Norris's attitude toward "Les Jeunes," see Don Graham, *The Fiction of Frank Norris* 4–7; McElrath, *Frank Norris Revisited* 6–10; Pizer, *Literary Criticism of Frank Norris* 20–25.

15. It is worthwhile to note Norris's use of indirect discourse, which establishes an ironic stance toward Mrs. Derrick's notion of a "positive affront." This contrasts sharply with the earlier passage criticizing the "flaccid banalities" of aestheticism, written in Norris's "straight" narrative voice.

16. In his introduction to *The Literary Criticism of Frank Norris,* Pizer summarizes Norris's stance:

> To Norris, as late as 1902 "literature" was characterized by the stylistics of Pater, by the "spirituality" of Ruskin, and most of all by Wilde's doctrines of art's moral neutrality and of the superiority of art to nature. "I was a man who stood in symbolic relations to the art and culture of my age," Wilde wrote, and one can see a rather twisted application of that statement in Norris's tendency to characterize "literature" in sexual terms as effeminate, with some suggestions of homosexuality. (20)

17. Norris's characterization of Shelgrim is based, at least in part, on Collis Huntington, president of the Southern Pacific Railroad, whom Norris interviewed in preparation for writing *The Octopus*. See Pizer, *Novels* 124.

18. This suggests a familial connection, by marriage at least, between Presley and Shelgrim, a possibility that Norris never fully explains.

19. See Charles Crow, "The Real Vanamee and His Influence on Frank Norris's *The Octopus*" 131, and Graham 105.

20. Vanamee's embrace of experience, in a sense, suggests what Leon Chai calls Oscar Wilde's "externalization of form" (*Aestheticism* 102). Unlike Pater, Wilde rejected a "subordination of life" to the demands of art and in fact sought ways to live that reflected his aesthetic principles. See also James Eli Adams, *Dandies and Desert Saints* 217–28.

21. Graham compares the state of contented passivity that Presley achieves with that expressed in Mallarmé's "Late Afternoon of a Faun" (68–71), and Hochman sees a parallel with Keats's "Ode to a Nightingale." Wordsworth is another obvious source for such creative reflection.

22. See Graham 95ff.

23. To allay his doubts about the poem, Presley then turns to Vanamee for support. Vanamee's response suggests the aesthetic problem with Presley's work: "It is an Utterance—a Message" (876). As Pizer points out, "The Toilers" is indeed a message, but "it is not art" (*Novels* 135).

24. In *Deconstructing Frank Norris's Fiction: The Male-Female Dialectic,* Lon West further explores Pizer's notion of the masculine-feminine relationship in Norris's popular fiction. West argues that the male-female "dialectic" forms a central trope in the development of Norris's fiction, from the early, simplistic view of male dominance and female submission in *McTeague* and *Vandover* to the more mature notion of a male-female union proposed by *The Octopus* and *The Pit*. The relationship between male and female, according to West, offers a synthetic model for the various binary tensions in Norris's writing, including romance-realism, life-literature, and primitive-civilized.

25. Obviously, as Hochman notes, "the image of a natural, growing plant, an organic whole, is a familiar image for the work of art" (*Art of Frank Norris* 34).

26. Pizer notes that "technology and the landscape are allied rather than opposed . . . so long as men use both landscape and machine (the means of production and distribution of wheat) in accordance with natural law" (*Realism and Naturalism* 161). This reading of the reproductive paradigm in Norris's novel contrasts with that provided by Seltzer, in *Bodies and Machines*. Seltzer usefully locates the centrality of reproduction to aesthetic and creative energies, but sees masculine and feminine reproductive forces as "linked but competing principles of creation" (27). Drawing upon Henry Adams's notion of the dynamo, Seltzer sees Norris's masculine "ma-

chine" opposing and defeating the female component in reproduction. Naturalist literary creation, Seltzer suggests, is "the product of a mechanistic and miraculous onanism" (31). The rape imagery in *The Octopus,* however, reinforces Norris's belief in the *union* of male and female forces—a union based on violence and instinct.

27. The most conventionally "tragic" element in the novel, the fall of Magnus Derrick—whose very name is almost perversely phallic—represents the final emasculating blow struck against the ranchers by the politicians, bankers, and the railroad trust. When Presley visits Derrick for the last time, he notices that, "all the old-time erectness was broken and bent" (Norris, *The Octopus* 1074). Derrick's "softened" appearance and manner contrasts sharply with his earlier potency, and, suggestively, his nervous hands are "the only members of his body that yet appeared to retain their activity" (1074).

28. This troubling notion reappears in the resolution of Vanamee's story. Vanamee, tortured over the loss of his fiancée, Angele, struggles to overcome death itself by recreating the relationship with Angele's daughter. Angele was mysteriously raped one night while waiting for Vanamee and subsequently died giving birth to the "product" of that rape, the daughter who will eventually appear to Vanamee in the wheat fields. Vanamee finds happiness eventually with Angele's daughter, who was conceived in the violence that disrupted Angele's and Vanamee's lives, whose birth caused Angele's death, and who submits to Vanamee's advances amid the ripening wheat.

29. See Norris, *Criticism* 99–103.

30. Presley's attitude toward the Mexican workers reinforces the simplistic stereotypes reflected in Norris's "Among Cliff Dwellers": "The Spanish-Mexicans, decayed, picturesque, vicious, and romantic, never failed to interest Presley . . . relics of a former generation, standing for a different order of things, absolutely idle, living God knew how, happy with their cigarette, their guitar, their glass of mescal, and their siesta" (*The Octopus* 593).

31. The name of the ship, perhaps modeled on an actual sailing vessel launched in 1890, or on a character in the ballet *Coppelia,* certainly suggests the Northern European "essence" that drives the westward march of the Teutonic races, according to Norris's conception of Anglo-Saxon destiny.

32. In his essay "A Neglected Epic," which suggests the importance of a new kind of writing that documents the expansion of the American empire, Norris predicts a similar mastery of the Orient: "As I have tried to point out once before in these pages, the Frontier has disappeared. The westward-moving course of empire has at last crossed the Pacific Ocean. Civilization has circled the globe and has come back to its starting point, the vague and mysterious East" (*Criticism* 119).

33. The wheat, much of it harvested from Derrick's "Los Muertos Ranch," is

sent to alleviate a famine in the Far East and serves as a physical manifestation of Kipling's "White Man's Burden," the paternalistic duty of the Anglo-Saxon to the less successful races.

34. See Michaels 183–86.

35. For a discussion of the relationship between social etiquette and Anglo-Saxon identity, see Maureen E. Montgomery, *Displaying Women* 7–9.

36. Several recent critics, including Wai-Chee Dimock and Kathy Miller Hadley, implicate Selden and Archer for their roles in the death of Lily and the banishment of Ellen, respectively. Dimock offers a critique of Wharton's "social marketplace," in which Selden is "a 'negative hero,' . . . not a high-minded dissident but very much 'one of them'" ("Debasing Exchange" 787). Hadley echoes this dismissal in her discussion of Newland Archer, who is "unable to truly help Ellen because he is so self-absorbed" ("Ironic Structure and Untold Stories in *The Age of Innocence*" 265). See also Michaels 225–30, and Amy Kaplan, "Edith Wharton's Profession of Authorship" in *The Social Construction of American Realism*. Alternately, others see these figures as unwitting dupes of the oppressive society who lack the ability or the awareness to transcend its influence. Blake Nevius locates Selden only slightly higher than Lily in this deterministic framework: "Through no fault of her own, [Lily] has—*can* have—only the loosest theoretical grasp of the principles which enable Selden to preserve his weak idealism from the corroding atmosphere in which they are both immersed" (*Edith Wharton* 57). Elaine Showalter argues that "[Selden's] failed effort to define himself as the New Man parallels Lily's futile effort to become a New Woman" ("The Death of the Lady (Novelist)" 149). Whereas deterministic readings view Lily's and Ellen's downfalls as symptomatic of female artistry in general, a number of contradictory feminist critiques construct quite different views of female creative power and accord Selden and Archer more sympathy than blame. Frances Restuccia, for example, criticizes Nevius's reading of Lily as a victim: "To retain his image of Lily as a helpless, victimized product of her society, Nevius must discount her movement, her oscillation" ("The Name of the Lily" 225). The view of Lily, not as helpless victim, but as frustrated artist, finds support in a wide range of criticism, from Cynthia Griffin Wolff's discussion of Art Nouveau to Candace Waid's interpretation of Lily as writer. Judith Fryer sees *The Age of Innocence* as not a critique of patriarchal values but a depiction of "a *female* society in decline" (*Felicitous Space* 140). Elizabeth Ammons identifies not Archer, but May, as "the author's title character" ("Cool Diana and Blood-Red Muse" 212), and sees her artistic performance as the central force of the novel. Appropriately enough, this focus on female artistry leaves Selden and Archer free from direct blame, perhaps, but ultimately irrelevant.

37. "Newland," Wharton notes, is in fact the maiden name of Mrs. Archer.

38. Elaine Showalter suggests that Wharton offers in Lily Bart a direct contrast to Wilde: "Wharton's major revision of a male text . . . was with relation to Oscar Wilde's *Picture of Dorian Gray*" (140).

39. For a discussion of the threat to normative sexuality posed by the first generation of "new women" in the late nineteenth century, see Carroll Smith-Rosenberg's *Disorderly Conduct: Visions of Gender in Victorian America* 253–80. As Smith-Rosenberg notes, the new woman's struggle to achieve some measure of intellectual and social autonomy alienated them also from the matriarchal matrix upon which their status relied: "Resentful words, lingering guilt, and consequent alienation divided the New Women from their mothers and their female kin" (257). In the end, of course, it is Mrs. Manson Mingott, May Welland, and the other women who decide Ellen Olenska's fate.

40. See the conclusion to Pater's *The Renaissance* 236–37.

41. Three sonnets from *The House of Life* appear in Wharton's collection *Eternal Passion in English Poetry.*

42. For a materialist analysis of Selden's behavior, see Dimock, for example.

43. Selden's attitude reflects what Regenia Gagnier calls the "natural aristocracy" advocated by Wilde in opposition to the vulgarity of British upper classes (*Idylls of the Marketplace* 98).

44. Archer's objectification of May after her death is consistent with his "use" of her as his wife. While he is walking with May in the park, Wharton notes, "Archer was proud of the glances turned on her and the simple joy of possessorship cleared away his underlying perplexities" (1080).

45. According to Deborah Barker, "Lily's imitation of *Mrs. Lloyd* reinforces the critical importance of how a woman, and especially a woman artist, acquires her name and her fame" (*Aesthetics and Gender in American Literature* 149).

46. May is compared to Diana four times in the novel.

47. Later Wharton places further emphasis on the serious "play" in which Lily is engaged, as well as her aunt's detachment from it:

> Mrs. Peniston disliked scenes, and her determination to avoid them had always led her to hold herself aloof from the details of Lily's life. In her youth, girls had not been supposed to require close supervision. They were generally assumed to be taken up with the legitimate business of courtship and marriage, and interference in such affairs on the part of their natural guardians was considered as unwarrantable as a spectator's suddenly joining in a game. (133)

48. Michael Oriard, in exploring "the conjunction of sportive and economic language" in *The House of Mirth,* observes that

Trenor's demand for "fair play" is in many ways a reasonable expectation of his due, yet Lily Bart is no more the stereotyped coquette than Trenor is the conventional rake. Although Lily willingly entered the game, only deluding herself that she would not have to play as well as he—or deluding herself about the nature of the stake—her decision to play was determined by factors over which she had no control. (*Sporting with the Gods* 40–41)

49. Selden's attitude is particularly ironic, given his onetime affair with Dorset's wife, let alone his attachment to Lily.

50. See R. W. B. Lewis's biography of Wharton 112–13.

51. *Active Service,* as Wharton must surely have known, is the title of one of Stephen Crane's novels.

52. R. W. B. Lewis notes that Wharton received her first royalty check, for *The Decoration of Houses,* in the summer of 1898 (79).

53. In *Aesthetics and Gender in American Literature,* Barker distinguishes between Henry James's outright disdain for the mass media and Wharton's more conflicted attitude. *The House of Mirth,* Barker notes, was a bestseller published serially in *Scribner's,* and its success afforded Wharton a degree of autonomy and influence taken for granted by men such as James. Barker writes, "Despite her own objections to the popular press, Wharton did not simply reject the mass media as James did, nor change her style to fit the demands of the illustrated and picture magazines; instead, she used her access to and knowledge of the popular press to satirize their practices in her own bestseller" (158).

54. See *Social Construction of American Realism* 96–98.

55. On the emergence of Lily and Ellen as artists, see, in particular, Candace Waid, *Edith Wharton's Letters from the Underworld* 17–21, and Cynthia Griffin Wolff, *A Feast of Words* 117–20.

Chapter Four

1. The use of the term "nadir" to describe this period can be traced to Rayford W. Logan's 1965 text, *The Betrayal of the Negro from Rutherford B. Hayes to Woodrow Wilson.*

2. For a full discussion of the role of *The Souls of Black Folk* in shaping the masculinist framework of African American intellectual work in the twentieth century, see Carby, *Race Men* 9–41. In "Both Sides of the Veil: Race, Science, and Mysticism in W. E. B. Du Bois," Cynthia Schrager provides a nuanced overview of the debate over the masculinist or feminist undertones of *Souls.*

3. For lynching data, see Robert L. Zangrando, *The NAACP Crusade against Lynching* 5–8. It is important to remember that these numbers reflect only officially

198 / Notes to Pages 141–146

recorded instances of lynching, or only a portion of the total number of violent acts of racist "justice" during this period.

4. In *Black Culture and Black Consciousness,* Lawrence Levine describes the essential role of sexuality in the profile of the outlaw folk hero in terms of the psychological impact of racism on African American notions of manhood: "The hypervirility of the bandit becomes a projection of the severely restricted masculine instincts and the 'severely dislocated ego' of the black male" (418). For more on Johnson as "Bad Nigger," see Roberts, 68–70.

5. For an account of the impact of *The Marrow of Tradition* on Chesnutt's career and the reaction of William Dean Howells to Chesnutt's naturalistic narrative, see Joseph McElrath's "W. D. Howells and Race: Charles W. Chesnutt's Disappointment of the Dean."

6. Gregory Candela in "We Wear the Mask: Irony in Dunbar's *The Sport of the Gods*" claims that the narrator "operates from behind the mask of his narrative . . . far removed from the Negro dialect of the Hamiltons but also clearly distinct from the stilted, over-ornate language of white Reconstruction aristocrats like the Oakleys" (64).

7. Kenny Williams, in "The Masking of the Novelist," argues that Dunbar's novel, imbued with a "spirit of pessimism," is "fundamentally a protest against the evil influence of the city" (195).

8. Kitty's fate, therefore, lies somewhere between Maggie's and Carrie's—neither utterly destroyed by the theatrical underworld nor a coldly successful survivor in it.

9. For accounts of the riots, see Leon Prather, *We Have Taken a City: The Wilmington Racial Massacre and Coup of 1898* and David Cecelski and Timothy Tyson, *Democracy Betrayed: The Wilmington Race Riot of 1898 and Its Legacy.*

10. As Frederick Wegener notes in "Charles W. Chesnutt and the Anti-Imperialist Matrix of African-American Writing, 1898–1905," Chesnutt mentions that the men joining Carteret in plotting the uprising, General Belmont and Captain McBane, have military experience "down in the American tropics" inciting violent revolutions. In the wake of the expansionist debate surrounding the Spanish-American War, Chesnutt's novel parallels oppression and imperialism at home and abroad: "Here and elsewhere in *The Marrow of Tradition,* Chesnutt conveys an unusually acute intuition of the essential and ominous kinship that linked domestic campaigns of racial terror and repression with the nation's swiftly multiplying expeditions overseas" ("Charles W. Chesnutt" 479).

11. This line of inquiry by no means represents the only approach to the problem of gender in the novel. Samina Najmi, for instance, in "Janet, Polly, and Olivia: Constructs of Blackness and White Femininity in Charles Chesnutt's *The Marrow of Tradition*" examines the connection between racial and sexual oppression in the

unacknowledged kinship among the three key women in the novel. This link between misogyny and masculinized racial identity is essential to the behavior of the men, white and black, in the novel. On black and white female bodies in *Marrow*, see Felipe Smith, *American Body Politics* 62–67. On the "doubling of Janet and Olivia," see Samira Kawash, *Dislocating the Color Line* 85–123.

12. In *To Wake the Nations*, which has significantly enhanced Chesnutt's visibility in the canon of American writers, Eric Sundquist offers the following overview of the conditions into which Chesnutt inserts his most controversial work:

> The mirroring images of male and female hysteria that Chesnutt examines in *The Marrow of Tradition* spring in part from the loss of economic and political power suffered by the South in the aftermath of the war and felt keenly by male leaders, and in part from the instability of gender relations that resulted. "Negro domination" did, in fact, threaten the manliness of the white southerner, though not in the way it was often represented. Male hysteria was not simply about rape: it was about votes and the loss of white southern virility, which in turn sprang from the region's prolonged economic deterioration which had reached the stage of depression by the end of the century. Rape was the mask behind which disfranchisement was hidden, but it was part of the larger charade of plantation mythology that set out to restore southern pride and revive a paradigm of white manliness that the legacy of the war and the economic and political rise of blacks during Reconstruction had called seriously into question. (425)

13. Houston Baker, in *Blues, Ideology, and Afro-American Literature: A Vernacular Theory*, connects Frank's weak aestheticism with Dunbar's critique of the literary plantation tradition: "The desire of Oakley and his confreres to elevate their provincial mode of life through art fosters a pallid and deceptive southern romanticism" (131).

14. In *To Wake the Nations*, Sundquist explores the notion of the cakewalk as the dominant trope that defines Chesnutt's work. The delicate balance between grotesque parody and free expression that characterizes black folklore of the period reflects the literary impact of Chesnutt and other African American writers on what has been perceived as a more broadly defined Eurocentric American culture (273–76).

15. In Dunbar's and Chesnutt's novels, the word *negro* is written in lower case, as was the publishing custom of the day. James Weldon Johnson, in fact, fought a successful battle with the publisher of *The Autobiography of an Ex-Colored Man* to ensure that the word *Negro* was capitalized throughout the book (see Eugene Levy, *James Weldon Johnson* 127).

16. Sundquist notes that "Josh is a figure of folk consciousness apparently drawn from no actual participant in the Wilmington riot" (*To Wake the Nations* 441).

17. Here Gilmore, like many critics, consciously calls to mind the surname of Alexander Manly, the black journalist whose editorializing on the subject of race and sexuality so angered the white establishment.

18. Referring to Skaggs as a "blues detective," Houston Baker claims, "The narrator . . . seems willing to recommend even the reportage of yellow journalism if it offers conditions of possibility for a just means of apprehending the world" (135).

19. For accounts of the involvement of the white and black press in the Wilmington riot, see Sundquist, *To Wake the Nations* 414–22, and Prather, "We Have Taken a City" 22–32.

20. See Glenda Gilmore, "Murder, Memory, and the Flight of the Incubus" 77–78, Sundquist, *To Wake the Nations* 419–25, and Prather, "We Have Taken a City" 23–30.

21. According to Rampersad, A. C. McClurg, publisher of *The Souls of Black Folk,* gave Du Bois the idea of writing a novel: "Struck by the lyric intensity of many of the essays, and perhaps by the power and effectiveness of the only short story in the collection 'Of the Coming of John,' McClurg had suggested that its author think of writing a novel to dramatize what Du Bois had called the 'problem' of being black in white America" (Foreword 5–6). The title of this novel alludes to the chapter of *Souls* entitled "Of the Quest of the Golden Fleece," an economic treatise on Southern cotton production which, in turn, alludes to the Greek legend of Jason and the Argonauts.

22. The title change from the chapter of *Souls* reflects concerns over David Graham Phillips's then-recent *Golden Fleece.* See Lewis, *W. E. B. Du Bois* 444–45.

23. In "Race and Romance: *The Quest of the Silver Fleece* as Utopian Narrative," Keith Byerman suggests that Du Bois's realistic message is undone by the romantic elements of the story.

24. One of many interesting parallels between Norris's and Du Bois's novels is the reference to death in the place names: "Los Muertos Ranch" and "Toomsville." In both cases, though with quite different degrees of sympathy, the narratives depict a way of life doomed to extinction.

25. The speech might be usefully compared with Presley's address to the Ranchers' League in *The Octopus,* into which he pours his passion and skill, and out of which he receives thunderous applause, but also a hollow sense of ineffectuality (1016–18).

26. In the course of the novel, "Caroline" Wynn becomes "Carrie"—perhaps an allusion to Dreiser's heroine and her role in the downfall of Hurstwood.

27. In fact, the most extended use of black dialect in the novel occurs in the

portrayal of the simple-minded and corrupt Preacher Jones, who condemns Zora as "de ebil one" when she enters his church to encourage the community's economic self-determination (Du Bois, *Quest* 373).

28. It is worth noting that Du Bois, like Norris, attended Harvard University, the epicenter of American upper-class masculinity. In "Manhood at Harvard: W. E. B. Du Bois," Kim Townsend explores the influence of Harvard on Du Bois's notion of muscular, virile manhood and its place in the advancement of the black race.

29. And, of the remaining three, only Chesnutt could easily pass for white, as he did on various occasions. Critics of the day, as Joseph McElrath has observed, were obsessed with the degree of "white blood" in black writers, and many early essays on Chesnutt, for instance, "were focusing on Chesnutt primarily for the purpose of gleaning the significance of his racial makeup rather than measuring the quality of his thought and art" (Introduction 7).

30. One of Du Bois's primary objections to Jack Johnson as cultural hero, in fact, stemmed from Johnson's marriages with white women, which Du Bois saw as evidence of racial shame.

31. I am using the American spelling of "Colored," as it appears in the 1912 edition. The 1927 reprint, which reached a much larger audience, uses the British "Coloured."

32. Several critics convincingly argue that Johnson's novel effectively dismantles the essentialized "scientific" assumptions about racial identity and demonstrates the porous nature of the color line. See, for example, Kawash 138–155, Neil Brooks, "On Becoming an Ex-Man" 18–19, and Cathy Boeckmann, *A Question of Character* 174–204. I would argue that, although Johnson's text clearly does support these readings, it also proposes a counterthesis, and the interplay of these two viewpoints gives the novel its resonance and value for understanding African American thought during this period.

33. There are, of course, multiple connotations of the word "yellow" in this context. Within the discourse of Anglo-Saxon racialism, the "yellow peril" of Asian immigration loomed as a constant concern, whereas the anti-aesthetic sensibilities of writers such as London and Norris invariably cautioned against the effete aestheticism epitomized by *The Yellow Book*.

34. For a discussion of the *Autobiography*'s relationship to the conventions of the slave narrative, see Lucinda MacKethan, "Black Boy and Ex-Colored Man: Version and Inversion of the Slave Narrator's Quest for Voice."

35. In his biography of Johnson, Eugene Levy points out the effect that his foreign service work in Venezuela had on Johnson's understanding of the race issue in the United States. In Venezuela, Johnson saw a far greater degree of equality be-

tween black and white races, but, in the process of achieving this laudable objective, Venezuelans of African descent had sacrificed an important part of their heritage and identity. See Levy 140–41.

36. For a discussion of Lee's influence on the notion of boy's play as "work" and a manly embrace of warlike tendencies, see Kett, *Rites of Passage* 225–28.

37. Joseph Skerrett examines the parallels between this "peculiar man" and an acquaintance of Johnson's, a "bachelor" millionaire, Dr. Summers ("Irony and Symbolic Action" 552–53).

38. For an overview of Johnson's musical career, see Levy 82–98.

39. MacKethan suggests that the blind preacher "Singing Johnson" reflects Johnson's own ideal of the expressiveness and integrity of art (146). For a detailed exploration of the relationship between the novel and Johnson's ambivalence about the "coon song" industry, see Cristina Ruotolo, "James Weldon Johnson and the *Autobiography of an Ex-Colored Musician.*"

40. In his study of the configurations of black and white female bodies and the notion of race, Felipe Smith draws several connections between Jack Johnson's professional downfall and James Weldon Johnson's concept of the "White Witch"—a white succubus who destroys the integrity of black men—as manifested in his poem of that name and in the *Autobiography.* See Felipe Smith 316–34.

41. Du Bois's censure of Chesnutt's choice of commerce over principle is itself reminiscent of Walter Camp's elitist critique of professional athletics: "A gentleman does not sell himself."

42. Despite the narrator's many insights on his own life and surroundings, critics have disagreed on the extent to which the ex-colored man speaks for Johnson. Levy, for instance, claims that "Johnson used the immediacy of the confession's first-person narrative to produce a largely didactic essay" (129). Robert Fleming, in contrast, focuses on Johnson's ironic characterization of an unreliable narrator and suggests that "the reader who keeps this in mind will appreciate *The Autobiography* as a novel rather than as a guidebook to Negro life" (*James Weldon Johnson* 31). Indeed, in assessing the protagonist's shortcomings, a reader might well approach the novel as a guidebook on pitfalls of a misguided life. For an overview of the critical dispute over Johnson's narrative stance and relationship between author and narrator, see Skerrett.

43. It is interesting to contrast these lynchings with the near-lynching of a *white* man in Crane's "Moonlight on the Snow," in which the potential victim talks his way out of trouble. Here, of course, mere words cannot save anyone.

44. Indeed, many readers of the 1912 edition took Johnson's conceit seriously, and its premise stuck close to home for some reviewers. Levy, for instance, cites the *Nashville Tennessean's* indignant denunciation of the books as a "lie" and an "insult to Southern womanhood" (127).

45. In addition to the references to the lynching of Sadness's father in *The Sport of the Gods* and the white uprising in *The Marrow of Tradition,* the climactic struggle in *The Quest of the Silver Fleece* occurs when the sheriff of Toomsville incites a white mob to attack the black infirmary run by Zora, and they murder an innocent black man who dares to carry a gun in self-defense.

Epilogue

1. Tellingly, despite his compassion for Jeff's fate, Dreiser never presents him as anything other than guilty of the crime itself.

2. As Pizer notes, Dreiser's claims to have based the story on an event he witnessed as a reporter for the St. Louis *Republic* do not match either the dates of his employment at the paper or any published accounts during that time. T. D. Nostwich, however, in "The Source of Dreiser's 'Nigger Jeff,'" established convincing links between the fictional story and another report published sometime later in the *Republic,* but not written by Dreiser.

Bibliography

Adams, James Eli. *Dandies and Desert Saints: Styles of Victorian Manhood.* Ithaca: Cornell UP, 1995.

Adams, William H. "New Orleans as the National Center of Boxing." *The Louisiana Historical Quarterly* 39.1 (1956): 92–112.

Adelman, Melvin L. *A Sporting Time: New York City and the Rise of Modern Athletics, 1820–70.* Urbana: U of Illinois P, 1990.

Ammons, Elizabeth. "Cool Diana and the Blood-Red Muse: Edith Wharton on Innocence and Art." *American Novelists Revisited: Essays in Feminist Criticism.* Ed. Fritz Fleischmann. Boston: Hall, 1982. 209–24.

———. "Men of Color, Women, and Uppity Art at the Turn of the Century." *American Realism and the Canon.* Ed. Tom Quirk and Gary Scharnhorst. Newark: U of Delaware P, 1994.

Andrews, William L. Introduction. *The Autobiography of an Ex-Colored Man.* New York: Penguin, 1990.

Baker, Houston A., Jr. *Blues, Ideology, and Afro-American Literature: A Vernacular Theory.* Chicago: U of Chicago P, 1984.

———. *Modernism and the Harlem Renaissance.* Chicago: U of Chicago P, 1987.

Barker, Deborah. *Aesthetics and Gender in American Literature.* Lewisburg: Bucknell UP, 2000.

Becker, George. *Documents of Modern Literary Realism.* Princeton: Princeton UP, 1963.

Bederman, Gail. *Manliness and Civilization: A Cultural History of Gender and Race in the United States, 1880–1917.* Chicago: U of Chicago P, 1995.

Bell, Michael Davitt. *The Problem of American Realism: Studies in the Cultural History of a Literary Idea.* Chicago: U of Chicago P, 1993.

Bender, Bert. *Sea Brothers: The Tradition of American Sea Fiction from Moby-Dick to the Present.* Philadelphia: U of Pennsylvania P, 1988.

Bergon, Frank. *Stephen Crane's Artistry.* New York: Columbia UP, 1975.

Betts, John Rickards. *America's Sporting Heritage: 1850–1950.* Reading: Addison-Wesley, 1974.

Boeckmann, Cathy. *A Question of Character: Scientific Racism and the Genres of American Fiction, 1892–1915.* Tuscaloosa: U of Alabama P, 2000.

Borus, Daniel H. *Writing Realism: Howells, James, and Norris in the Mass Market.* Chapel Hill: U of North Carolina P, 1989.

Brooks, Neil. "On Becoming an Ex-Man: Postmodern Irony and the Extinguishing Certainties in the *Autobiography of An Ex-Colored Man.*" *College Literature* 22.3 (1995): 17–29.

Brown, Bill. "Interlude: The Agony of Play in 'The Open Boat.'" *Arizona Quarterly* 45:3 (1989): 23–46.

Brown, Charles H. *The Correspondents' War: Journalists in the Spanish-American War.* New York: Charles Scribner's Sons, 1967.

Bruce, Dickson D. *Black American Writing from the Nadir: The Evolution of a Literary Tradition, 1877–1915.* Baton Rouge: Louisiana State U Press, 1992.

Byerman, Keith. "Race and Romance: *The Quest of the Silver Fleece* as Utopian Narrative." *American Literary Realism* 24.3 (1992): 58–71.

Cady, Edwin H. *Stephen Crane.* New York: Twayne, 1962.

Campbell, Donna. *Resisting Regionalism: Gender and Naturalism in American Fiction, 1885–1915.* Athens: Ohio UP, 1997.

Candela, Gregory. "We Wear the Mask: Irony in Dunbar's *The Sport of the Gods.*" *American Literature* 48.1 (1976): 60–72.

Carby, Hazel. *Race Men.* Cambridge: Harvard UP, 1998.

Cassuto, Leonard. "'Keeping Company' with the Old Folks: Unravelling the Edges of *McTeague*'s Deterministic Fabric." *American Literary Realism* 25.2 (1995): 46–55.

Cecelski, David S., and Timothy B. Tyson, eds. *Democracy Betrayed: The Wilmington Race Riot of 1898 and Its Legacy.* Chapel Hill: U of North Carolina Press, 1998.

Chai, Leon. *Aestheticism: The Religion of Art in Post-Romantic Literature.* New York: Columbia UP, 1990.

Chesnutt, Charles Waddell. *The Marrow of Tradition.* New York: Penguin, 1993.

Collins, Michael. "Realism and Romance in the Western Stories of Stephen Crane." *Under the Sun: Myth and Realism in Western American Literature.* Ed. Barbara Meldrum. Troy: Whitston, 1985. 139–48.

Crane, Stephen. *Stephen Crane in the West and Mexico*. Ed. Joseph Katz. Kent: Kent State UP, 1970.

———. *Stephen Crane: Letters*. Ed. R. W. Stallman and Lillian Gilkes. New York: New York UP, 1960.

———. *The University of Virginia Edition of the Works of Stephen Crane*. Ed. Fredson Bowers. 10 vols. Charlottesville: U of Virginia P, 1969–76.

Crow, Charles L. "The Real Vanamee and His Influence on Frank Norris' *The Octopus*." *Western American Literature* 9 (1974): 131–39.

Davis, Richard Harding. *The Cuban and Porto Rican Campaigns*. New York: Charles Scribner's Sons, 1898.

———. *Soldiers of Fortune*. 1897. New York: Charles Scribner's Sons, 1905.

Davison, Richard Allen. "Frank Norris and the Arts of Social Criticism." *American Literary Realism* 14.1 (1981): 77–89.

Den Tandt, Cristophe. *The Urban Sublime in American Literary Naturalism*. Urbana: U of Illinois P, 1998.

Derrick, Scott. "Making a Heterosexual Man: Gender, Sexuality, and Narrative in the Fiction of Jack London." *Rereading Jack London*. Ed. Leonard Cassuto and Jeanne Campbell Reesman. Stanford: Stanford UP, 1996. 110–29.

———. *Monumental Anxieties: Homoerotic Desire and Feminine Influence in Nineteenth-Century U.S. Literature*. New Brunswick: Rutgers UP, 1997.

Dijkstra, Bram. *Idols of Perversity: Fantasies of Feminine Evil in Fin-De-Siècle Culture*. New York: Oxford UP, 1986.

Dillingham, William B. "Frank Norris and the Genteel Tradition." *Critical Essays on Frank Norris*. Ed. Don Graham. Boston: Hall, 1980. 194–204.

———. "The Old Folks of McTeague." *Nineteenth Century Fiction* 9 (1961): 169–73.

Dimock, Wai-chee. "Debasing Exchange: Edith Wharton's *House of Mirth*." *PMLA* 100 (1985): 783–92.

Dooley, Patrick K. *The Pluralistic Philosophy of Stephen Crane*. Urbana: U of Illinois P, 1993.

———. "Young Frank Norris As a Sports Journalist." *Frank Norris Studies* 27 (Spring 1999): 6–8.

Douglas, Ann. *The Feminization of American Culture*. New York: Knopf, 1977.

Douglass, Frederick. *Narrative of the Life of Frederick Douglass, An American Slave*. Boston: Anti-Slavery Office, 1845.

Dowling, Linda. *Language and Decadence in the Victorian Fin De Siècle*. Princeton: Princeton UP, 1986.

Dreiser, Theodore. "Nigger Jeff." *The Best Short Stories of Theodore Dreiser*. 1918. New York: Fawcett, 1961. 142–65.

———. *Sister Carrie*. 1900. Ed. Donald Pizer. 2nd ed. New York: Norton, 1991.

Dubbert, Joe L. *A Man's Place: Masculinity in Transition.* Englewood Cliffs: Prentice, 1979.

Du Bois, W. E. B. *The Quest of the Silver Fleece.* 1911. Boston: Northeastern UP, 1989.

———. *The Souls of Black Folk: Essays and Sketches. Writings.* New York: Library of America, 1986.

———. *Writings.* Ed. Nathan Huggins. New York: Library of America, 1986.

Dunbar, Paul Laurence. *The Sport of the Gods.* New York: Dodd, Mead and Co., 1981.

Early, Gerald. *The Culture of Bruising: Essays on Prizefighting, Literature, and Modern American Culture.* Hopewell: Ecco, 1994.

———. "Three Notes toward a Cultural Definition of the Harlem Renaissance." *Callaloo* 14.1 (1991): 136–49.

Ellmann, Richard. *Oscar Wilde.* New York: Knopf, 1988.

Emery, Edwin. *The Press and America: An Interpretive History of Journalism.* 2nd ed. Englewood Cliffs: Prentice, 1962.

Farr, Finis. *Black Champion: The Life and Times of Jack Johnson.* New York: Scribner's, 1964.

Fisher, Philip. *Hard Facts: Setting and Form in the American Novel.* New York: Oxford UP, 1985.

Fleming, Robert E. *James Weldon Johnson.* Boston: Twayne, 1987.

Freedman, Jonathan. *Professions of Taste: Henry James, British Aestheticism and Commodity Culture.* Stanford: Stanford UP, 1990.

Fryer, Judith. *Felicitous Space: The Imaginative Structures of Edith Wharton and Willa Cather.* Chapel Hill: U of North Carolina P, 1986.

Gagnier, Regenia. *Idylls of the Marketplace: Oscar Wilde and the Victorian Public.* Stanford: Stanford UP, 1986.

Gates, Henry Louis, Jr. *The Signifying Monkey: A Theory of African-American Literary Criticism.* New York: Oxford UP, 1988.

Gilmore, Al-Tony. *Bad Nigger! The National Impact of Jack Johnson.* Port Washington: Kennikat, 1975.

Gilmore, Glenda Elizabeth. *Gender and Jim Crow: Women and the Politics of White Supremacy in North Carolina, 1896–1920.* Chapel Hill: U of North Carolina P, 1996.

———. "Murder, Memory, and the Flight of the Incubus." *Democracy Betrayed: The Wilmington Race Riot of 1898 and Its Legacy.* Ed. David S. Cecelski and Timothy B. Tyson. Chapel Hill: U of North Carolina P, 1998. 73–93.

Gleason, William. *The Leisure Ethic: Work and Play in American Literature, 1840–1940.* Stanford: Stanford UP, 1999.

Goldberg, David Theo. *Anatomy of Racism*. Minneapolis: U of Minnesota P, 1990.

Gorn, Elliot J. *The Manly Art: Bare-Knuckle Prize Fighting in America*. Ithaca: Cornell UP, 1986.

Gould, Stephen Jay. *The Mismeasure of Man*. New York: Norton, 1981.

Graham, Don. *The Fiction of Frank Norris: The Aesthetic Context*. Columbia: U of Missouri P, 1978.

Green, Carol Hurd. "Stephen Crane and the Fallen Women." *American Novelists Revisited: Essays in Feminist Criticism*. Ed. Fritz Fleischmann. Boston: Hall, 1982.

Green, Martin. *The Adventurous Male: Chapters in the History of the White Male Mind*. University Park: Pennsylvania State UP, 1993.

Guttman, Allen. *A Whole New Ball Game: An Interpretation of American Sports*. Chapel Hill: U of North Carolina P, 1988.

Habegger, Alfred. "Fighting Words: The Talk of Men at War in *The Red Badge of Courage*." In *Fictions of Masculinity: Crossing Cultures, Crossing Sexualities*. Ed. Peter F. Murphy. New York: New York UP, 1994. 185–203.

Hadley, Kathy Miller. "Ironic Structure and Untold Stories in *The Age of Innocence*." *Studies in the Novel* 23 (1991): 262–71.

Hagemann, E. R. "'Sadder than the End': Another Look at 'The Open Boat.'" *Stephen Crane in Transition: Centenary Essays*. Ed. Joseph Katz. DeKalb: Northern Illinois UP, 1972.

Haller, John S. *Outcasts from Evolution: Scientific Attitudes of Racial Inferiority, 1859–1900*. Carbondale: S Illinois UP, 1995.

Halliburton, David. *The Color of the Sky: A Study of Stephen Crane*. New York: Cambridge UP, 1989.

Hantover, Jeffery. "The Boy Scouts and the Validation of Masculinity." *The American Man*. Ed. Elizabeth H. Pleck and Joseph H. Pleck. Englewood Cliffs: Prentice, 1980. 285–301.

Harper, Phillip Brian. *Are We Not Men: Masculine Anxiety and the Problem of African-American Identity*. New York: Oxford UP, 1996.

Hochman, Barbara. *The Art of Frank Norris, Storyteller*. Columbia: U of Missouri P, 1988.

——. "The Rewards of Representation: Edith Wharton, Lily Bart and the Writer/Reader Interchange." *Novel* 24 (1991): 147–61.

Holbrook, David. *Edith Wharton and the Unsatisfactory Man*. New York: St. Martin's, 1991.

Howard, June. *Form and History in American Literary Naturalism*. Chapel Hill: U of North Carolina P, 1985.

Isenberg, Michael T. *John L. Sullivan and His America*. Urbana: U of Illinois P, 1994.

James, Henry. *The Art of Fiction and Other Essays*. New York: Oxford UP, 1948.

Johnson, James Weldon. *Along This Way.* 1933. New York: Penguin, 1990.

——. *The Autobiography of an Ex-Colored Man. The Selected Writings of James Weldon Johnson.* Vol. 2. 273–362.

——. *Black Manhattan.* New York: Atheneum, 1977.

——. *The Selected Writings of James Weldon Johnson.* Ed. Sondra Kathryn Wilson. 2 vols. New York: Oxford UP, 1995.

Joslin, Katherine. *Edith Wharton.* New York: St. Martin's, 1991.

Kaplan, Amy. "Romancing the Empire: The Embodiment of American Masculinity in the Popular Historical Novel of the 1890s." *American Literary History* 2.4 (1990): 659–90.

——. *The Social Construction of American Realism.* Chicago: U of Chicago P, 1988.

Kaplan, Harold. *Power and Order: Henry Adams and the Naturalist Tradition in American Fiction.* Chicago: U of Chicago P, 1981.

Kassanoff, Jennie A. "Extinction, Taxidermy, Tableaux Vivants: Staging Race and Class in *The House of Mirth.*" *PMLA* 115 (2000): 60–74.

Kawash, Samira. *Dislocating the Color Line: Identity, Hybridity, and Singularity in African-American Literature.* Stanford: Stanford UP, 1997.

Kent, Thomas L. "The Problem of Knowledge in 'The Open Boat' and 'The Blue Hotel.'" *American Literary Realism* 15.2 (1982): 262–68.

Kett, Joseph. *Rites of Passage: Adolescence in America, 1790 to the Present.* New York: Basic, 1977.

Kimmel, Michael. *Manhood in America: A Cultural History.* New York: Free Press, 1996.

Kingsdale, Jon M. "'The Poor Man's Club': Social Functions of the Urban Working-Class Saloon." *The American Man.* Ed. Elizabeth H. Pleck and Joseph H. Pleck. Englewood Cliffs: Prentice, 1980. 255–83.

Kipling, Rudyard. *Captains Courageous.* New York: Century, 1896.

——. *The Light That Failed.* 1891. New York: Penguin, 1988.

Kooistra, Lorraine Janzen. *The Artist as Critic: Bitextuality in Fin-de-Siècle Illustrated Books.* Aldershot, UK: Scolar, 1995.

Kozloff, Sarah. "Complicity in *The Age of Innocence.*" *Style* 35.2 (2001): 270–88.

LaFrance, Marston. *A Reading of Stephen Crane.* Oxford: Oxford UP, 1971.

Levine, Lawrence. *Black Culture and Black Consciousness: Afro-American Folk Thought from Slavery to Freedom.* New York: Oxford UP, 1977.

Levy, Eugene. *James Weldon Johnson: Black Leader, Black Voice.* Chicago: U of Chicago P, 1973.

Lewis, David Levering. *W. E. B. Du Bois: Biography of a Race, 1868–1919.* New York: Holt, 1993.

Lewis, R. W. B. *Edith Wharton: A Biography.* New York: Harper, 1975.

Logan, Rayford W. *The Betrayal of the Negro from Rutherford B. Hayes to Woodrow Wilson.* New York: Collier Books, 1965.

London, Jack. *The Game.* New York: MacMillan, 1905.

———. *Jack London Reports: War Correspondence, Sports Articles, and Miscellaneous Writings.* Ed. King Hendricks and Irving Shepard. Garden City: Doubleday, 1970.

———. *The Sea-Wolf.* New York: MacMillan, 1904.

MacKethan, Lucinda. "Black Boy and Ex-Colored Man: Version and Inversion of the Slave Narrator's Quest for Voice." *College Language Association Journal* 32 (1988): 123–47.

Martin, Jay. *Harvests of Change: American Literature, 1865–1914.* Englewood Cliffs: Prentice, 1967.

Martin, Ronald E. *American Literature and the Universe of Force.* Durham: Duke UP, 1981.

McElrath, Joseph R. *Frank Norris Revisited.* New York: Twayne, 1992.

———. Introduction. *Critical Essays on Charles W. Chesnutt.* Ed. Joseph R. McElrath. New York: Hall, 1999. 1–25.

———. "W. D. Howells and Race: Charles W. Chesnutt's Disappointment of the Dean." *Critical Essays on Charles W. Chesnutt.* Ed. Joseph R. McElrath. New York: Hall, 1999. 242–60.

Mencken, H. L. Introduction. *An American Tragedy.* By Theodore Dreiser. New York: World, 1948.

Messenger, Christian. *Sport and the Spirit of Play in American Fiction.* New York: Columbia UP, 1981.

Michaels, Walter Benn. *The Gold Standard and the Logic of Naturalism.* Berkeley: U of California P, 1987.

Mitchell, S. Weir. *Doctor and Patient.* 1887. Philadelphia: Lippincott, 1904.

Moers, Ellen. *Two Dreisers.* New York: Viking, 1969.

Montgomery, Maureen E. *Displaying Women: Spectacles of Leisure in Edith Wharton's New York.* New York: Routledge, 1998.

Mott, Frank Luther. *American Journalism, A History: 1690–1960.* 3rd ed. New York: Macmillan, 1962.

Mrozek, Donald J. *Sport and American Mentality, 1880–1910.* Knoxville: U of Tennessee P, 1983.

Nagel, James. *Stephen Crane and Literary Impressionism.* University Park: Pennsylvania State UP, 1980.

Najmi, Samina. "Janet, Polly, and Olivia: Constructs of Blackness and White Femininity in Charles Chesnutt's *The Marrow of Tradition.*" *Southern Literary Journal* 32.1 (1999): 1–19.

Nettels, Elsa. *Language and Gender in American Fiction.* Charlottesville: U of Virginia P, 1997.

Nevius, Blake. *Edith Wharton: A Study of Her Fiction.* Berkeley: U of California P, 1953.

Norris, Frank. *Blix. A Novelist in the Making.* Ed. James D. Hart. Cambridge: Harvard UP, 1970.

———. *Collected Letters.* Ed. Jesse Crisler. San Francisco: Book Club of California, 1986.

———. *The Complete Edition of Frank Norris.* Garden City: Doubleday, 1928.

———. *The Literary Criticism of Frank Norris.* Ed. Donald Pizer. Austin: U of Texas P, 1964.

———. *McTeague.* Ed. Donald Pizer. New York: Norton, 1977.

———. *McTeague. Novels and Essays.* Ed. Donald Pizer. New York: Library of America, 1986.

———. *The Octopus. Novels and Essays.* Ed. Donald Pizer. New York: Library of America, 1986.

———. *The Surrender of Santiago.* San Francisco: Elder, 1917.

Nostwich, T. D. "The Source of Dreiser's 'Nigger Jeff.'" *Resources for American Literary Study* 8 (1978): 174–87.

O'Reilly, John Boyle. *Ethics of Boxing and Manly Sport.* Boston: Ticknor, 1888.

Oriard, Michael. *Reading Football: How the Popular Press Created an American Spectacle.* Chapel Hill: U of North Carolina P, 1993.

———. *Sporting with the Gods: The Rhetoric of Play and Game in American Culture.* New York: Cambridge UP, 1991.

Orlando, Emily J. "Rereading Wharton's 'Poor Archer': A Mr. 'Might-Have-Been' in the Age of Innocence." *American Literary Realism* 30.2 (1998): 56–77.

Paredes, Raymund. "Stephen Crane and the Mexican." *Western American Literature* 6.1 (1971): 31–38.

Pater, Walter. *The Renaissance.* Chicago: Academy, 1982.

Pizer, Donald. *The Novels of Frank Norris.* Bloomington: Indiana UP, 1966.

———. *Realism and Naturalism in Nineteenth-Century American Literature.* Rev. ed. Carbondale: Southern Illinois UP, 1984.

———. "Stephen Crane's 'The Monster' and Tolstoy's What to Do?: A Neglected Allusion." *Studies in Short Fiction* 20.2–3 (1983): 127–29.

———. "Theodore Dreiser's 'Nigger Jeff': The Development of an Aesthetic." *American Literature* 41.3 (1969): 331–41.

Pleck, Elizabeth H., and Joseph H. Pleck, eds. *The American Man.* Englewood Cliffs: Prentice, 1980.

Prather, Leon. "We Have Taken a City: A Centennial Essay." *Democracy Betrayed: The Wilmington Race Riot of 1898 and Its Legacy.* Ed. David S. Cecelski and Timothy B. Tyson. Chapel Hill: U of North Carolina P, 1998. 15–41.

———. *We Have Taken a City: The Wilmington Racial Massacre and Coup of 1898.* Cranbury: Associated UP, 1984.

Rader, Benjamin G. *American Sports: From the Age of Folk Games to the Age of Televised Sports.* 2nd ed. Englewood Cliffs, N.J.: Prentice Hall, 1990.

———. *Baseball: A History of America's Game.* Urbana: U of Illinois P, 1992.

Rahv, Philip. "Notes on the Decline of Naturalism." *Image and Idea.* Norfolk: New Directions, 1949.

Rampersad, Arnold. Foreword. *The Quest of the Silver Fleece.* Boston: Northeastern UP, 1989. 1–11.

———. "W. E. B. Du Bois as a Man of Literature." *Critical Essays on W. E. B. Du Bois.* Ed. William L. Andrews. Boston: Hall, 1985. 57–72.

Restuccia, Frances L. "The Name of the Lily: Edith Wharton's Feminism(s)." *Contemporary Literature* 28.2 (1987): 223–38.

Riess, Stephen. *City Games: The Evolution of American Urban Society and the Rise of Sports.* Urbana: U of Illinois P, 1991.

Riis, Jacob. *How the Other Half Lives.* 1890. New York: Penguin, 1997.

Roberts, Randy. *Papa Jack: Jack Johnson and the Era of White Hopes.* New York: Free Press, 1983.

Robertson, Jamie. "Stephen Crane, Eastern Outsider in the West and Mexico." *Western American Literature* 13 (1978): 243–57.

Robertson, Michael. *Stephen Crane, Journalism, and the Making of Modern American Literature.* New York: Columbia UP, 1997.

Roosevelt, Theodore. *The Strenuous Life.* New York: Century, 1900.

Rotundo, E. Anthony. *American Manhood: Transformations in Masculinity from the Revolution to the Modern Era.* New York: Basic, 1993.

Ruotolo, Cristina L. "James Weldon Johnson and the Autobiography of an Ex-Colored Musician." *American Literature* 72.2 (2000): 249–74.

Ruskin, John. "Of Modern Landscape." *The Victorian Age.* Ed. Robert Langbaum. Chicago: Academy, 1983.

Sammons, Jeffrey T. *Beyond the Ring: The Role of Boxing in American Society.* Urbana: U of Illinois P, 1988.

Samuels, Peggy, and Harold Samuels. *Teddy Roosevelt at San Juan: The Making of a President.* College Station: Texas A & M UP, 1997.

Schrager, Cynthia D. "Both Sides of the Veil: Race, Science, and Mysticism in W. E. B. Du Bois." *American Quarterly* 48.4 (1996): 551–86.

Schriber, MarySue. "Darwin, Wharton, and 'The Descent of Man': Blueprints of American Society." *Studies in Short Fiction* 17 (1980): 31–38.

Seltzer, Mark. *Bodies and Machines.* New York: Routledge, 1992.

Sensibar, Judith. "Edith Wharton Reads the Bachelor Type: Her Critique of Modernism's Representative Man." *American Literature* 60 (1988): 575–90.

Seton, Ernest Thompson. *Boy Scouts of America: A Handbook of Woodcraft, Scouting, and Life Craft.* New York: Doubleday, 1910.

Showalter, Elaine. "The Death of the Lady (Novelist): Wharton's *House of Mirth.*" *Representations* 9 (1985): 133–49.

Silbajoris, Rimvydas. *Tolstoy's Aesthetics and His Art.* Columbus: Slavica, 1991.

Skerrett, Joseph T., Jr. "Irony and Symbolic Action in James Weldon Johnson's *The Autobiography of an Ex-Coloured Man.*" *American Quarterly* 32.5 (1980): 540–58.

Smith, Felipe. *American Body Politics: Race, Gender, and Black Literary Renaissance.* Athens: U of Georgia P, 1998.

Smith, Ronald A. *Sports and Freedom.* New York: Oxford UP, 1988.

Smith-Rosenberg, Carroll. *Disorderly Conduct: Visions of Gender in Victorian America.* New York: Knopf, 1985.

Spurr, David. *The Rhetoric of Empire: Colonial Discourse in Journalism, Travel Writing, and Imperial Administration.* Durham: Duke UP, 1993.

Stallman, R. W. *Stephen Crane: A Biography.* New York: Braziller, 1968.

Stepto, Robert B. *From Behind the Veil: A Study of Afro-American Narrative.* 2nd ed. Urbana: U of Illinois P, 1991.

Sundquist, Eric. *The Hammers of Creation: Folk Culture in Modern African-American Fiction.* Athens: U of Georgia P, 1992.

———. *To Wake the Nations: Race in the Making of American Literature.* Cambridge: Harvard UP, 1993.

Thompson, Albert W. "I Helped Raise the Rough Riders." *New Mexico Historical Review* 14.3 (1939): 287–99.

Tolstoy, Leo. *The Complete Works of Count Tolstoy.* 14 vols. Ed. and trans. Leo Wiener. Boston: Page, 1904.

———. *I Cannot Be Silent: Writings on Politics, Art and Religion.* Bristol: Bristol, 1989.

———. *"What Is Art" and Essays on Art.* Trans. Alymer Maude. London: Oxford UP, 1930.

Turner, Frederick Jackson. *The Significance of the Frontier in American History.* New York: Holt, 1921.

Veblen, Thorstein. *The Theory of the Leisure Class.* 1899. New York: Penguin, 1994.

Waid, Candace. *Edith Wharton's Letters from the Underworld: Fictions of Women and Writing.* Chapel Hill: U of North Carolina P, 1991.

Warren, Kenneth. "Troubled Black Humanity in *The Souls of Black Folk* and *The Autobiography of an Ex-Colored Man.*" *The Cambridge Companion to American Realism and Naturalism.* Ed. Donald Pizer. New York: Cambridge UP, 1995. 263–77.

Wegener, Frederick. "Charles W. Chesnutt and the Anti-Imperialist Matrix of African-American Writing, 1898–1905." *Criticism* 41.4 (1999): 465–93.

———. "'Rabid Imperialist': Edith Wharton and the Obligations of Empire in Modern American Fiction." *American Literature* 72.4 (2000): 783–812.

Weiss, Daniel. "The Blue Hotel." *The Critic Agonistes: Psychology, Myth, and the Art of Fiction.* Ed. Eric Solomon and Stephen Arkin. Seattle: U of Washington P, 1985.

Wertheim, Stanley. "Two Yellow Kids: Frank Norris and Stephen Crane." *Frank Norris Studies* 27 (Spring 1999): 2–6.

Wertheim, Stanley, and Paul Sorrentino. *The Crane Log: A Documentary Life of Stephen Crane, 1871–1900.* New York: Hall, 1994.

West, Lon. *Deconstructing Frank Norris's Fiction: The Male-Female Dialectic.* New York: Lang, 1998.

Wharton, Edith. *The Age of Innocence. Edith Wharton: Novels.* Ed. R. W. B. Lewis. New York: Library of America, 1985.

———. *The Descent of Man and Other Stories.* 1904. New York: Charles Scribner's Sons, 1914.

———. *The House of Mirth. Edith Wharton: Novels.* Ed. R. W. B. Lewis. New York: Library of America, 1985.

———. *The Letters of Edith Wharton.* Ed. R. W. B. Lewis and Nancy Lewis. New York: Scribners, 1988.

———. *The Uncollected Critical Writings.* Ed. Frederick Wegener. Princeton: Princeton UP, 1996.

———. "The Valley of Childish Things, and Other Emblems." *Century Magazine* 52 (1896): 467–69.

———. *The Writing of Fiction.* New York: Scribner's, 1925.

Wharton, Edith, and Ogden Codman, Jr. *The Decoration of Houses.* 1897. New York: Norton, 1997.

Wharton, Edith, and Robert Norton, eds. *Eternal Passion in English Poetry.* Freeport: Books for Libraries, 1969.

Williams, Kenny J. "The Masking of the Novelist." *A Singer in the Dawn: Reinterpretations of Paul Laurence Dunbar.* Ed. Jay Martin. New York: Dodd, 1975. 152–207.

Wilson, Christopher. *The Labor of Words: Literary Professionalism in the Progressive Era.* Athens: U of Georgia P, 1985.

Winwar, Frances. *Oscar Wilde and the Yellow 'Nineties.* New York: Harper, 1940.

Wolff, Cynthia Griffin. *A Feast of Words: The Triumph of Edith Wharton.* New York: Oxford UP, 1977.

Wolford, Chester. *Stephen Crane: A Study of the Short Fiction.* Boston: Twayne, 1989.

Yeazell, Ruth Bernard. "The Conspicuous Wasting of Lily Bart." *ELH* 59 (1992): 713–34.

Zangrando, Robert L. *The NAACP Crusade against Lynching, 1909–1950.* Philadelphia: Temple UP, 1980.

Ziff, Larzer. *The American 1890s.* New York: Viking, 1966.

Index

tragic mulatto, 165–66
Turner, Frederick Jackson, 57
Twain, Mark, 181n. 9, 190n. 26
Tyson, Timothy, 198n. 9

Veblen, Thorstein, 28

Waid, Candace, 89–90, 115, 197n. 55
Walcutt, Charles, 180n. 6
Warren, Kenneth, 168
Wegener, Frederick, 95, 191nn. 3, 10,
    198n. 10
Weiss, Daniel, 190n. 23
Wertheim, Stanley, 185n. 28, 191n. 5
West, Lon, 193n. 24
Wharton, Edith: *The Age of Innocence,* 17,
    89, 111–21, 124–29, 132–33, 136–
    37; and architecture, 117–18, 120–21;
    and British aestheticism, 118–19; anti-
    Semitism in, 112–13; "The Descent of
    Man," 1–3; *The Decoration of Houses,*
    3, 117; *Eternal Passion in English Poetry*
    (ed.), 116–17, 196n. 41; "The Great
    American Novel," 87–88; *The House
    of Mirth,* 17, 89, 111–12, 114–18,
    121–24, 126–27, 129–32, 135–37,

197n. 53; relationship to Roosevelt,
    133, 191n. 3; relationship to women
    writers, 89–90, 136; "The Valley of
    Childish Things," 134–35; *The Writing
    of Fiction,* 95
Wilde, Oscar, 9–10, 22, 189n. 16, 192n. 16,
    193n. 20, 196n. 38
Willard, Jess, 52, 169
Williams, Kenny, 198n. 7
Wilmington Daily Record, 157
Wilmington *Messenger,* 155
Wilson, Christopher, 7, 61, 188n. 12
Wolff, Cynthia Griffin, 195n. 36, 197n. 55
Wolford, Chester, 65
Wood, Leonard, 93
Wright, Richard, 156, 158

yellow, 201n. 33; as cowardice, 187n. 41;
    as mixed race, 53, 165
Yellow Book, The, 4, 51, 201n. 33
yellow journalism, 51–52, 154–57
Yellow Kid, The, 52

Zangrando, Robert L., 140–41, 197n. 3
Ziff, Larzer, 180n. 8
Zola, Émile, 9, 11, 33, 52; *L'Assommoir,* 153